# Bizenghast

Volume 6

By M. Alice LeGrow

HAMBURG // LONDON // LOS ANGELES // TOKYO

# Bizenghast

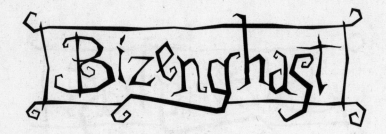

Contents

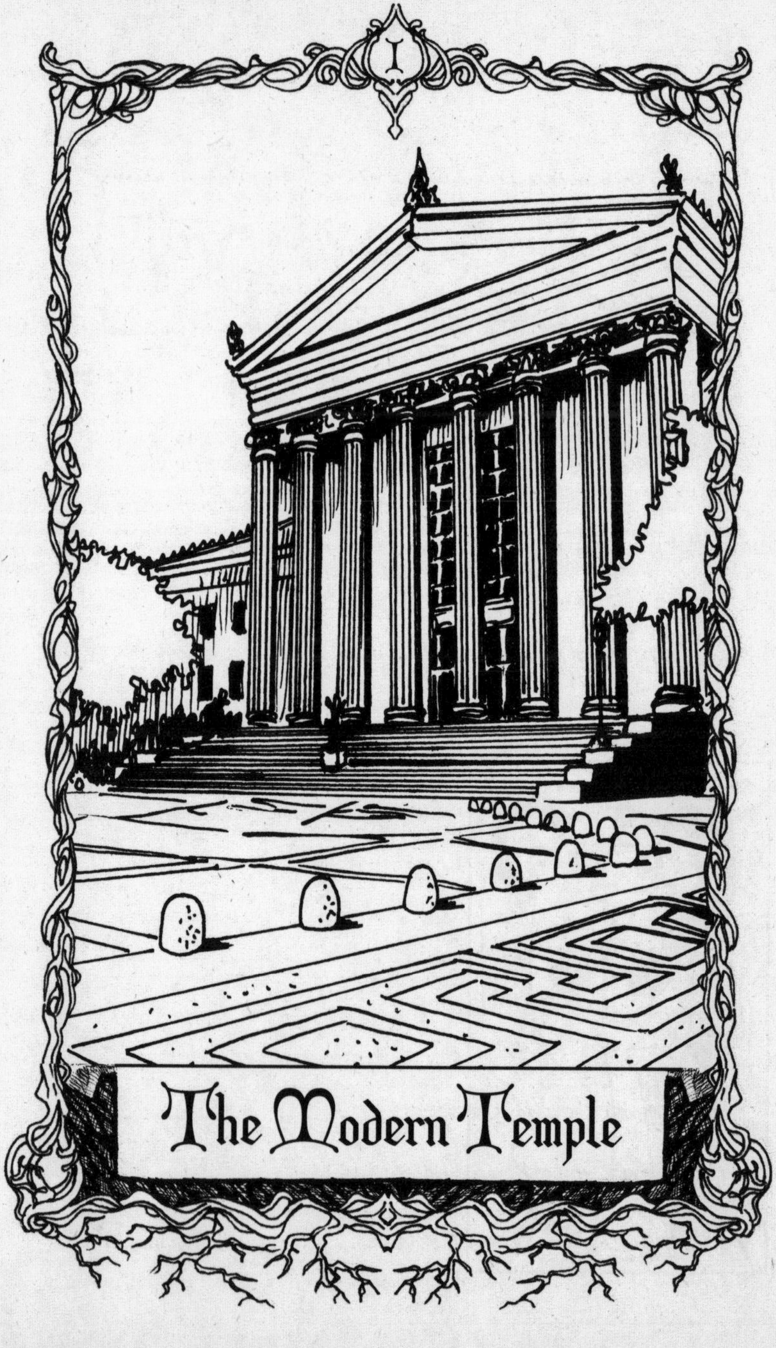
I
The Modern Temple

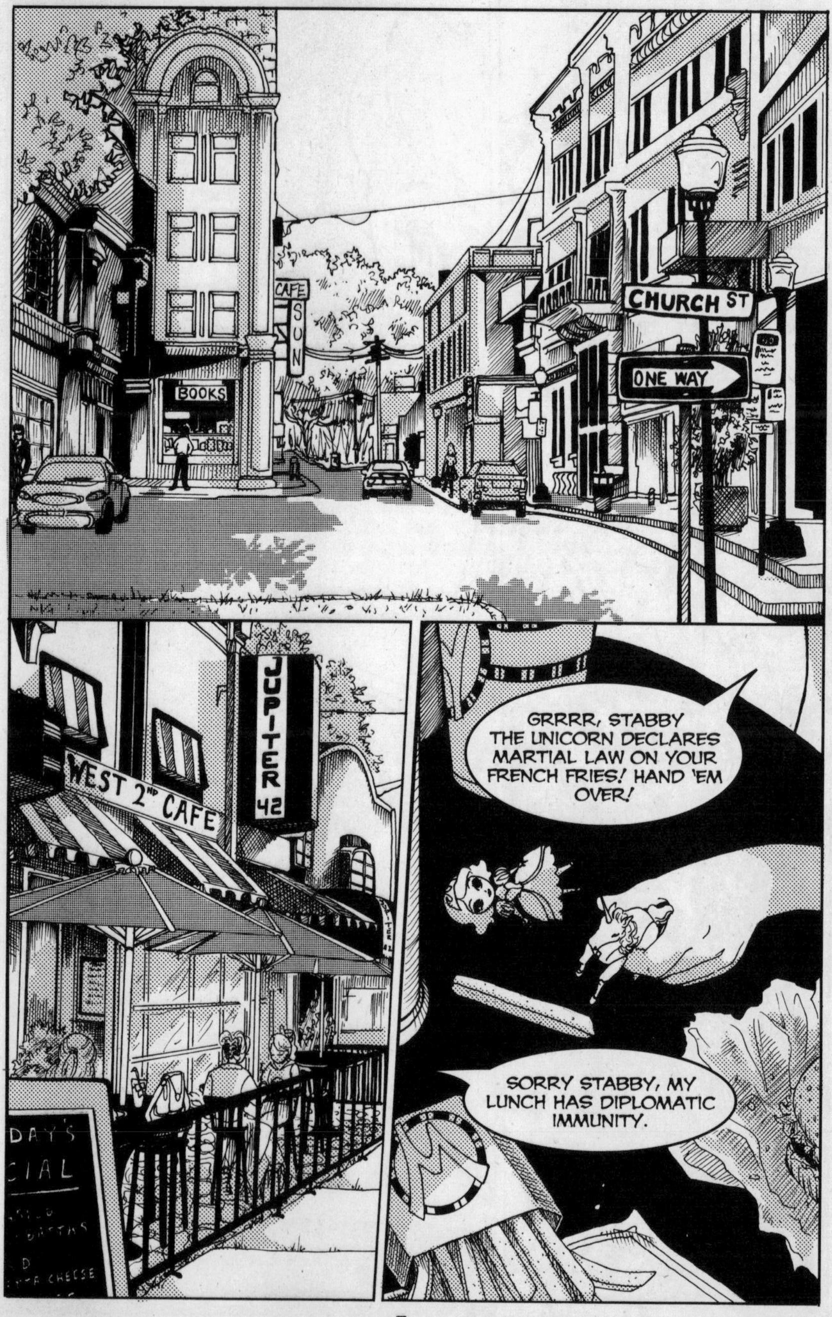
CAFE
SUN
BOOKS
CHURCH ST
ONE WAY
WEST 2ND CAFE
JUPITER 42
GRRRR, STABBY THE UNICORN DECLARES MARTIAL LAW ON YOUR FRENCH FRIES! HAND 'EM OVER!
SORRY STABBY, MY LUNCH HAS DIPLOMATIC IMMUNITY.

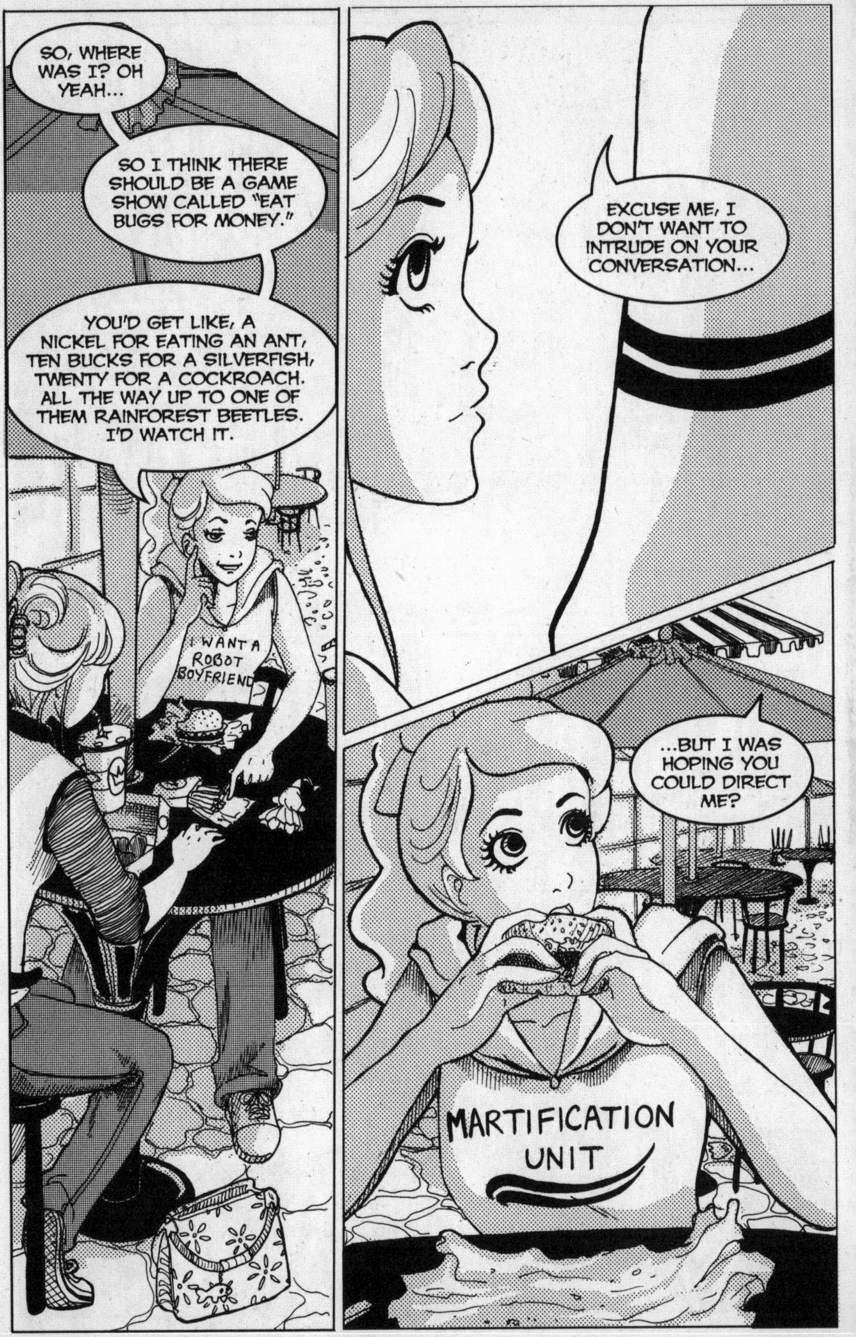
SO, WHERE WAS I? OH YEAH...
SO I THINK THERE SHOULD BE A GAME SHOW CALLED "EAT BUGS FOR MONEY."
YOU'D GET LIKE, A NICKEL FOR EATING AN ANT, TEN BUCKS FOR A SILVERFISH, TWENTY FOR A COCKROACH. ALL THE WAY UP TO ONE OF THEM RAINFOREST BEETLES. I'D WATCH IT.
I WANT A ROBOT BOYFRIEND
EXCUSE ME, I DON'T WANT TO INTRUDE ON YOUR CONVERSATION...
...BUT I WAS HOPING YOU COULD DIRECT ME?
MARTIFICATION UNIT

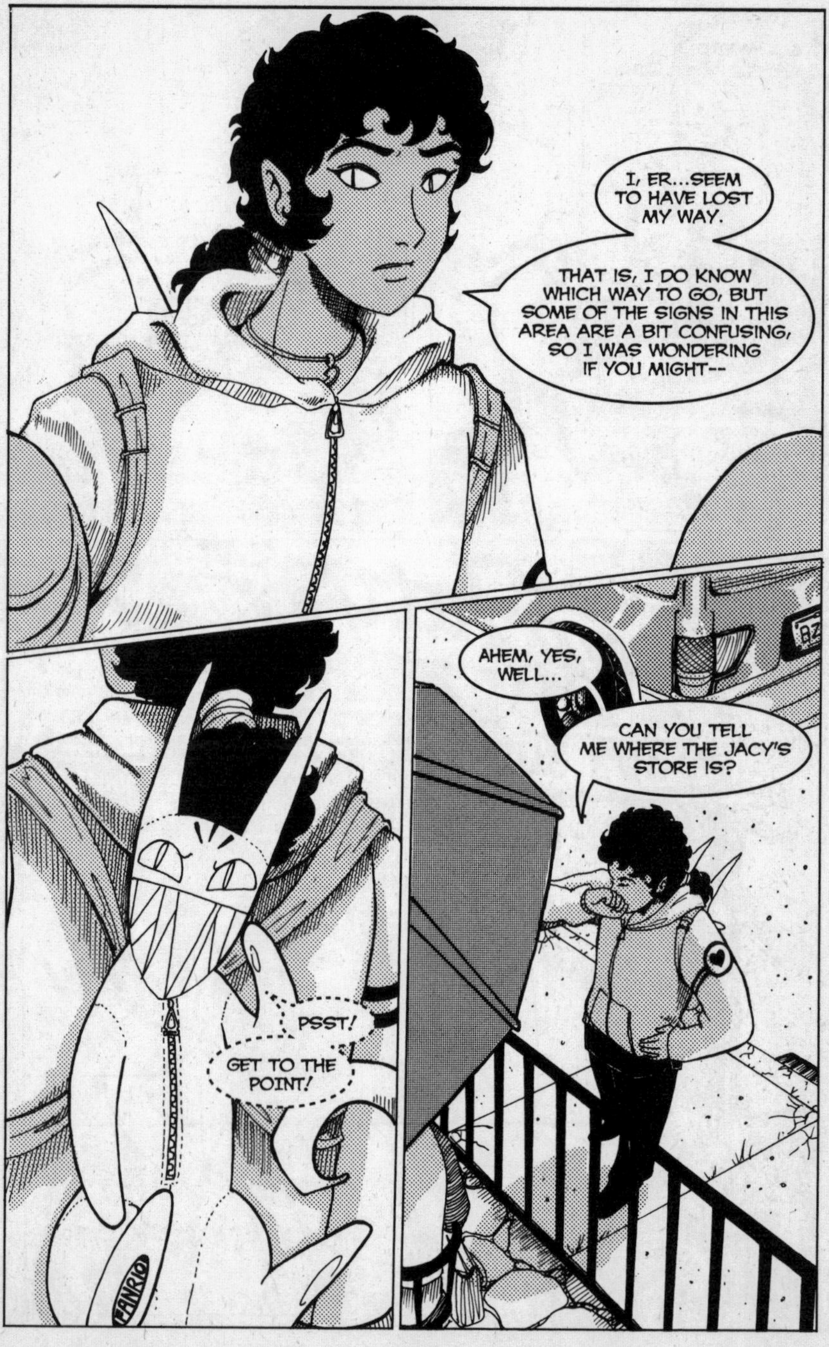
I, ER...SEEM TO HAVE LOST MY WAY.
THAT IS, I DO KNOW WHICH WAY TO GO, BUT SOME OF THE SIGNS IN THIS AREA ARE A BIT CONFUSING, SO I WAS WONDERING IF YOU MIGHT--
PSST!
GET TO THE POINT!
FANRIO
AHEM, YES, WELL...
CAN YOU TELL ME WHERE THE JACY'S STORE IS?

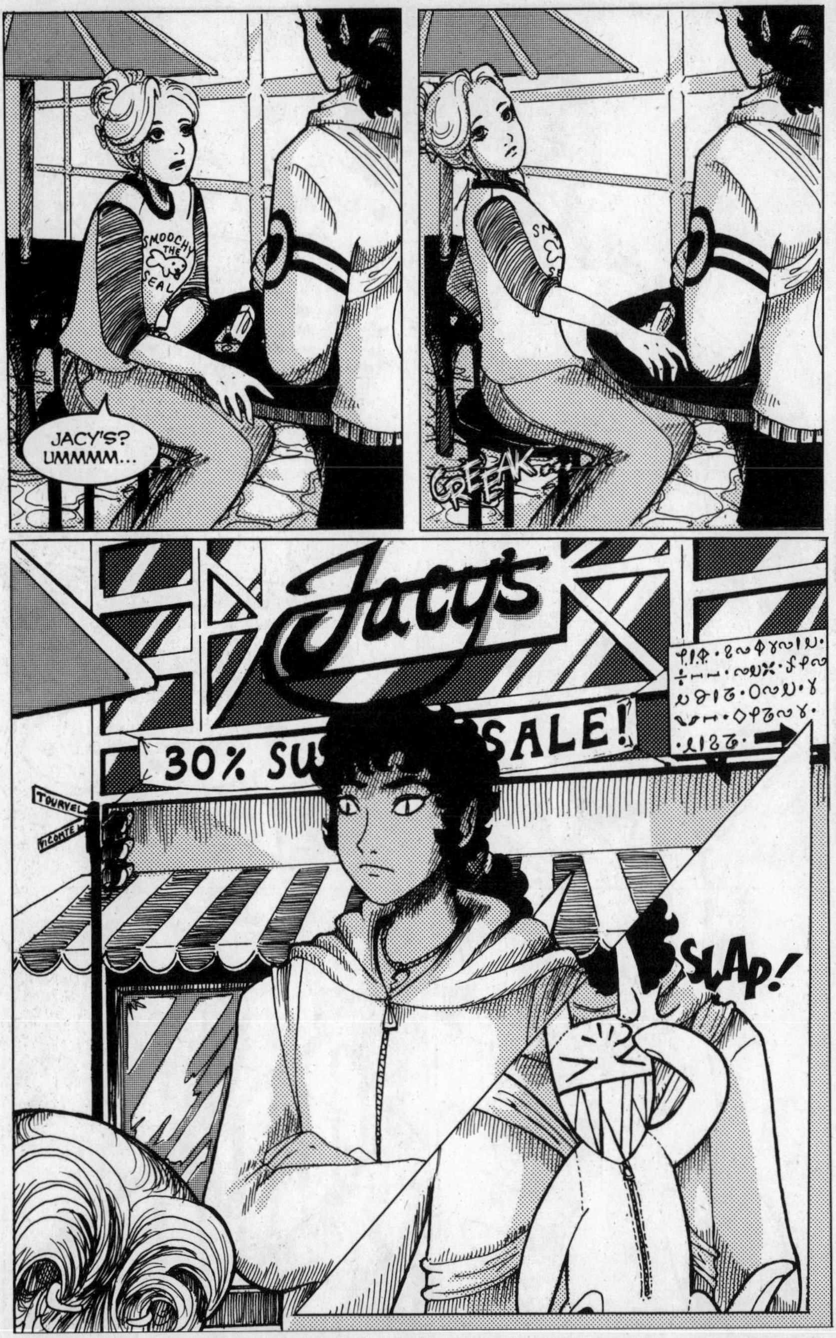
SMOOCHY THE SEAL
JACY'S? UMMMM...
CREEAK...
Jacy's
30% SU SALE!
TOURVEL
VICOMTE
SLAP!

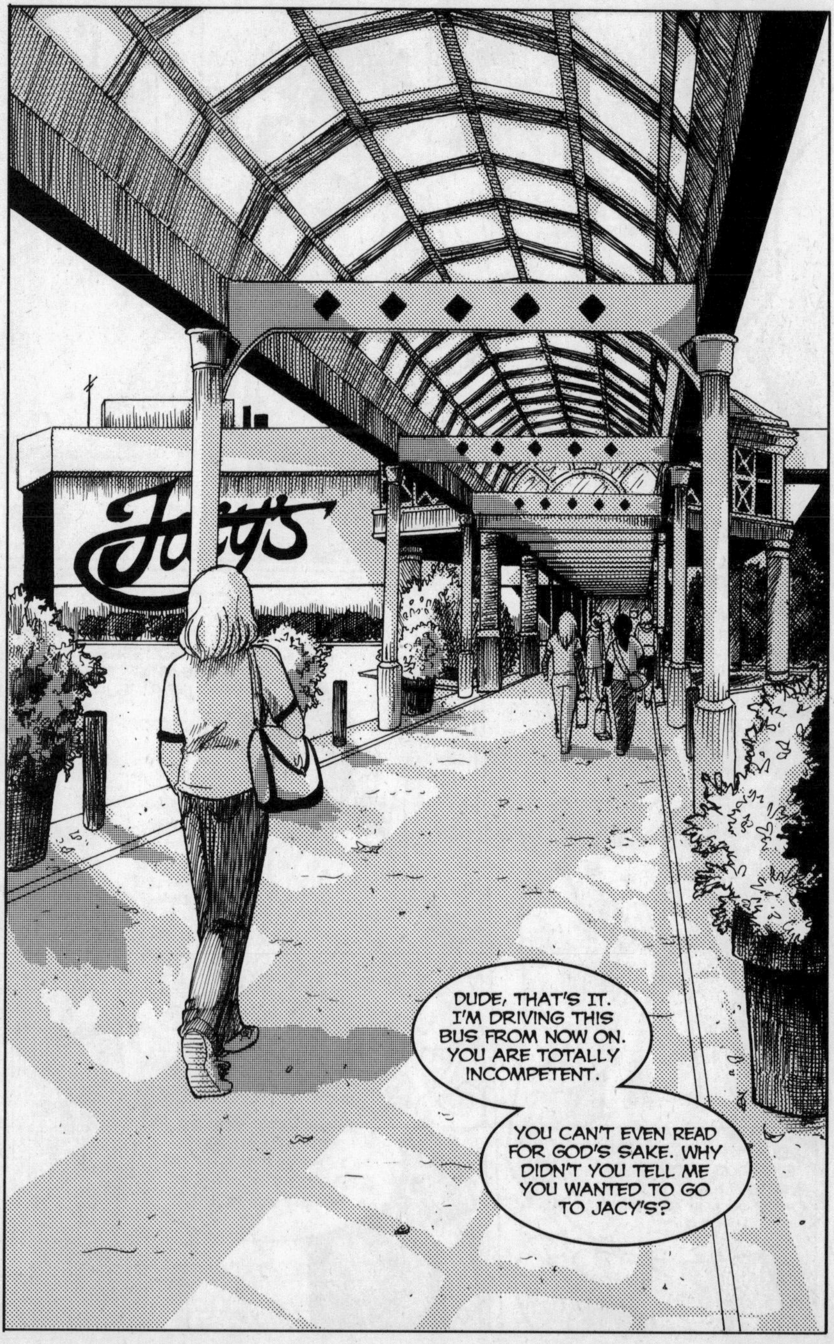

DUDE, THAT'S IT. I'M DRIVING THIS BUS FROM NOW ON. YOU ARE TOTALLY INCOMPETENT.
YOU CAN'T EVEN READ FOR GOD'S SAKE. WHY DIDN'T YOU TELL ME YOU WANTED TO GO TO JACY'S?

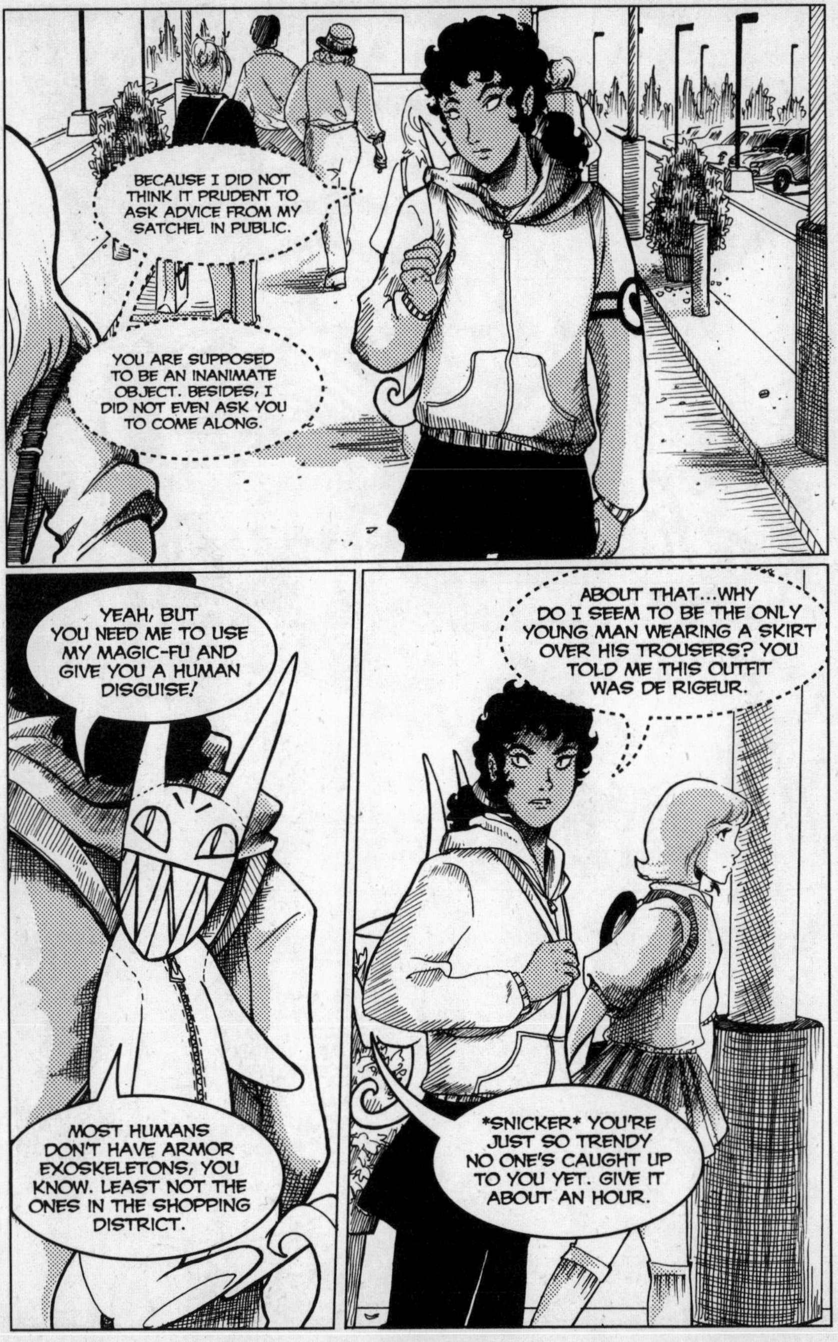
BECAUSE I DID NOT THINK IT PRUDENT TO ASK ADVICE FROM MY SATCHEL IN PUBLIC.
YOU ARE SUPPOSED TO BE AN INANIMATE OBJECT. BESIDES, I DID NOT EVEN ASK YOU TO COME ALONG.
YEAH, BUT YOU NEED ME TO USE MY MAGIC-FU AND GIVE YOU A HUMAN DISGUISE!
MOST HUMANS DON'T HAVE ARMOR EXOSKELETONS, YOU KNOW. LEAST NOT THE ONES IN THE SHOPPING DISTRICT.
ABOUT THAT...WHY DO I SEEM TO BE THE ONLY YOUNG MAN WEARING A SKIRT OVER HIS TROUSERS? YOU TOLD ME THIS OUTFIT WAS DE RIGEUR.
*SNICKER* YOU'RE JUST SO TRENDY NO ONE'S CAUGHT UP TO YOU YET. GIVE IT ABOUT AN HOUR.

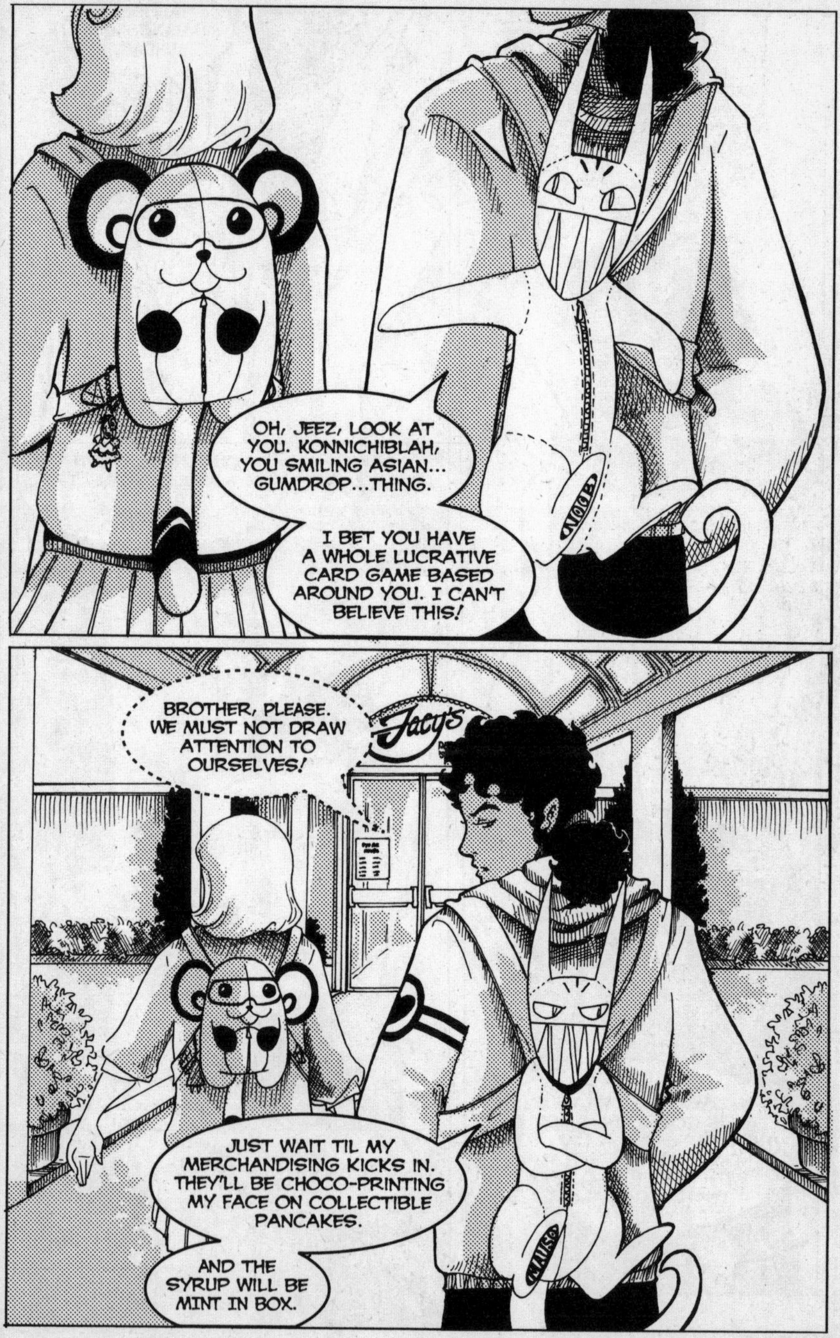
OH, JEEZ, LOOK AT YOU. KONNICHIBLAH, YOU SMILING ASIAN... GUMDROP...THING.
I BET YOU HAVE A WHOLE LUCRATIVE CARD GAME BASED AROUND YOU. I CAN'T BELIEVE THIS!
BROTHER, PLEASE. WE MUST NOT DRAW ATTENTION TO OURSELVES!
Jacy's
JUST WAIT TIL MY MERCHANDISING KICKS IN. THEY'LL BE CHOCO-PRINTING MY FACE ON COLLECTIBLE PANCAKES.
AND THE SYRUP WILL BE MINT IN BOX.

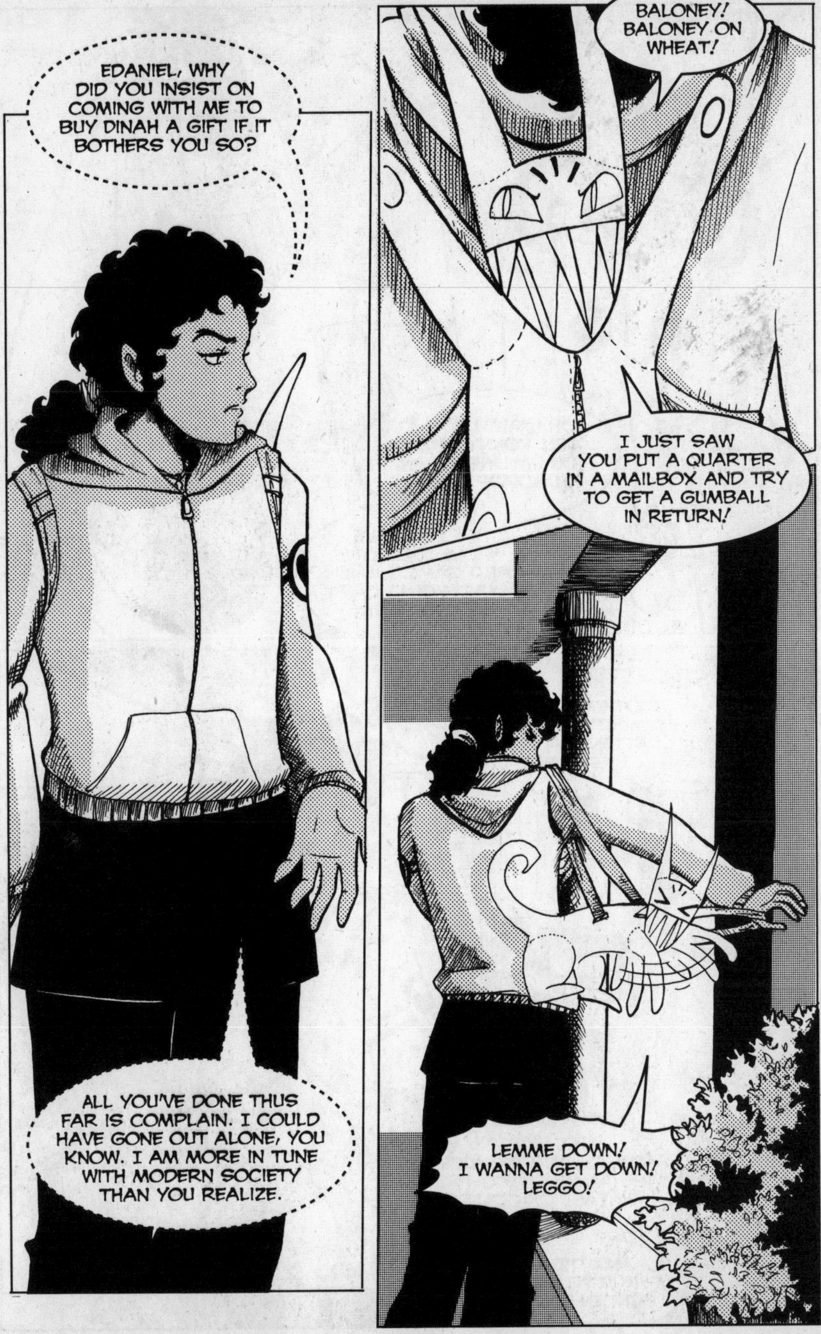
EDANIEL, WHY DID YOU INSIST ON COMING WITH ME TO BUY DINAH A GIFT IF IT BOTHERS YOU SO?
ALL YOU'VE DONE THUS FAR IS COMPLAIN. I COULD HAVE GONE OUT ALONE, YOU KNOW. I AM MORE IN TUNE WITH MODERN SOCIETY THAN YOU REALIZE.
BALONEY! BALONEY ON WHEAT!
I JUST SAW YOU PUT A QUARTER IN A MAILBOX AND TRY TO GET A GUMBALL IN RETURN!
LEMME DOWN! I WANNA GET DOWN! LEGGO!

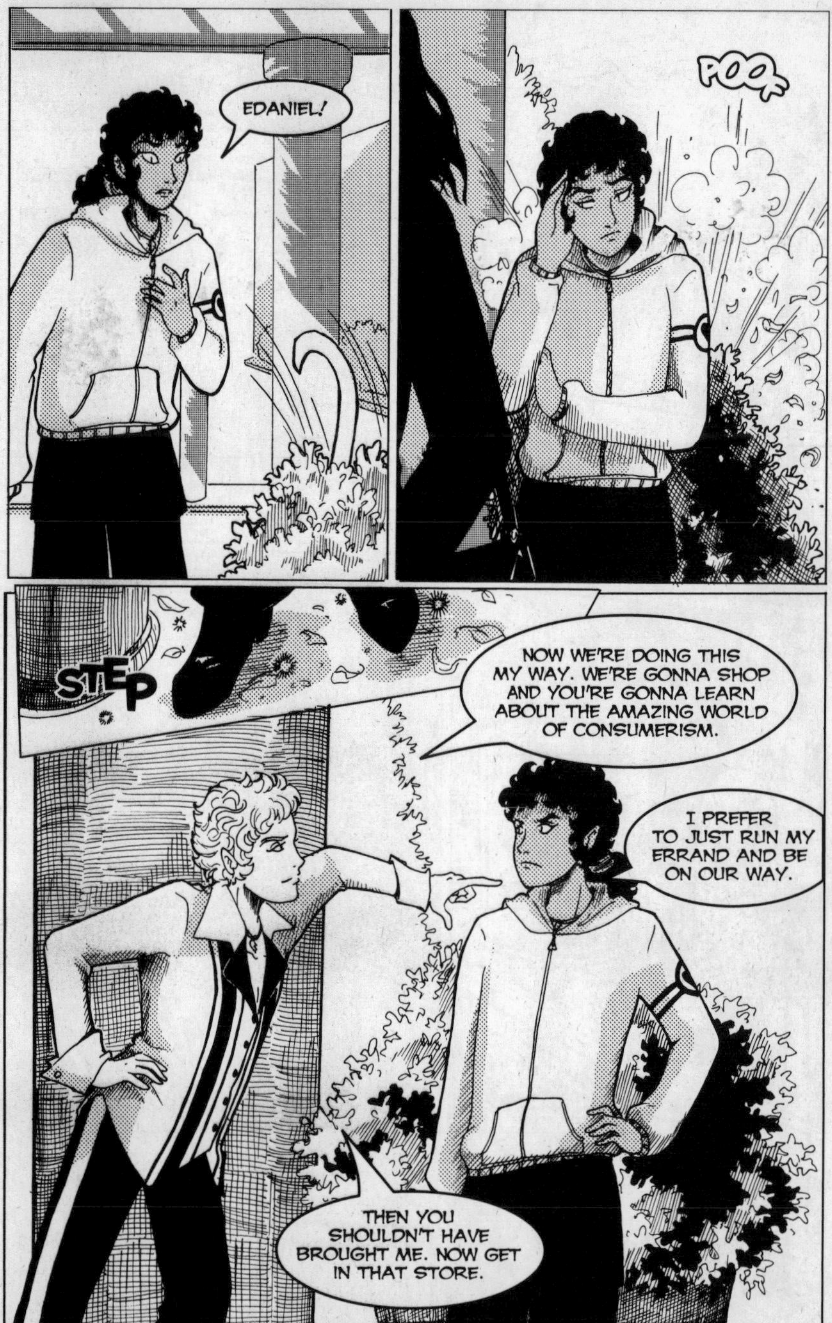
EDANIEL!
POOF
STEP
NOW WE'RE DOING THIS MY WAY. WE'RE GONNA SHOP AND YOU'RE GONNA LEARN ABOUT THE AMAZING WORLD OF CONSUMERISM.
I PREFER TO JUST RUN MY ERRAND AND BE ON OUR WAY.
THEN YOU SHOULDN'T HAVE BROUGHT ME. NOW GET IN THAT STORE.

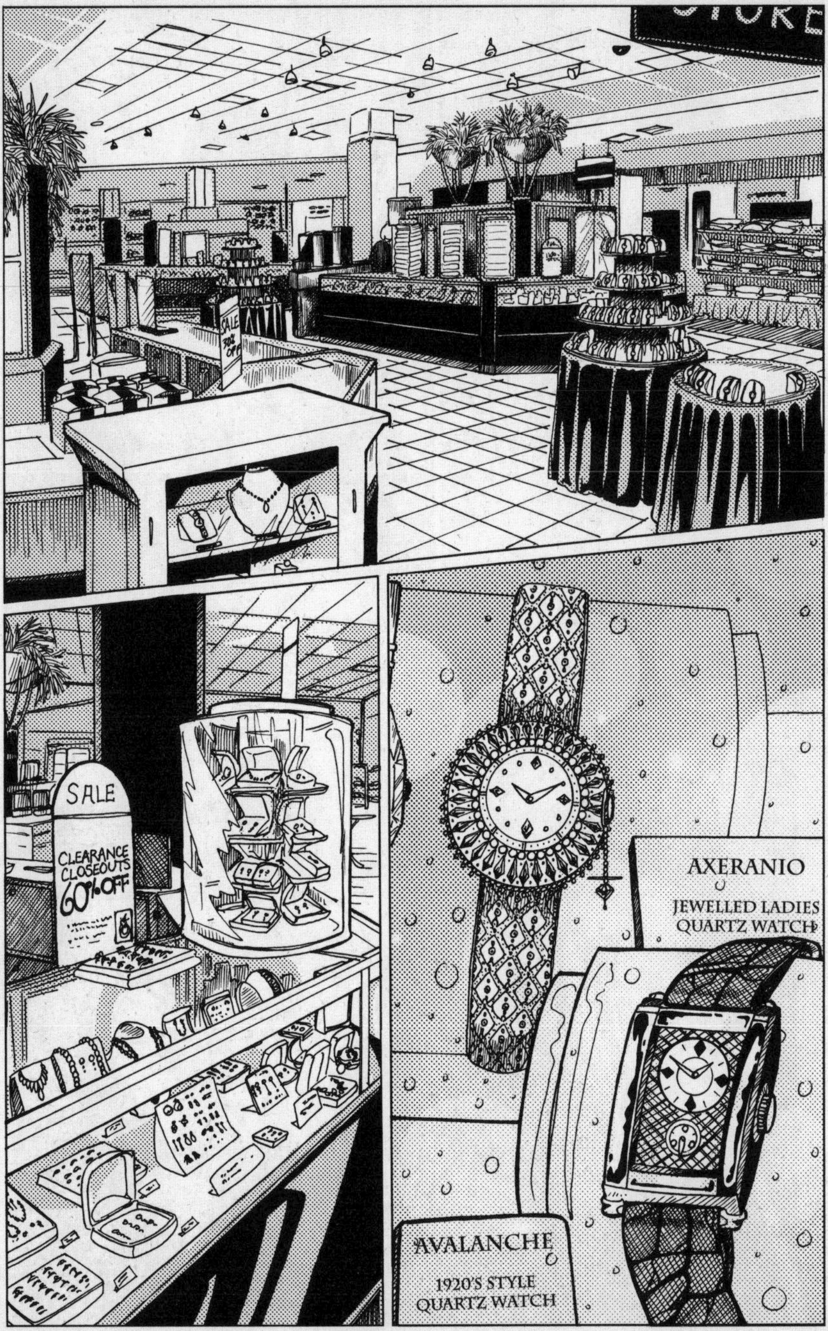
SALE
SALE
CLEARANCE
CLOSEOUTS
60% OFF
AXERANIO
JEWELLED LADIES
QUARTZ WATCH
AVALANCHE
1920'S STYLE
QUARTZ WATCH

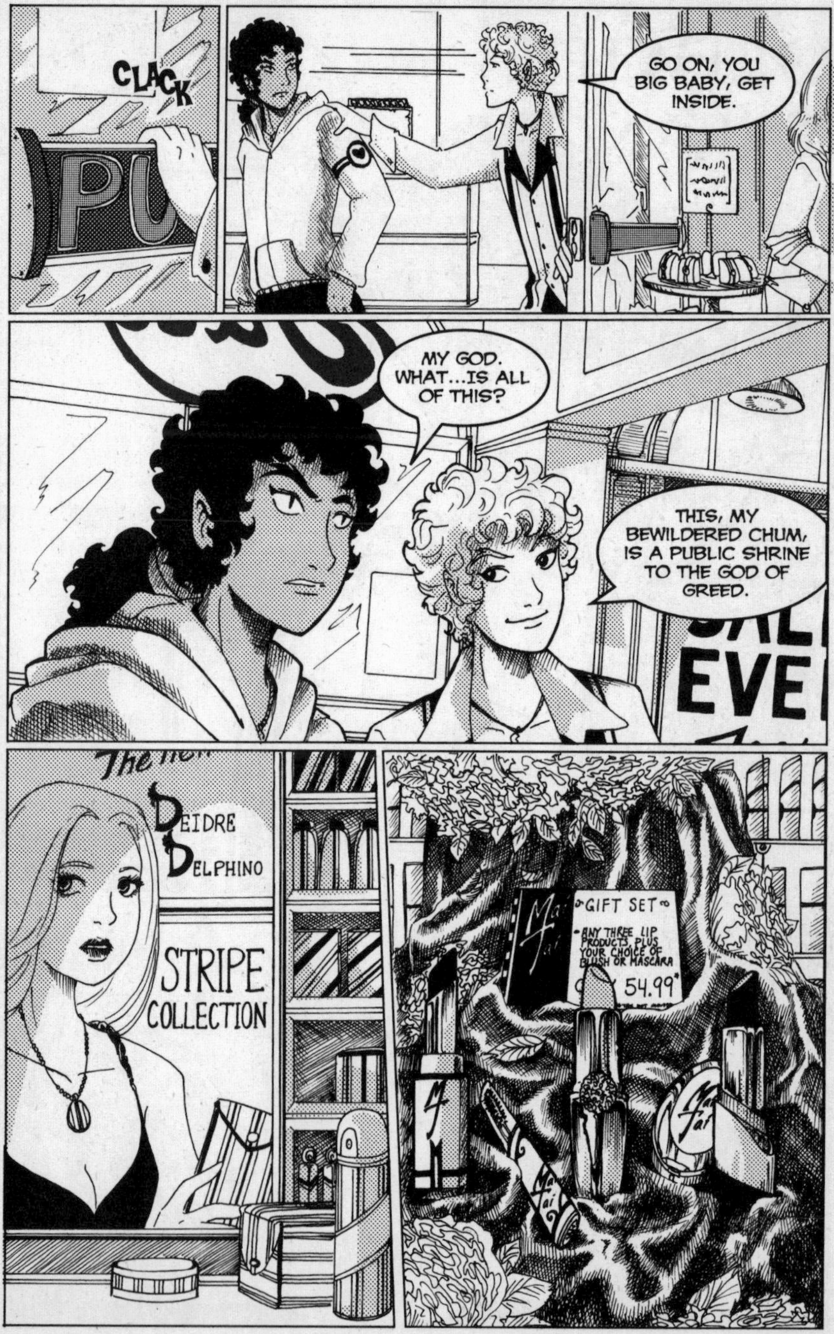
CLACK
GO ON, YOU BIG BABY, GET INSIDE.
MY GOD. WHAT...IS ALL OF THIS?
THIS, MY BEWILDERED CHUM, IS A PUBLIC SHRINE TO THE GOD OF GREED.
DEIDRE DELPHINO
STRIPE COLLECTION
GIFT SET
ANY THREE LIP PRODUCTS, PLUS YOUR CHOICE OF BLUSH OR MASCARA
54.99*

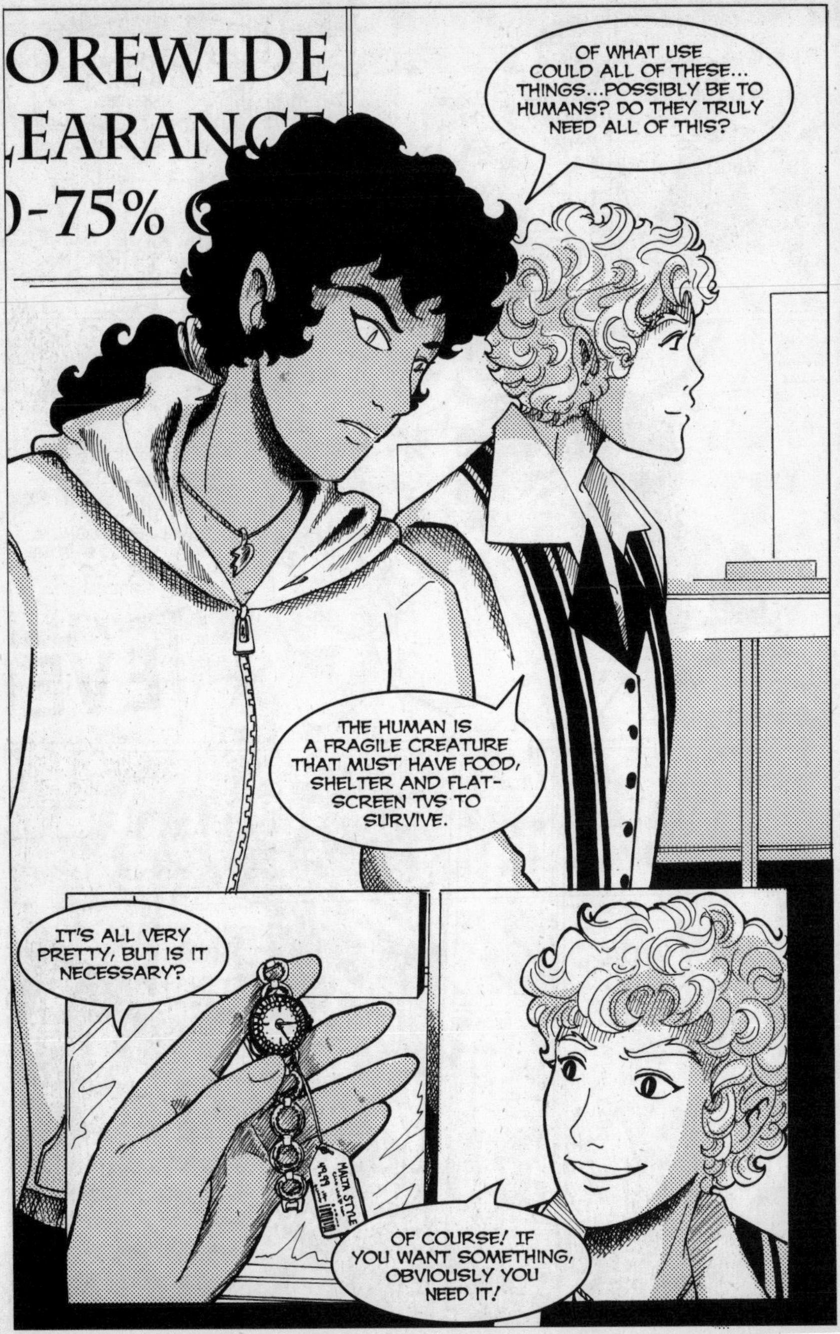
OREWIDE
LEARANCE
0-75%
OF WHAT USE COULD ALL OF THESE... THINGS...POSSIBLY BE TO HUMANS? DO THEY TRULY NEED ALL OF THIS?
THE HUMAN IS A FRAGILE CREATURE THAT MUST HAVE FOOD, SHELTER AND FLAT-SCREEN TVS TO SURVIVE.
IT'S ALL VERY PRETTY, BUT IS IT NECESSARY?
MALTA STYLE
OF COURSE! IF YOU WANT SOMETHING, OBVIOUSLY YOU NEED IT!

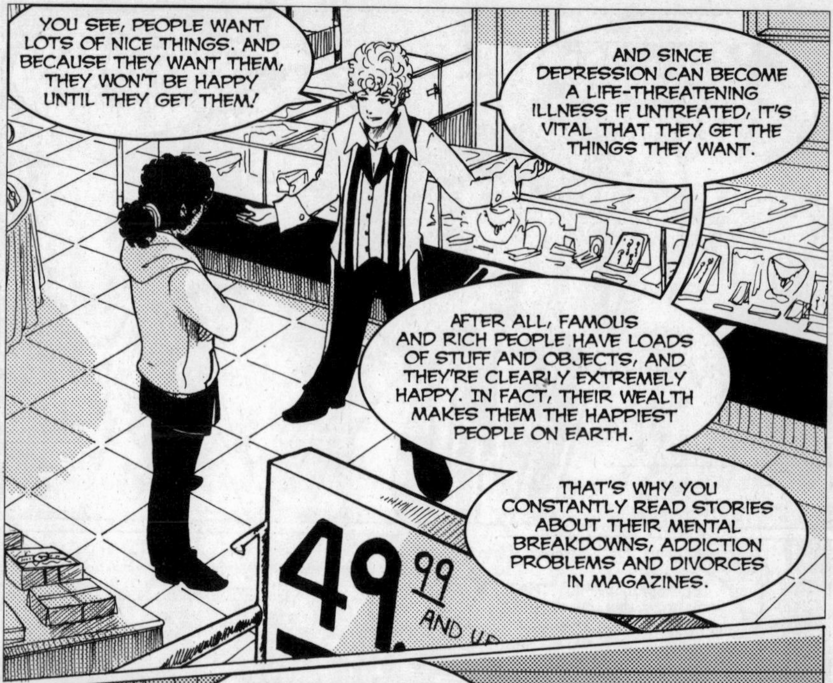
YOU SEE, PEOPLE WANT LOTS OF NICE THINGS. AND BECAUSE THEY WANT THEM, THEY WON'T BE HAPPY UNTIL THEY GET THEM!
AND SINCE DEPRESSION CAN BECOME A LIFE-THREATENING ILLNESS IF UNTREATED, IT'S VITAL THAT THEY GET THE THINGS THEY WANT.
AFTER ALL, FAMOUS AND RICH PEOPLE HAVE LOADS OF STUFF AND OBJECTS, AND THEY'RE CLEARLY EXTREMELY HAPPY. IN FACT, THEIR WEALTH MAKES THEM THE HAPPIEST PEOPLE ON EARTH.
THAT'S WHY YOU CONSTANTLY READ STORIES ABOUT THEIR MENTAL BREAKDOWNS, ADDICTION PROBLEMS AND DIVORCES IN MAGAZINES.
49.99
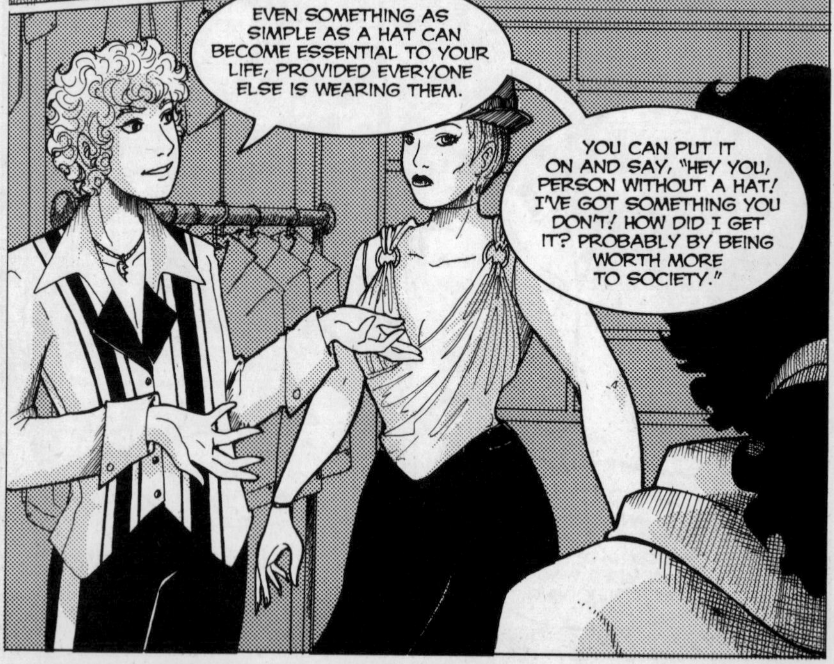
EVEN SOMETHING AS SIMPLE AS A HAT CAN BECOME ESSENTIAL TO YOUR LIFE, PROVIDED EVERYONE ELSE IS WEARING THEM.
YOU CAN PUT IT ON AND SAY, "HEY YOU, PERSON WITHOUT A HAT! I'VE GOT SOMETHING YOU DON'T! HOW DID I GET IT? PROBABLY BY BEING WORTH MORE TO SOCIETY."

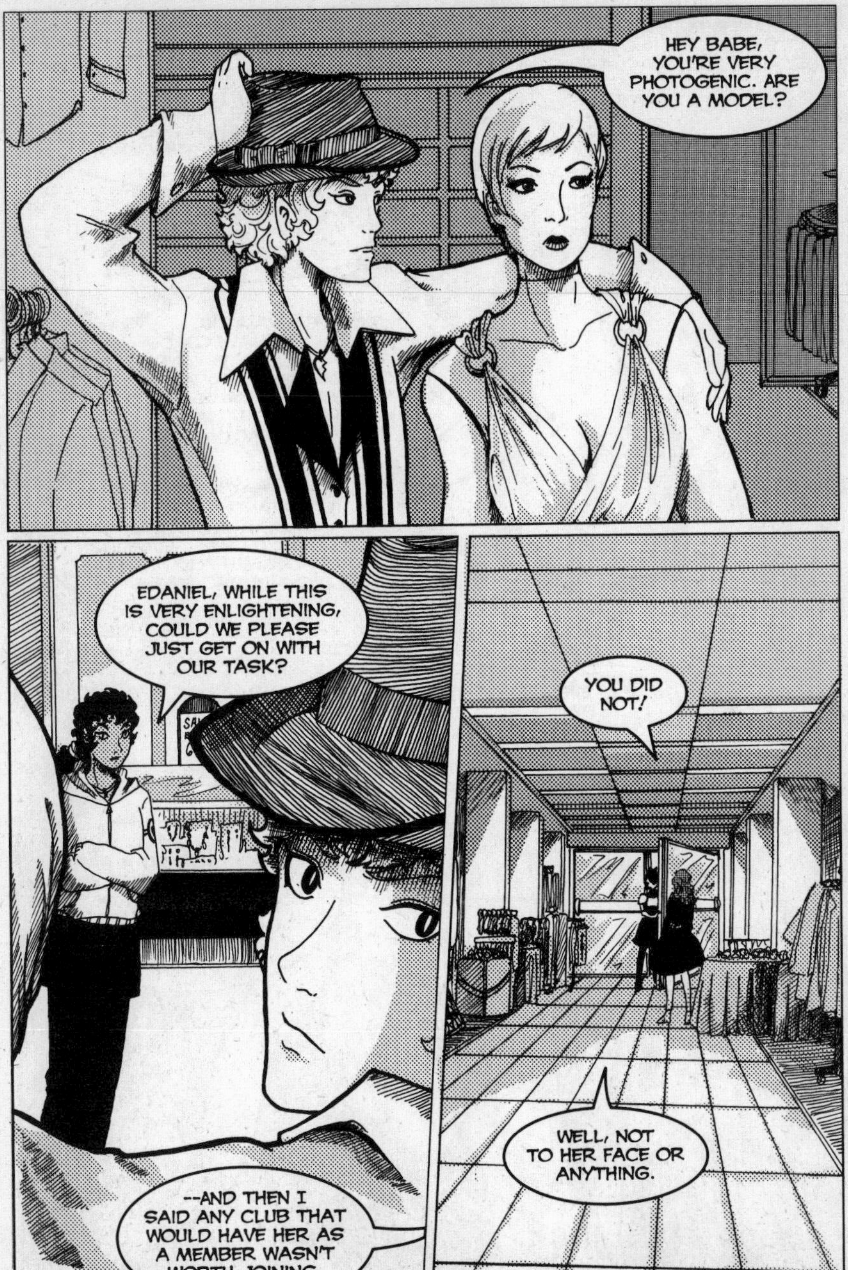
HEY BABE, YOU'RE VERY PHOTOGENIC. ARE YOU A MODEL?
EDANIEL, WHILE THIS IS VERY ENLIGHTENING, COULD WE PLEASE JUST GET ON WITH OUR TASK?
--AND THEN I SAID ANY CLUB THAT WOULD HAVE HER AS A MEMBER WASN'T WORTH JOINING.
YOU DID NOT!
WELL, NOT TO HER FACE OR ANYTHING.

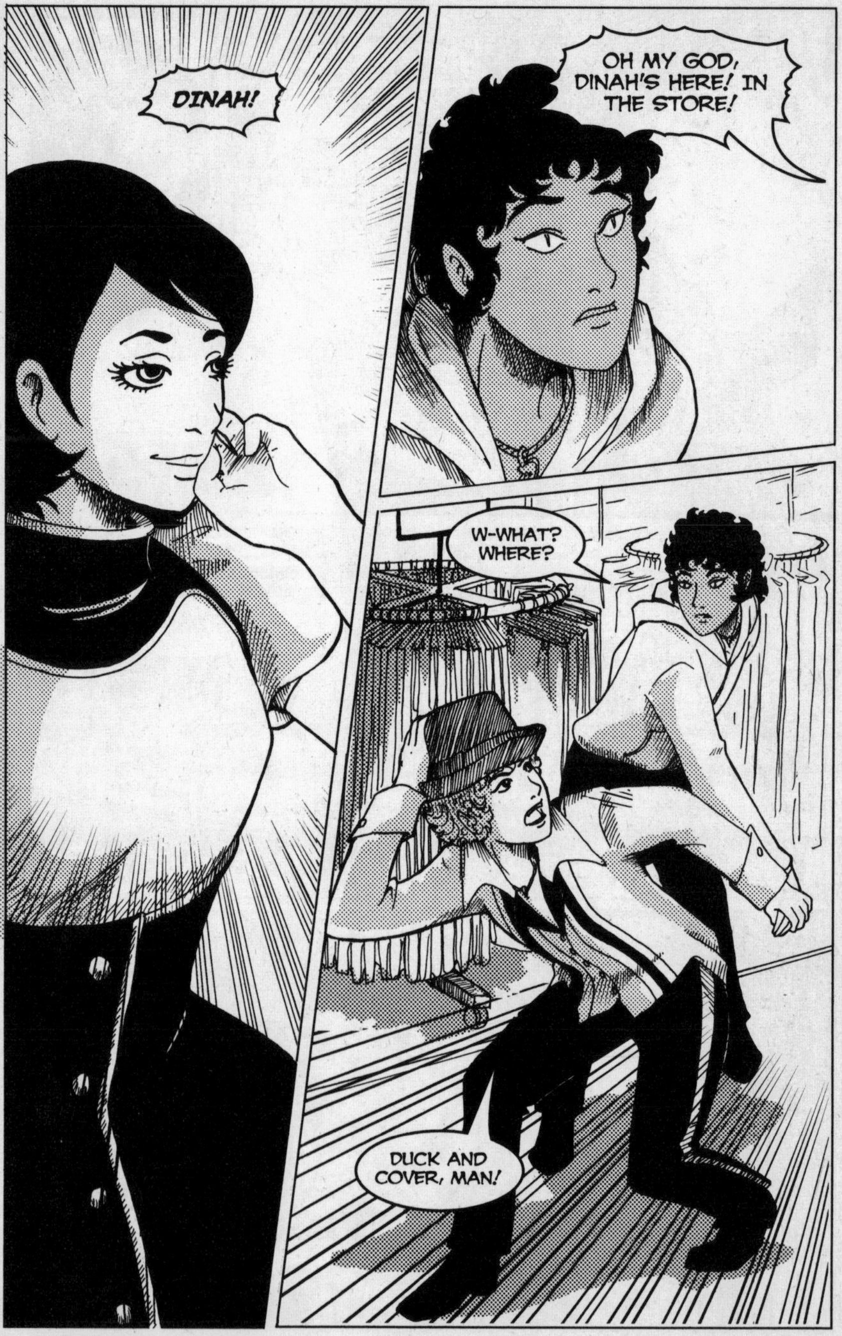
DINAH!
OH MY GOD, DINAH'S HERE! IN THE STORE!
W-WHAT? WHERE?
DUCK AND COVER, MAN!

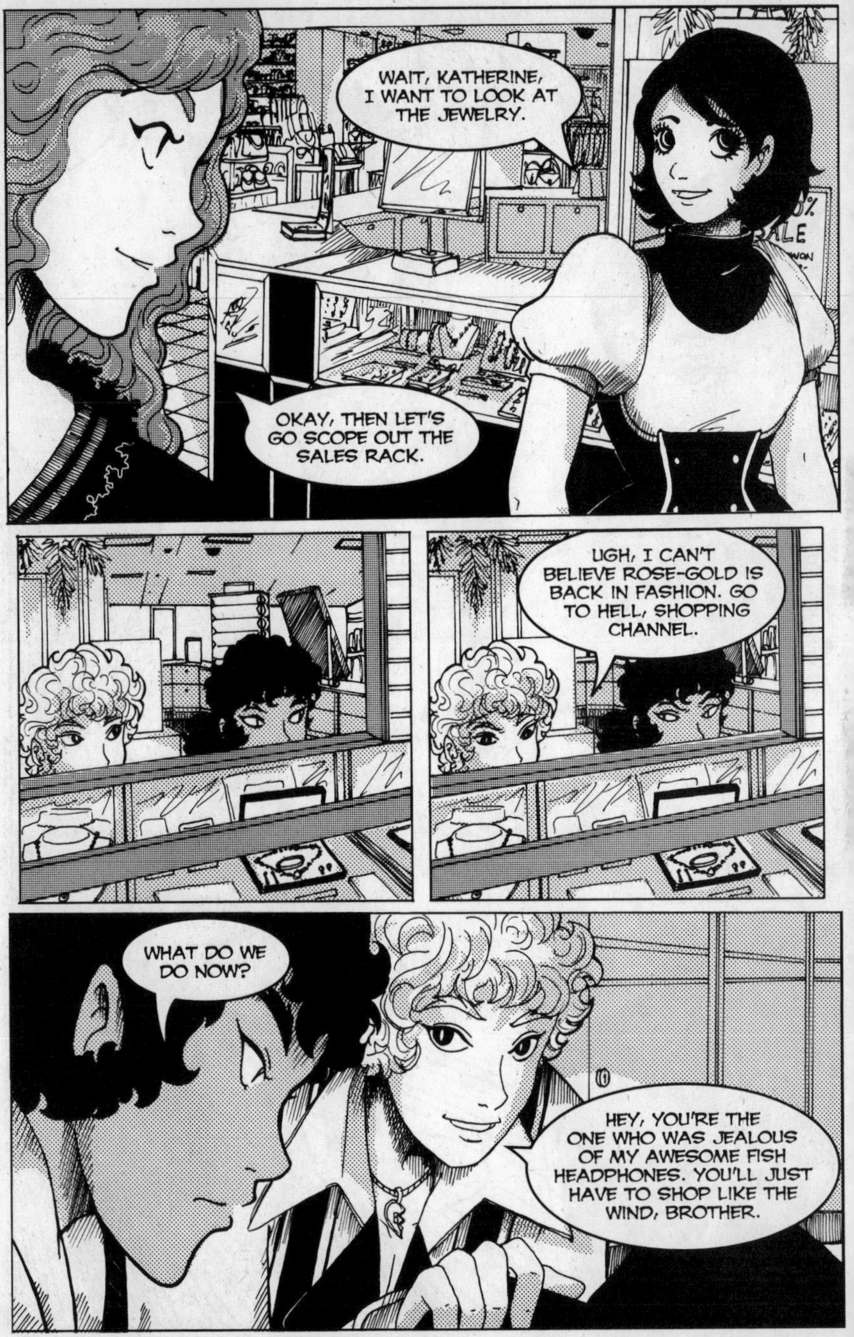
WAIT, KATHERINE, I WANT TO LOOK AT THE JEWELRY.
OKAY, THEN LET'S GO SCOPE OUT THE SALES RACK.
UGH, I CAN'T BELIEVE ROSE-GOLD IS BACK IN FASHION. GO TO HELL, SHOPPING CHANNEL.
WHAT DO WE DO NOW?
HEY, YOU'RE THE ONE WHO WAS JEALOUS OF MY AWESOME FISH HEADPHONES. YOU'LL JUST HAVE TO SHOP LIKE THE WIND, BROTHER.

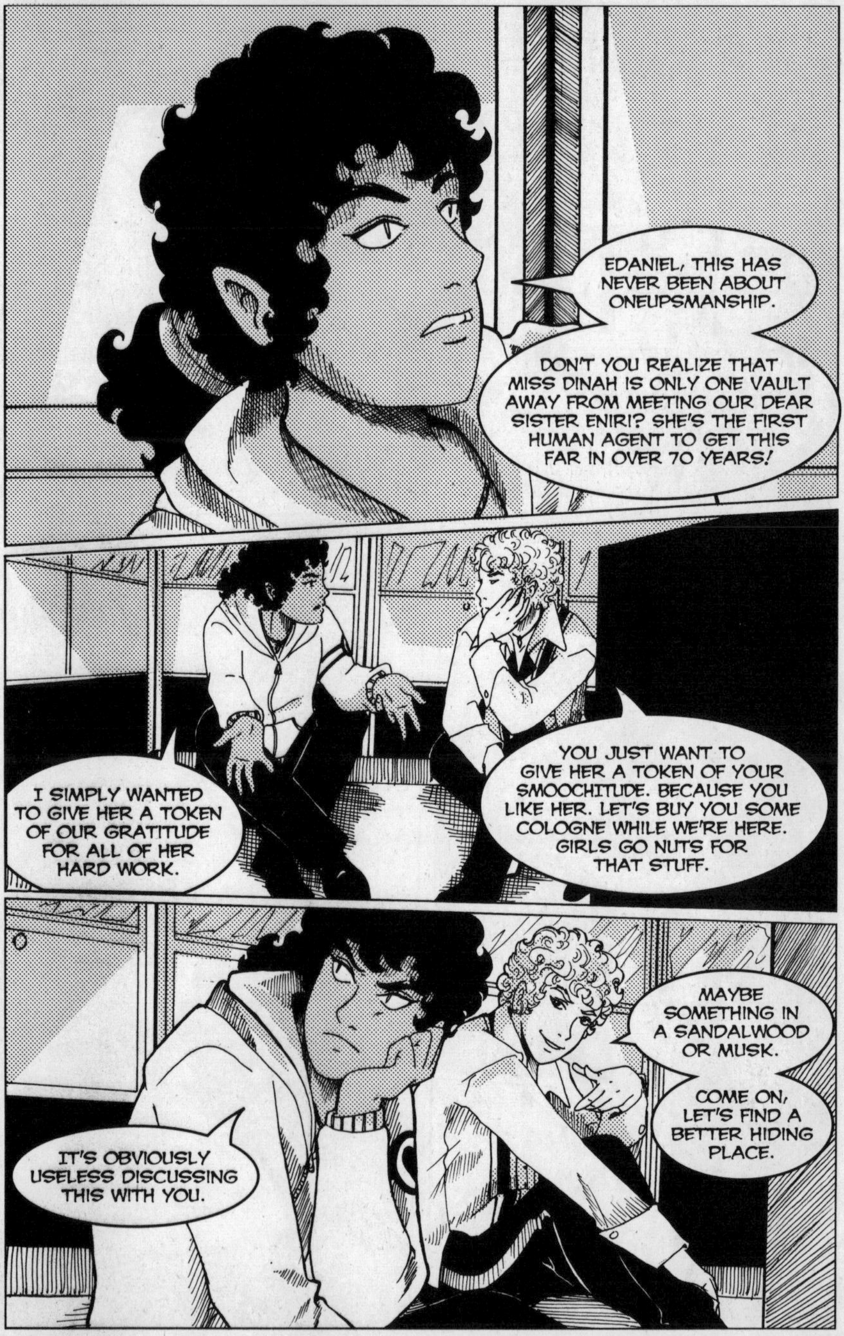
EDANIEL, THIS HAS NEVER BEEN ABOUT ONEUPSMANSHIP.
DON'T YOU REALIZE THAT MISS DINAH IS ONLY ONE VAULT AWAY FROM MEETING OUR DEAR SISTER ENIRI? SHE'S THE FIRST HUMAN AGENT TO GET THIS FAR IN OVER 70 YEARS!
I SIMPLY WANTED TO GIVE HER A TOKEN OF OUR GRATITUDE FOR ALL OF HER HARD WORK.
YOU JUST WANT TO GIVE HER A TOKEN OF YOUR SMOOCHITUDE. BECAUSE YOU LIKE HER. LET'S BUY YOU SOME COLOGNE WHILE WE'RE HERE. GIRLS GO NUTS FOR THAT STUFF.
IT'S OBVIOUSLY USELESS DISCUSSING THIS WITH YOU.
MAYBE SOMETHING IN A SANDALWOOD OR MUSK.
COME ON, LET'S FIND A BETTER HIDING PLACE.

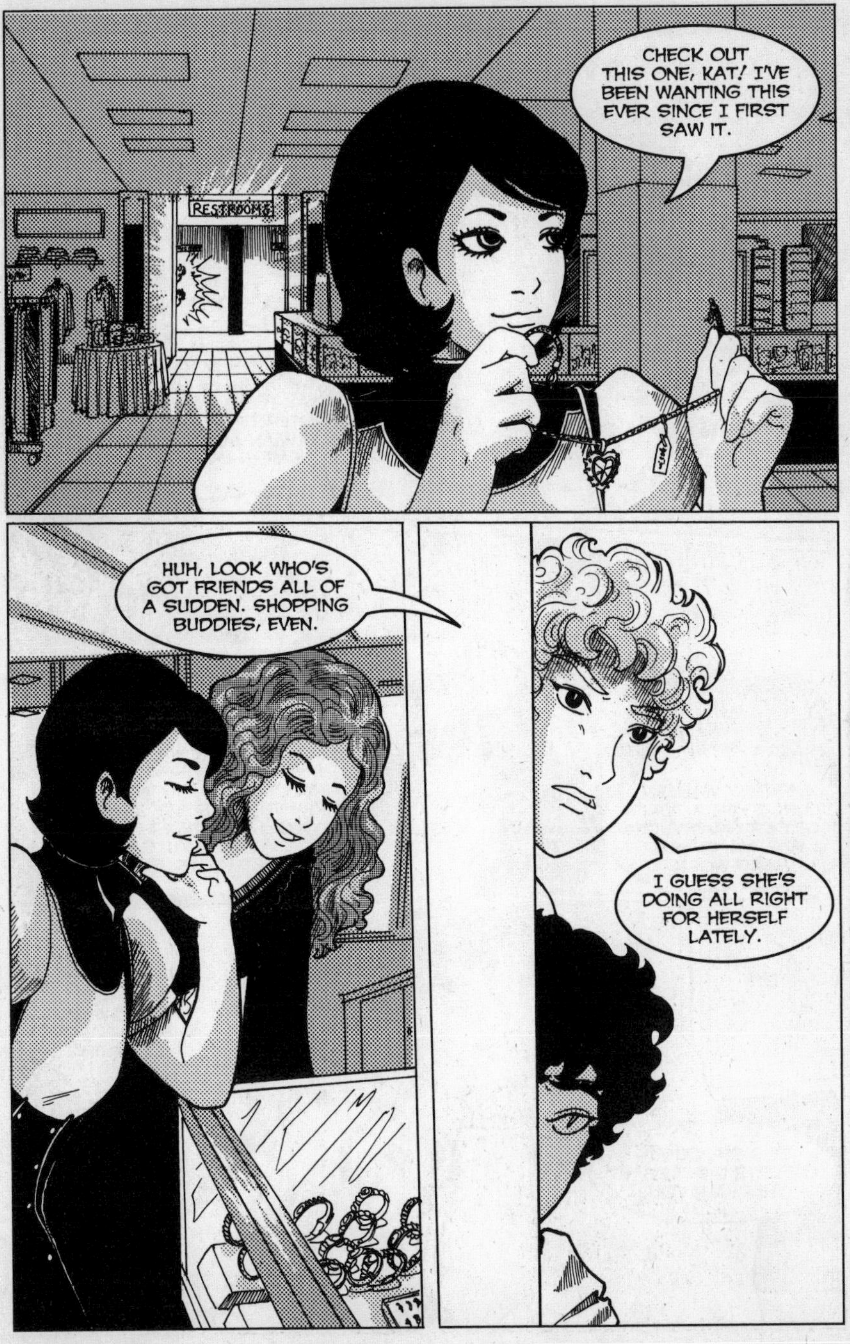
CHECK OUT THIS ONE, KAT! I'VE BEEN WANTING THIS EVER SINCE I FIRST SAW IT.
RESTROOMS
HUH, LOOK WHO'S GOT FRIENDS ALL OF A SUDDEN. SHOPPING BUDDIES, EVEN.
I GUESS SHE'S DOING ALL RIGHT FOR HERSELF LATELY.

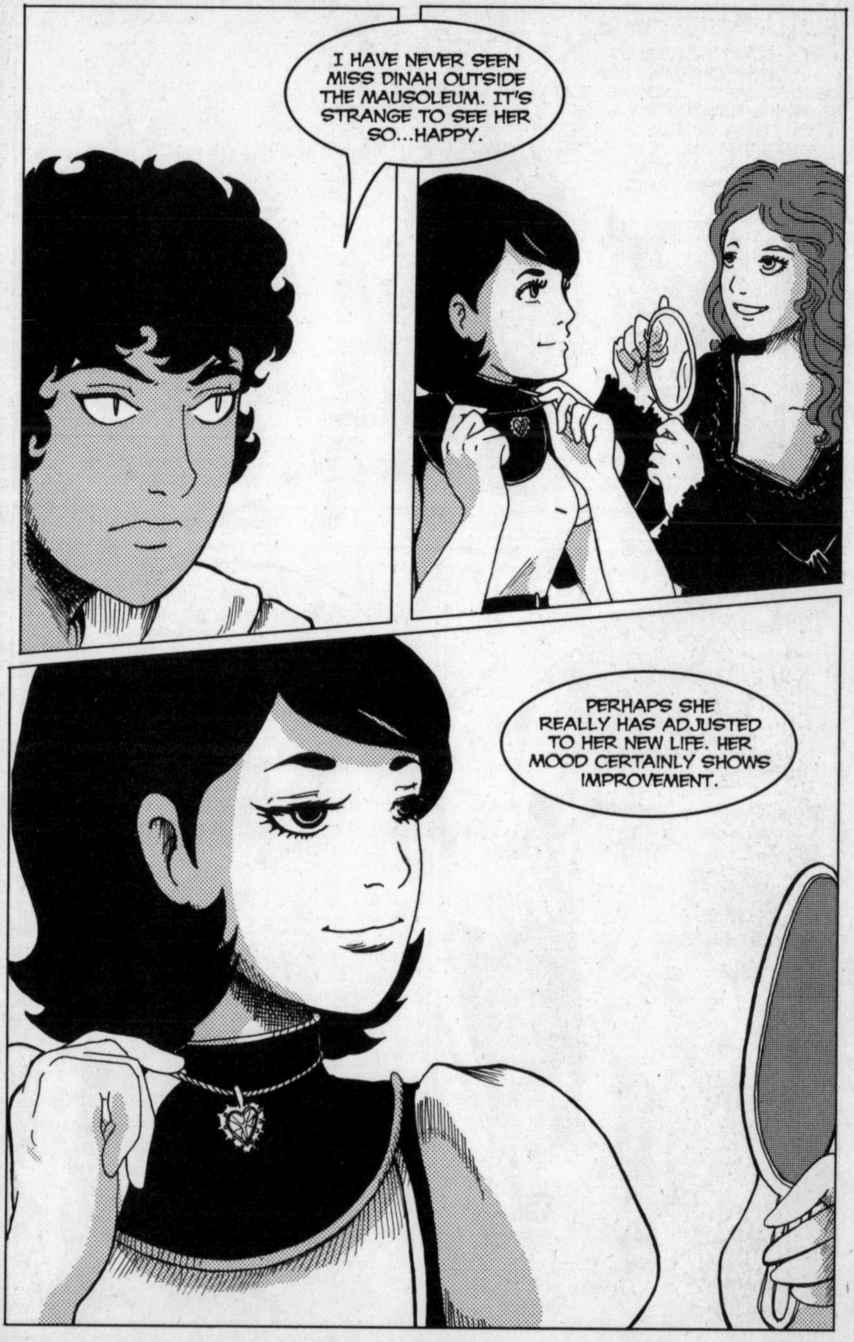
I HAVE NEVER SEEN MISS DINAH OUTSIDE THE MAUSOLEUM. IT'S STRANGE TO SEE HER SO...HAPPY.
PERHAPS SHE REALLY HAS ADJUSTED TO HER NEW LIFE. HER MOOD CERTAINLY SHOWS IMPROVEMENT.

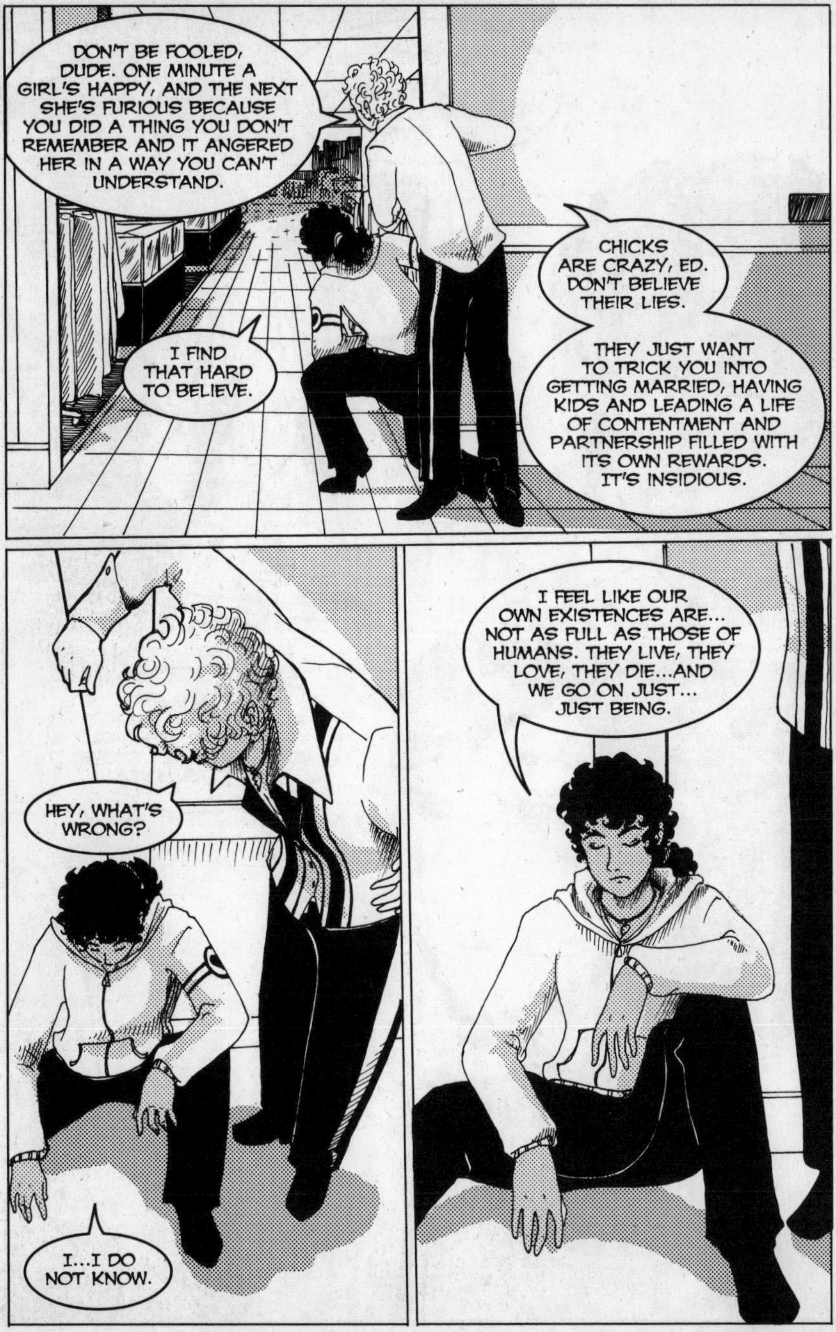
DON'T BE FOOLED, DUDE. ONE MINUTE A GIRL'S HAPPY, AND THE NEXT SHE'S FURIOUS BECAUSE YOU DID A THING YOU DON'T REMEMBER AND IT ANGERED HER IN A WAY YOU CAN'T UNDERSTAND.
I FIND THAT HARD TO BELIEVE.
CHICKS ARE CRAZY, ED. DON'T BELIEVE THEIR LIES.
THEY JUST WANT TO TRICK YOU INTO GETTING MARRIED, HAVING KIDS AND LEADING A LIFE OF CONTENTMENT AND PARTNERSHIP FILLED WITH ITS OWN REWARDS. IT'S INSIDIOUS.
HEY, WHAT'S WRONG?
I...I DO NOT KNOW.
I FEEL LIKE OUR OWN EXISTENCES ARE... NOT AS FULL AS THOSE OF HUMANS. THEY LIVE, THEY LOVE, THEY DIE...AND WE GO ON JUST... JUST BEING.

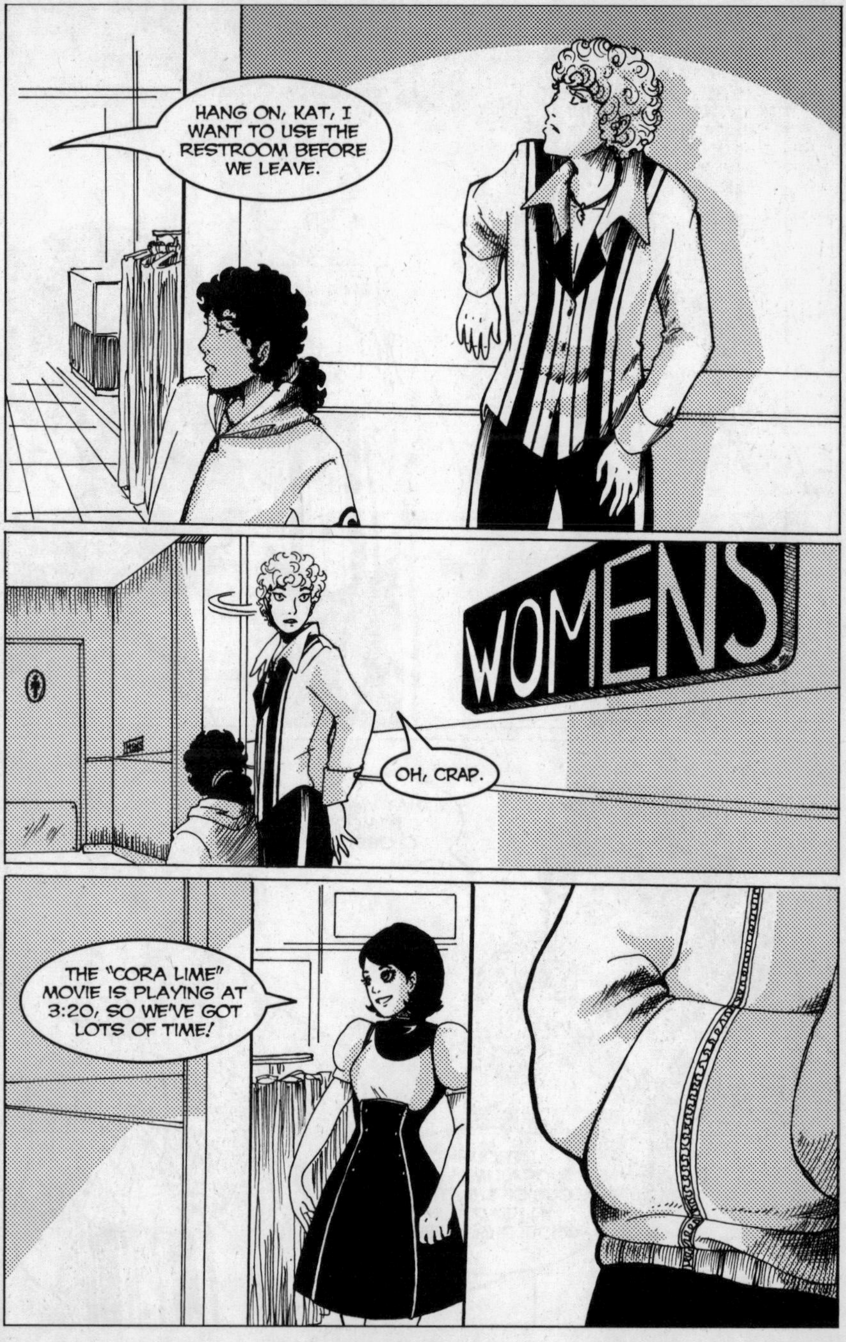
HANG ON, KAT, I WANT TO USE THE RESTROOM BEFORE WE LEAVE.
WOMENS
OH, CRAP.
THE "CORA LIME" MOVIE IS PLAYING AT 3:20, SO WE'VE GOT LOTS OF TIME!

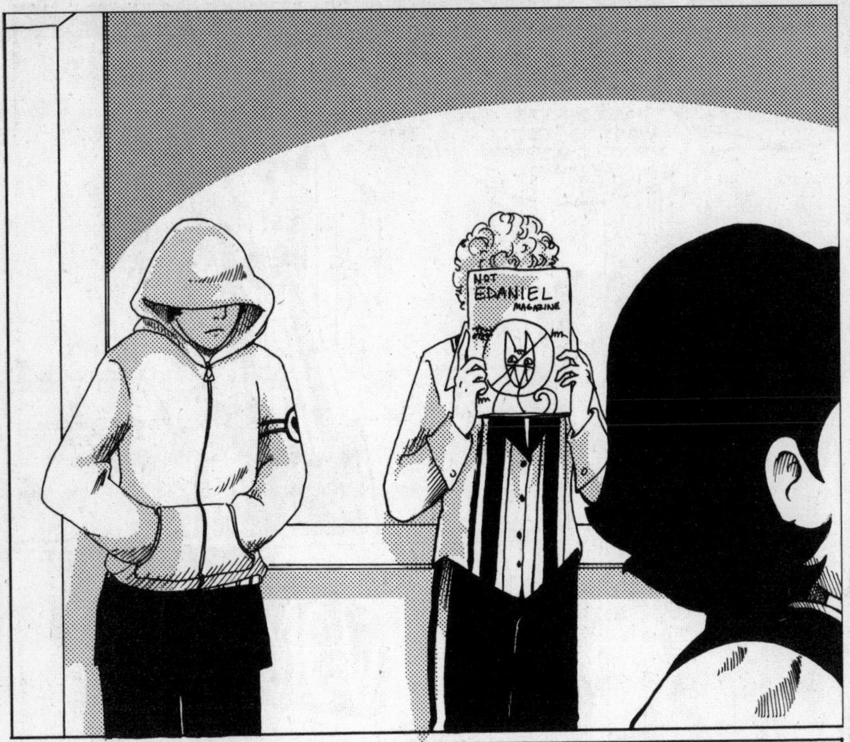
NOT EDANIEL MAGAZINE

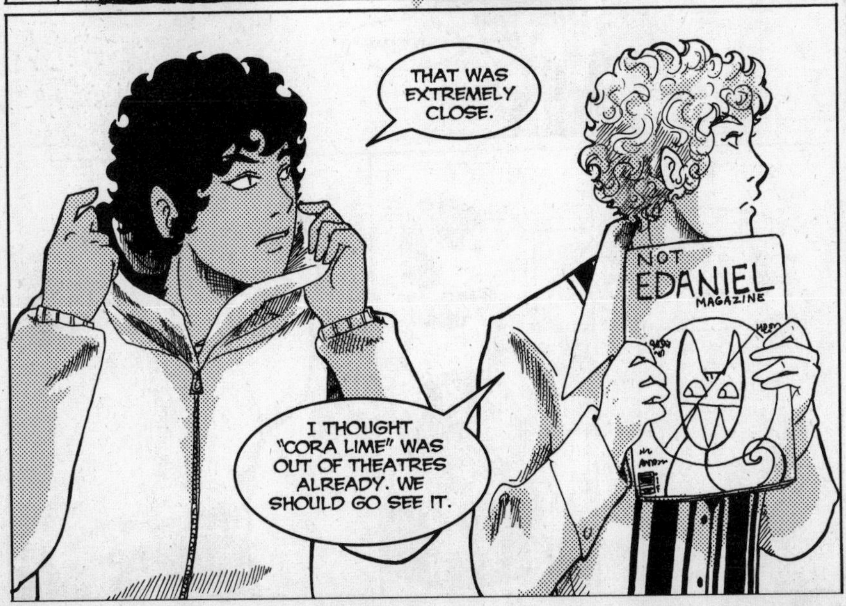
THAT WAS EXTREMELY CLOSE.
NOT EDANIEL MAGAZINE
I THOUGHT "CORA LIME" WAS OUT OF THEATRES ALREADY. WE SHOULD GO SEE IT.

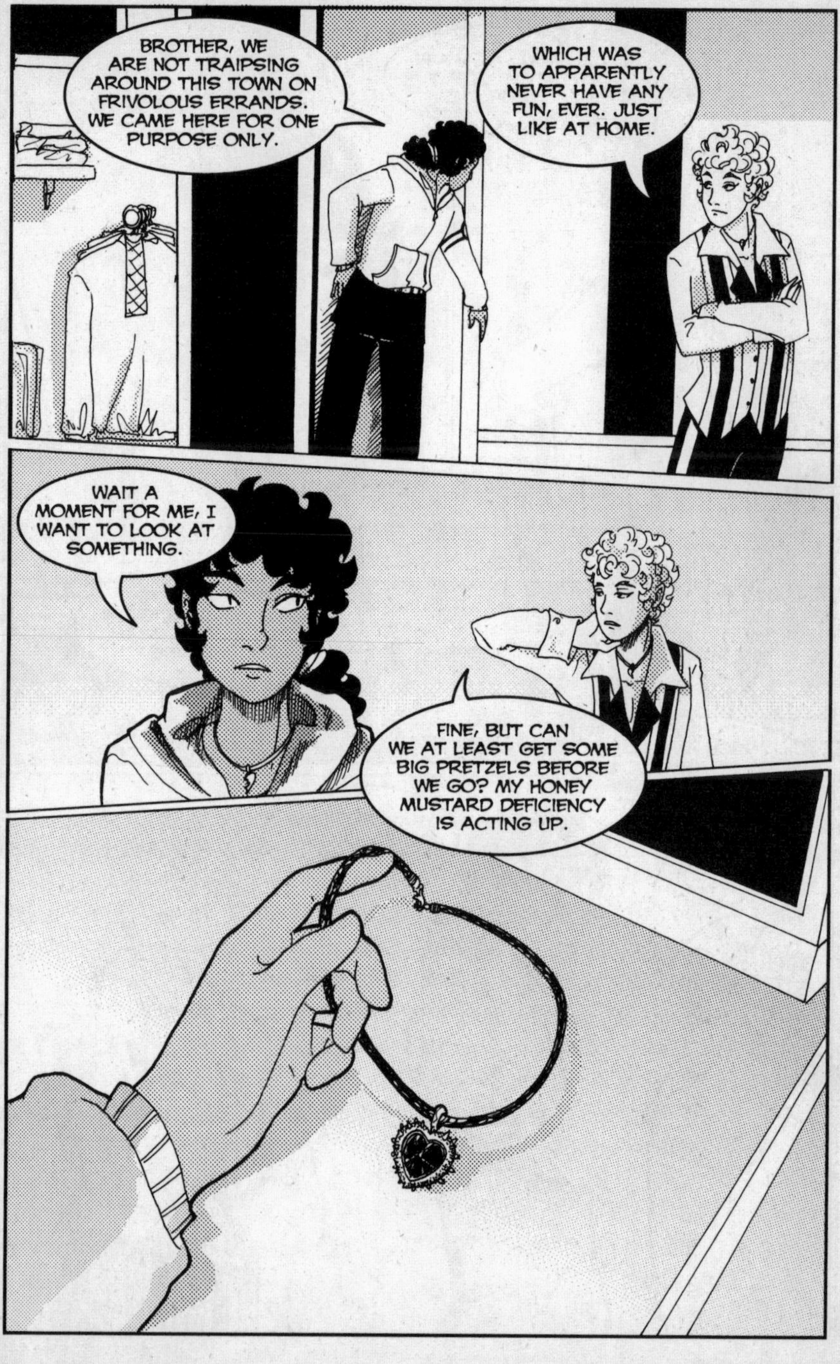
BROTHER, WE ARE NOT TRAIPSING AROUND THIS TOWN ON FRIVOLOUS ERRANDS. WE CAME HERE FOR ONE PURPOSE ONLY.
WHICH WAS TO APPARENTLY NEVER HAVE ANY FUN, EVER. JUST LIKE AT HOME.
WAIT A MOMENT FOR ME, I WANT TO LOOK AT SOMETHING.
FINE, BUT CAN WE AT LEAST GET SOME BIG PRETZELS BEFORE WE GO? MY HONEY MUSTARD DEFICIENCY IS ACTING UP.

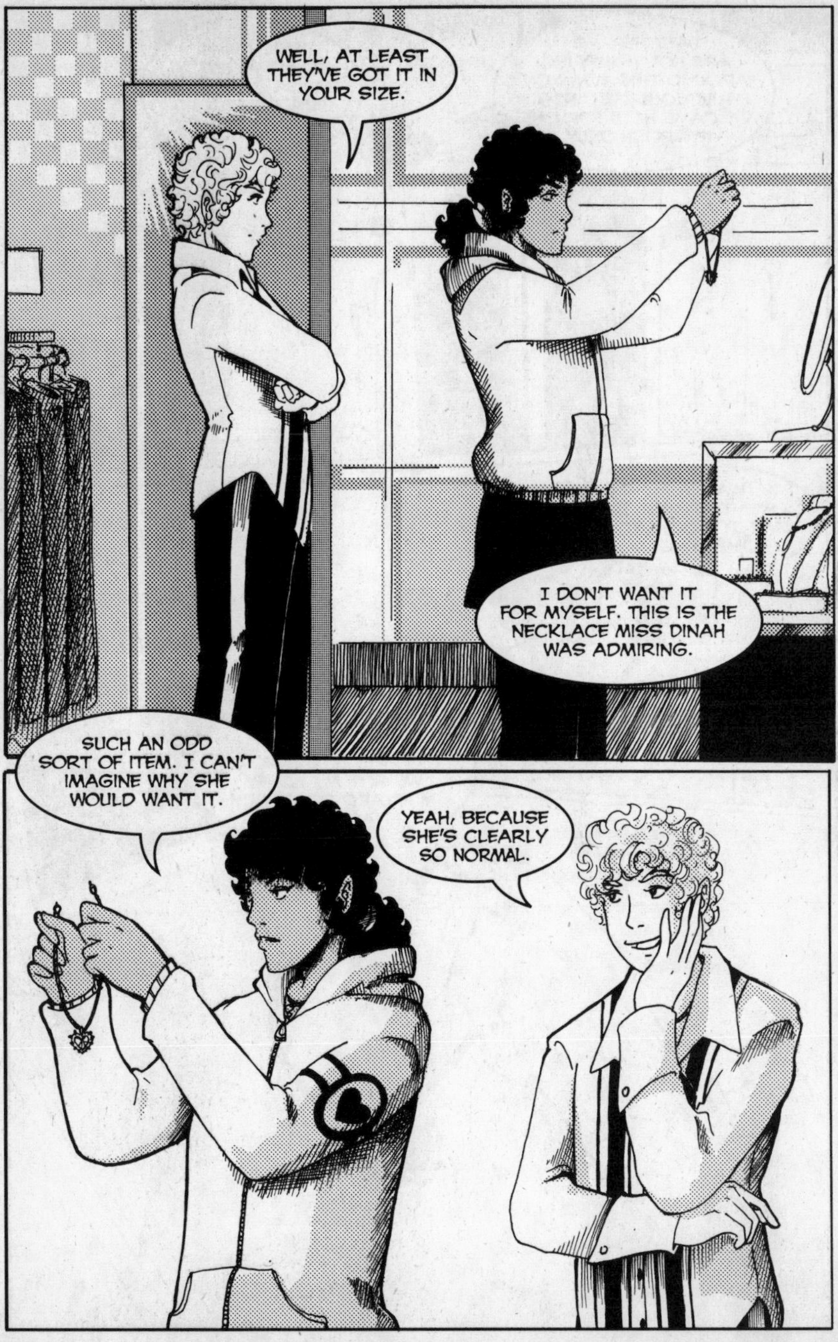
WELL, AT LEAST THEY'VE GOT IT IN YOUR SIZE.
I DON'T WANT IT FOR MYSELF. THIS IS THE NECKLACE MISS DINAH WAS ADMIRING.
SUCH AN ODD SORT OF ITEM. I CAN'T IMAGINE WHY SHE WOULD WANT IT.
YEAH, BECAUSE SHE'S CLEARLY SO NORMAL.

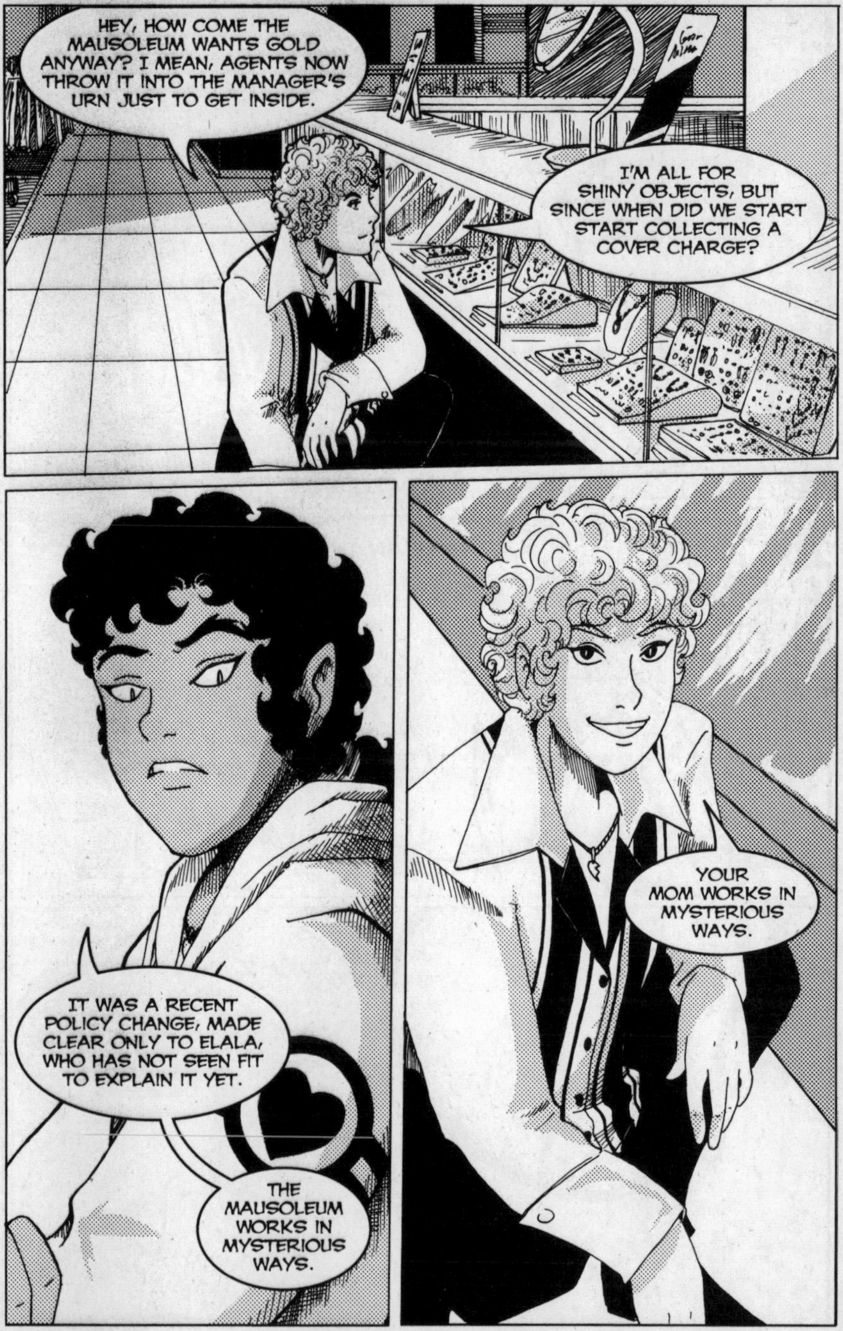
HEY, HOW COME THE MAUSOLEUM WANTS GOLD ANYWAY? I MEAN, AGENTS NOW THROW IT INTO THE MANAGER'S URN JUST TO GET INSIDE.
I'M ALL FOR SHINY OBJECTS, BUT SINCE WHEN DID WE START START COLLECTING A COVER CHARGE?
IT WAS A RECENT POLICY CHANGE, MADE CLEAR ONLY TO ELALA, WHO HAS NOT SEEN FIT TO EXPLAIN IT YET.
THE MAUSOLEUM WORKS IN MYSTERIOUS WAYS.
YOUR MOM WORKS IN MYSTERIOUS WAYS.

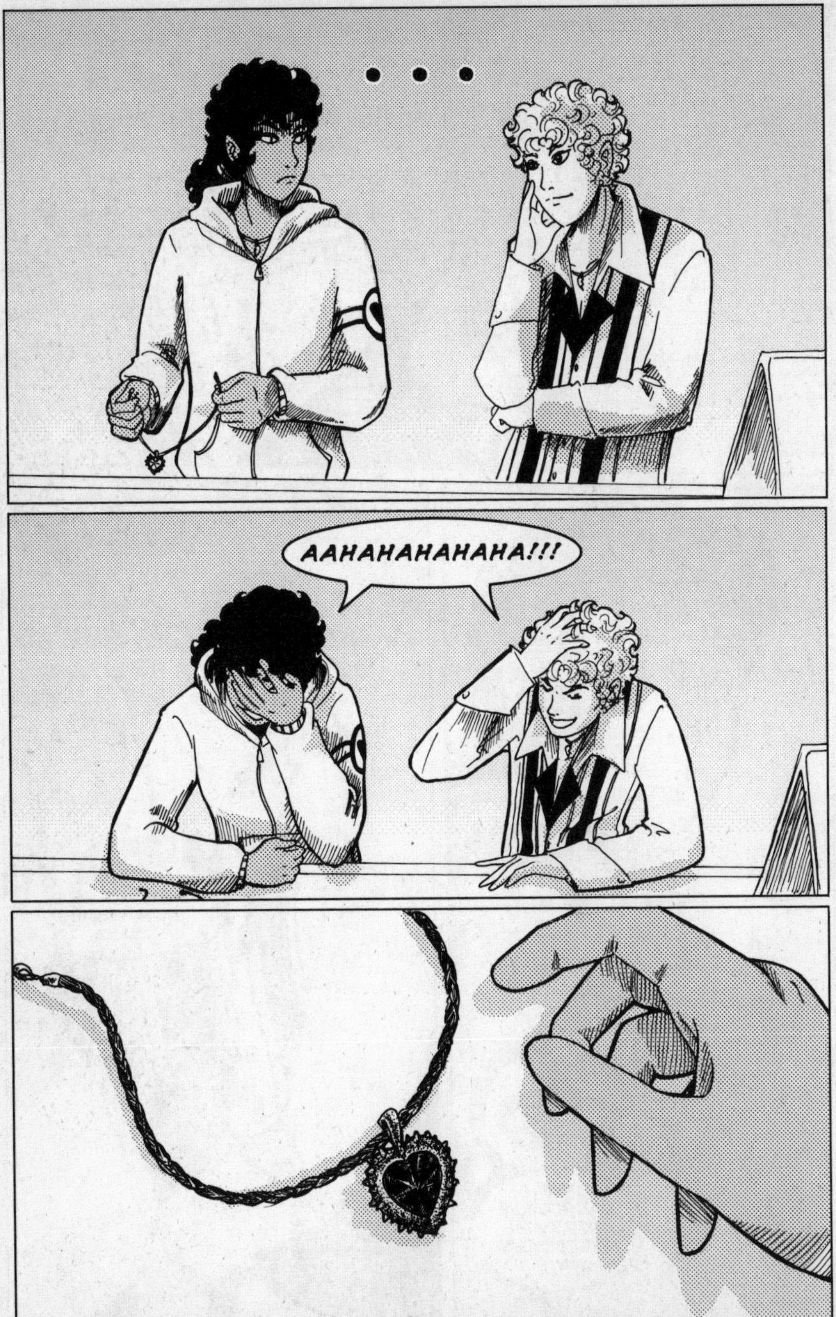
• • •
AAHAHAHAHAHA!!!

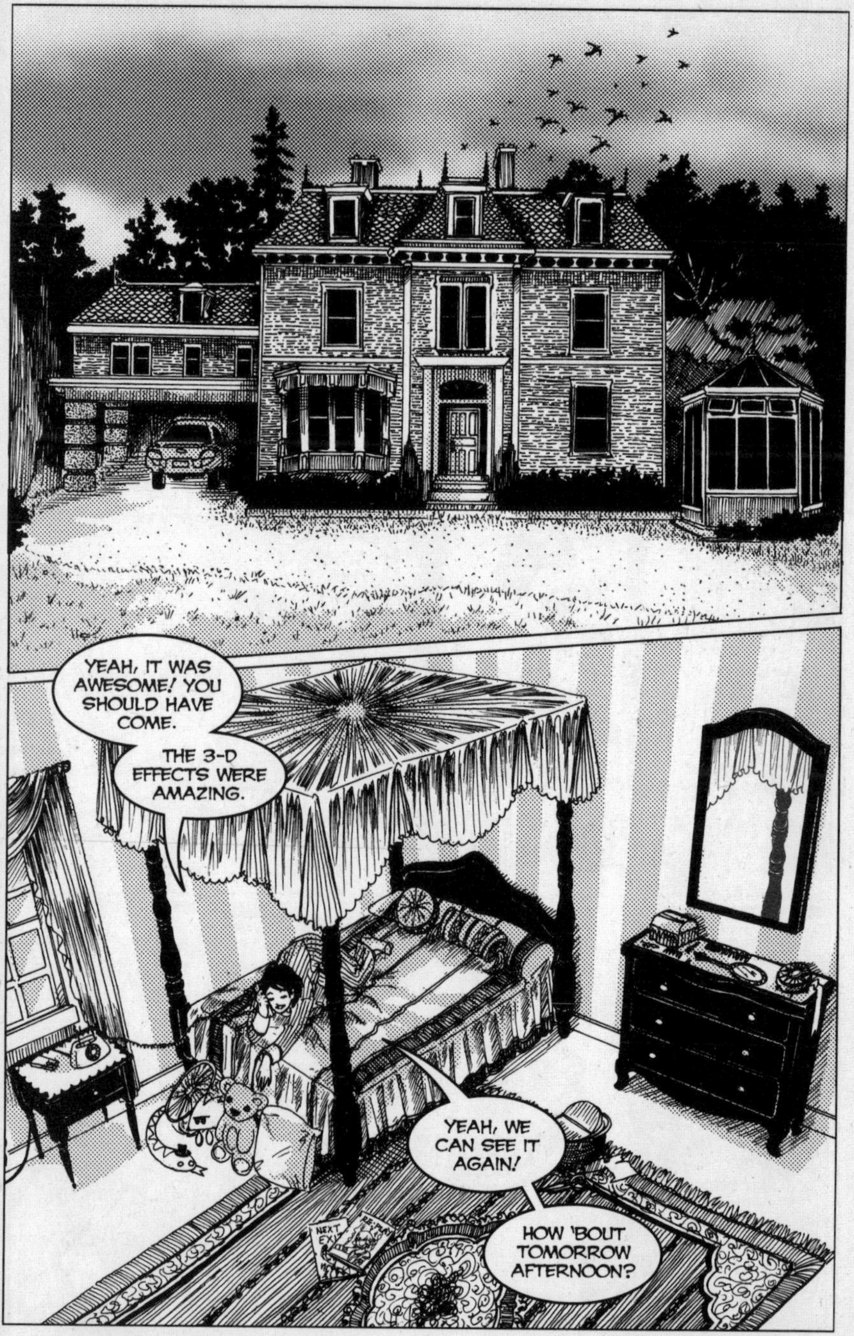
YEAH, IT WAS AWESOME! YOU SHOULD HAVE COME.
THE 3-D EFFECTS WERE AMAZING.
YEAH, WE CAN SEE IT AGAIN!
HOW 'BOUT TOMORROW AFTERNOON?

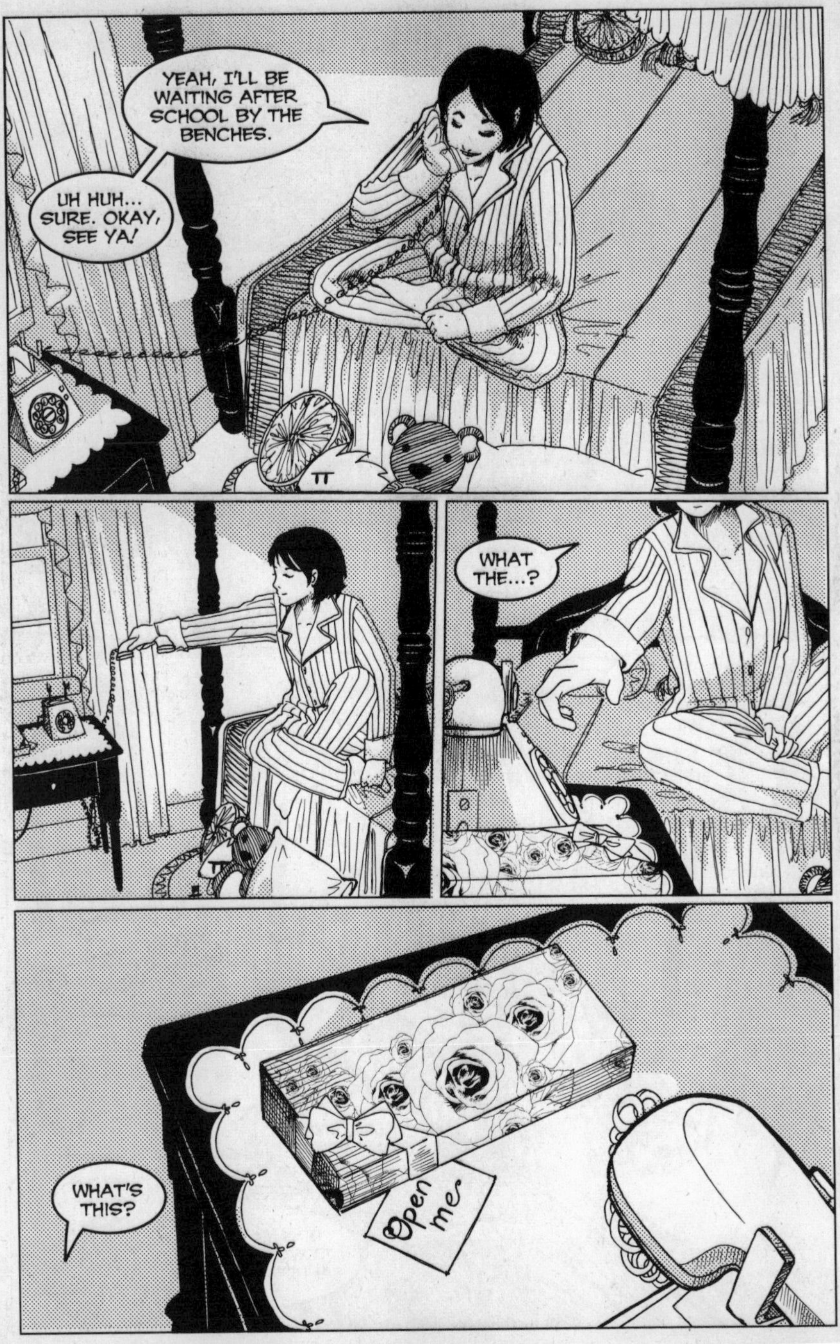
YEAH, I'LL BE WAITING AFTER SCHOOL BY THE BENCHES.
UH HUH... SURE. OKAY, SEE YA!
WHAT THE...?
WHAT'S THIS?
Open me

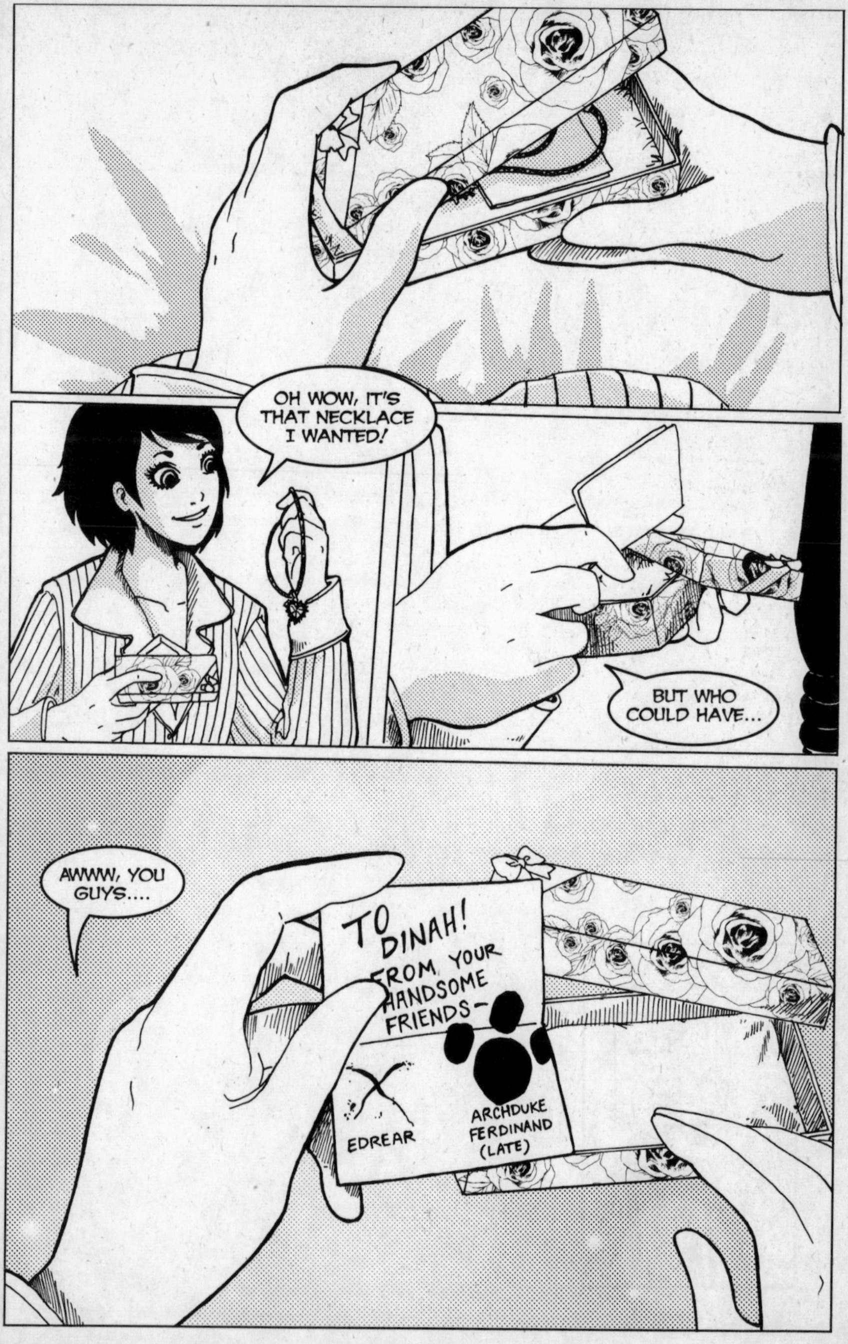
OH WOW, IT'S THAT NECKLACE I WANTED!
BUT WHO COULD HAVE...
AWWW, YOU GUYS....
TO DINAH! FROM YOUR HANDSOME FRIENDS-
EDREAR
ARCHDUKE FERDINAND (LATE)

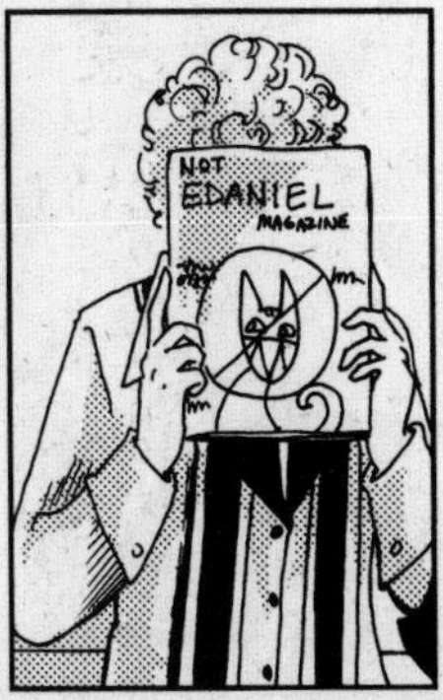
NOT
EDANIEL
MAGAZINE

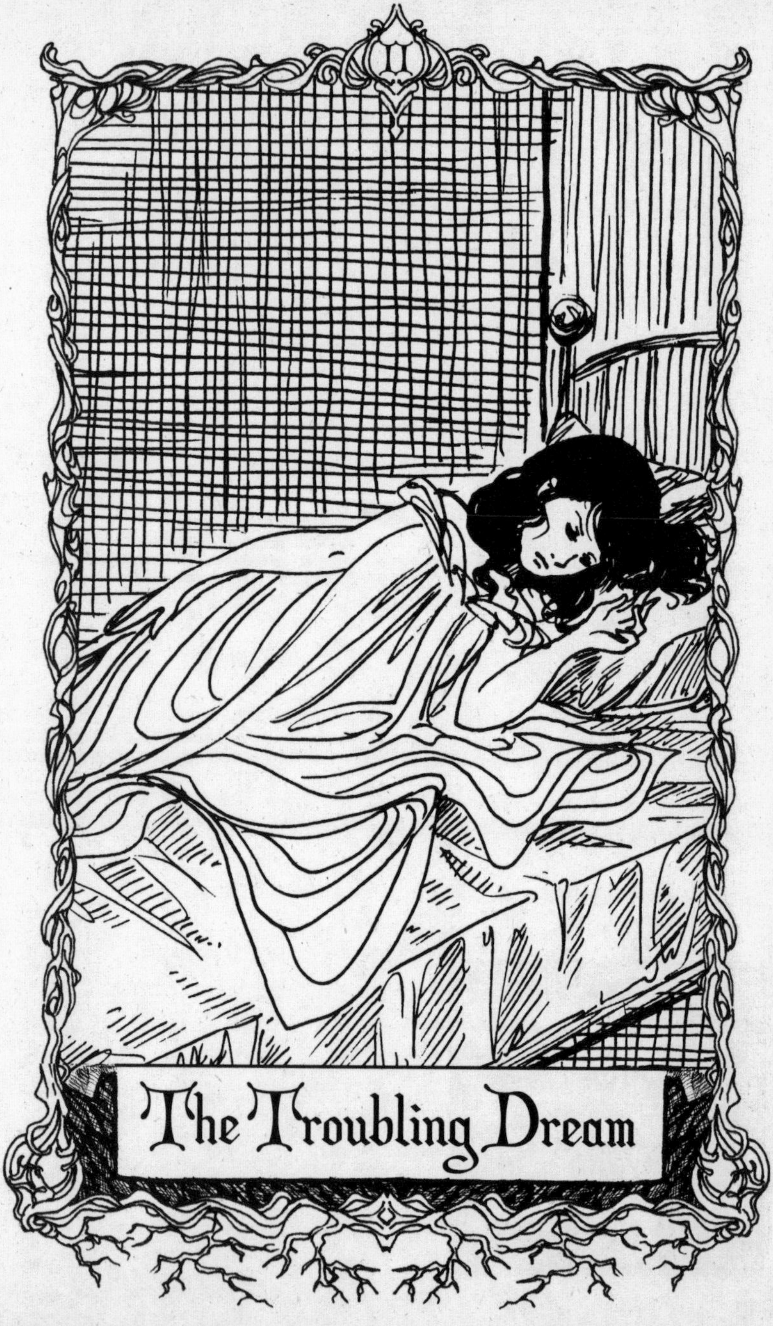
II
The Troubling Dream

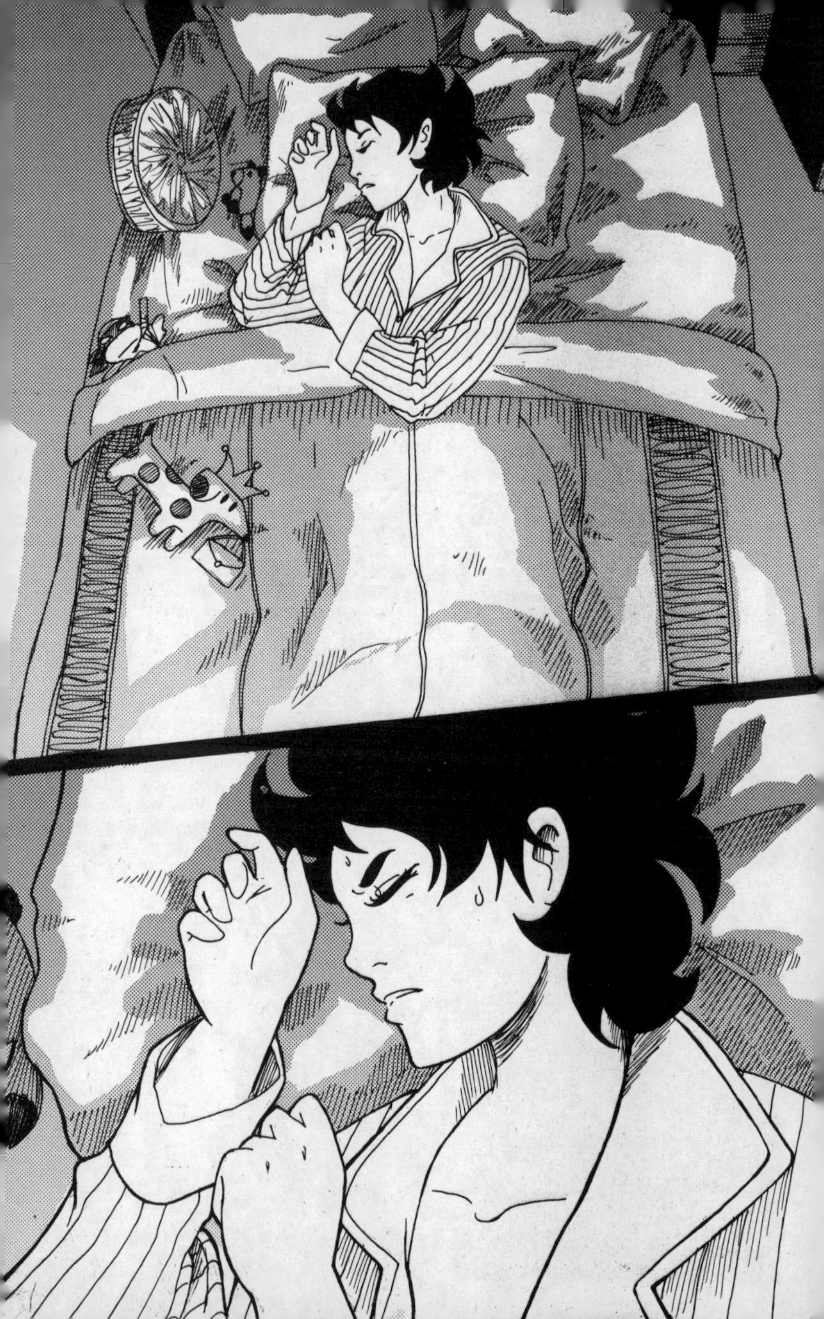

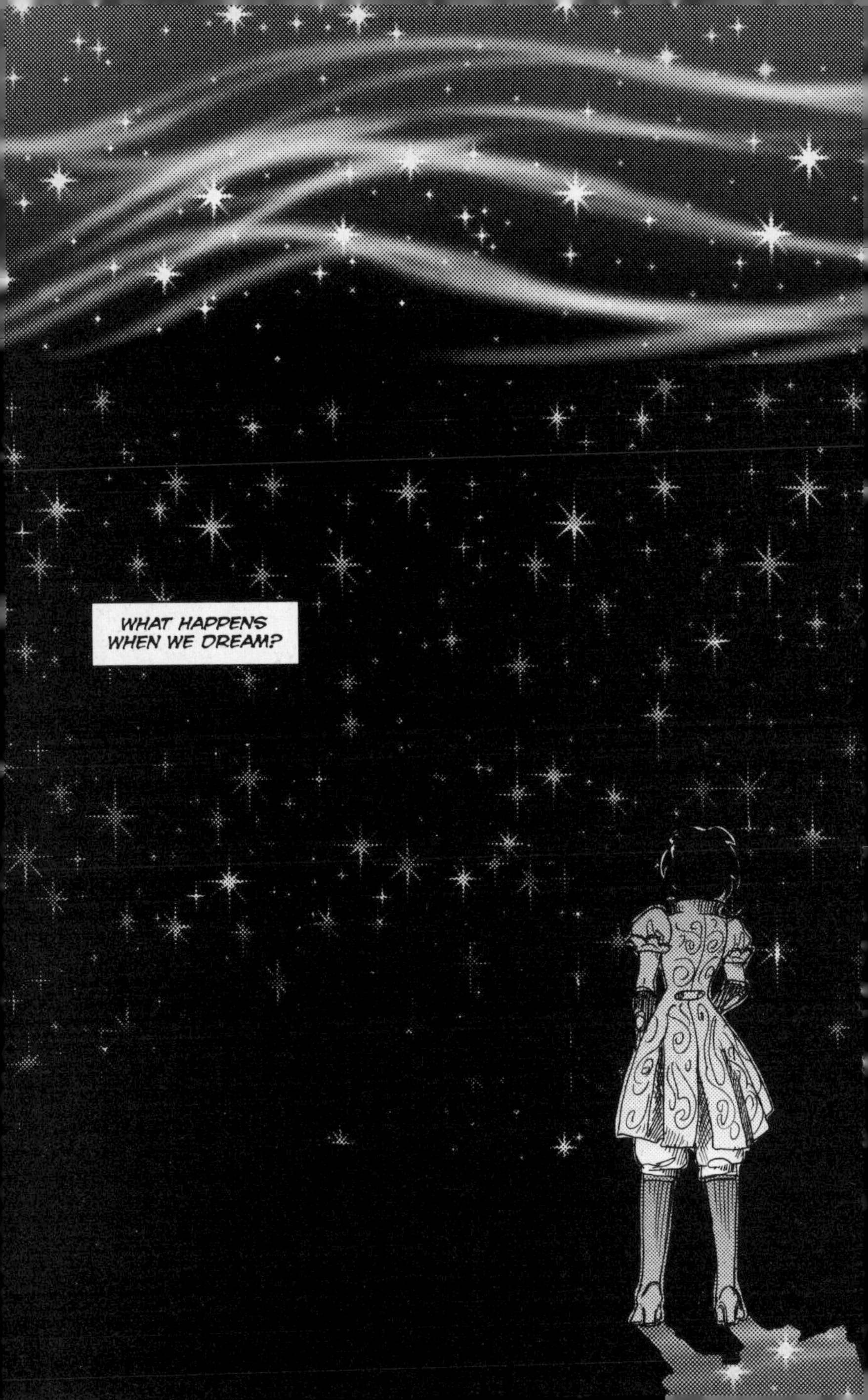
WHAT HAPPENS WHEN WE DREAM?

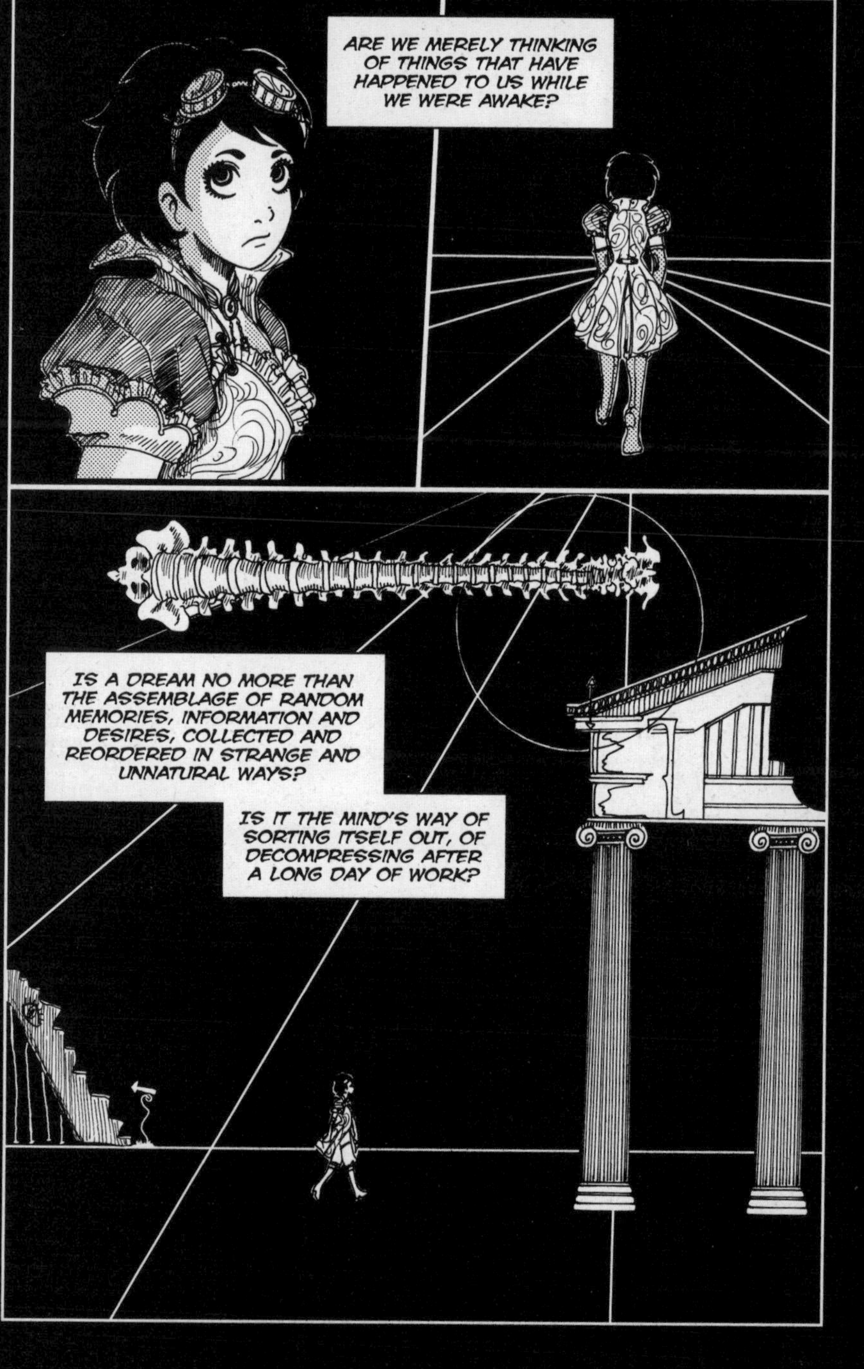
ARE WE MERELY THINKING OF THINGS THAT HAVE HAPPENED TO US WHILE WE WERE AWAKE?
IS A DREAM NO MORE THAN THE ASSEMBLAGE OF RANDOM MEMORIES, INFORMATION AND DESIRES, COLLECTED AND REORDERED IN STRANGE AND UNNATURAL WAYS?
IS IT THE MIND'S WAY OF SORTING ITSELF OUT, OF DECOMPRESSING AFTER A LONG DAY OF WORK?

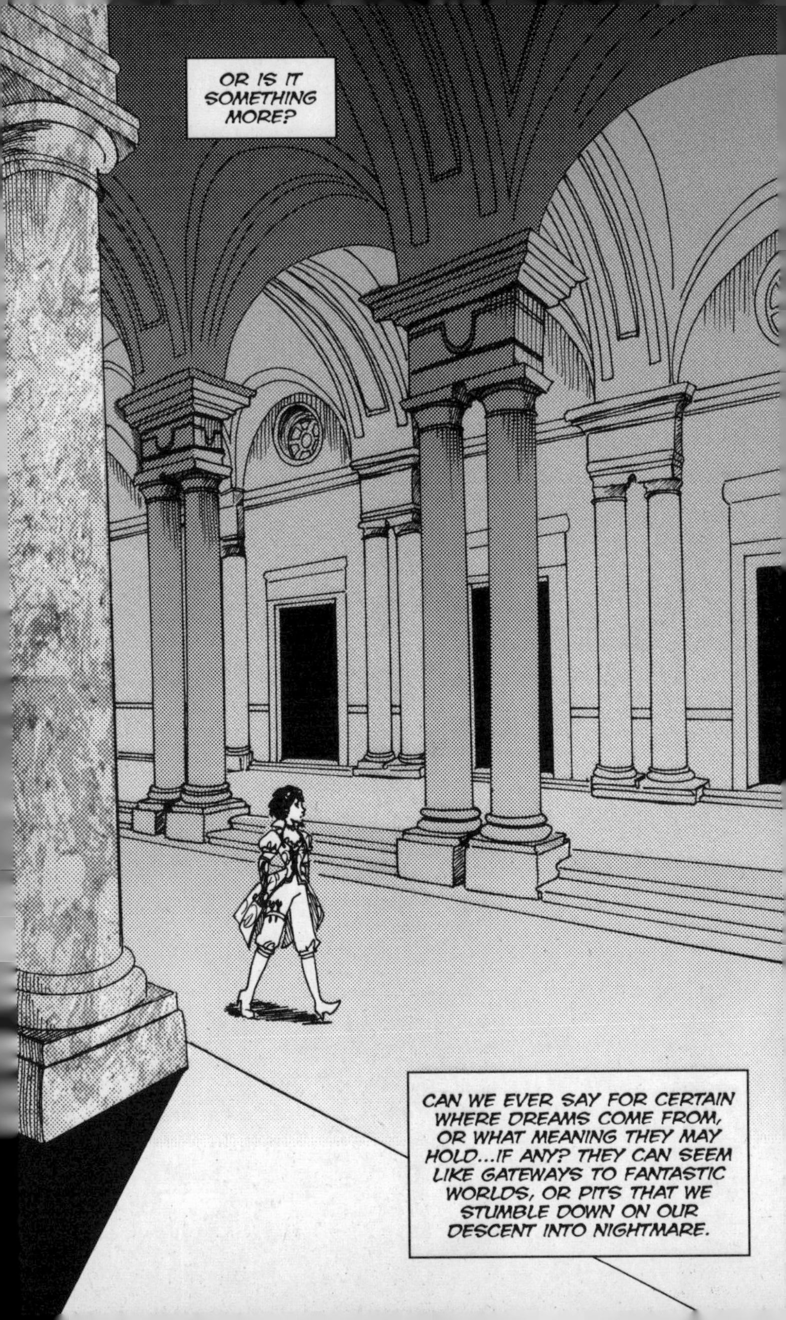
OR IS IT SOMETHING MORE?
CAN WE EVER SAY FOR CERTAIN WHERE DREAMS COME FROM, OR WHAT MEANING THEY MAY HOLD...IF ANY? THEY CAN SEEM LIKE GATEWAYS TO FANTASTIC WORLDS, OR PITS THAT WE STUMBLE DOWN ON OUR DESCENT INTO NIGHTMARE.

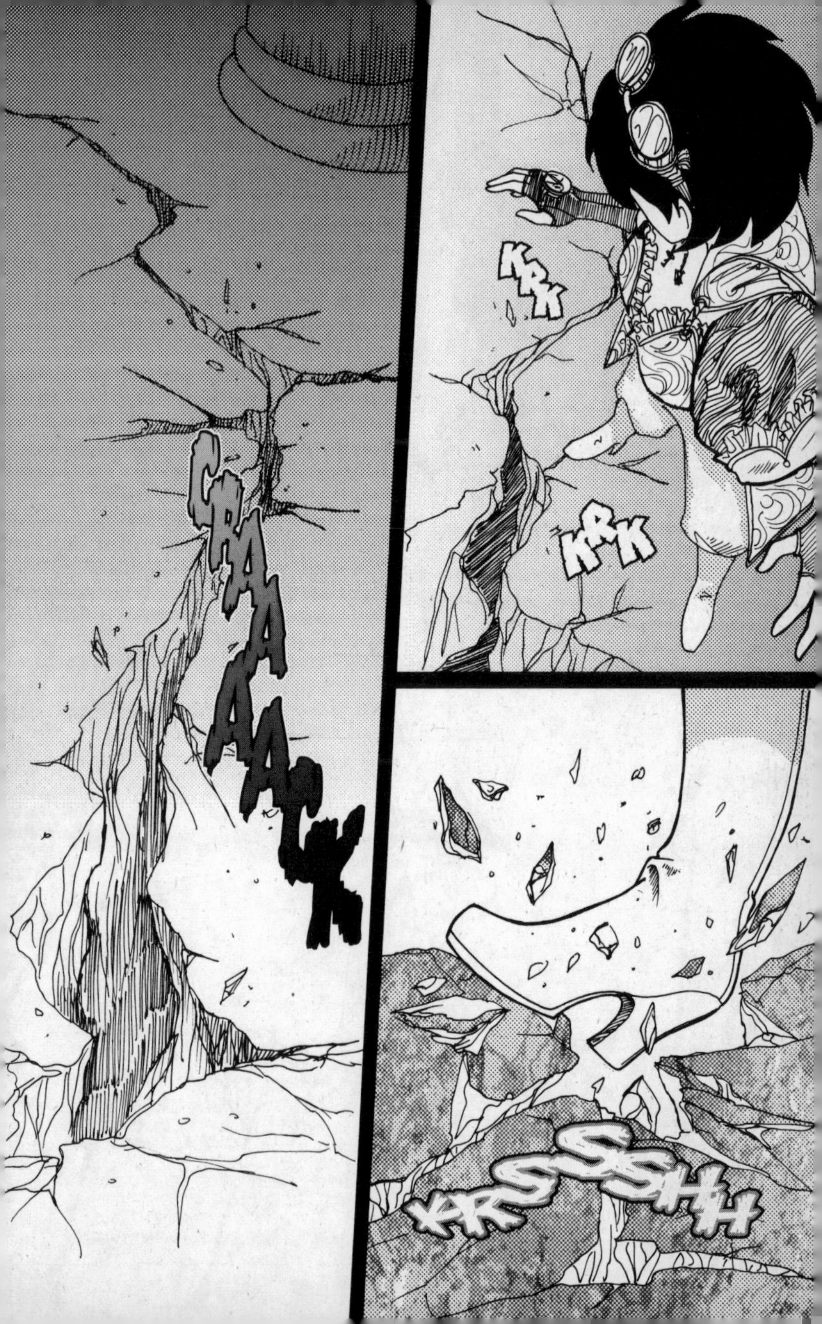
CRAAAACK
KRK
KRK
KRSSSHH

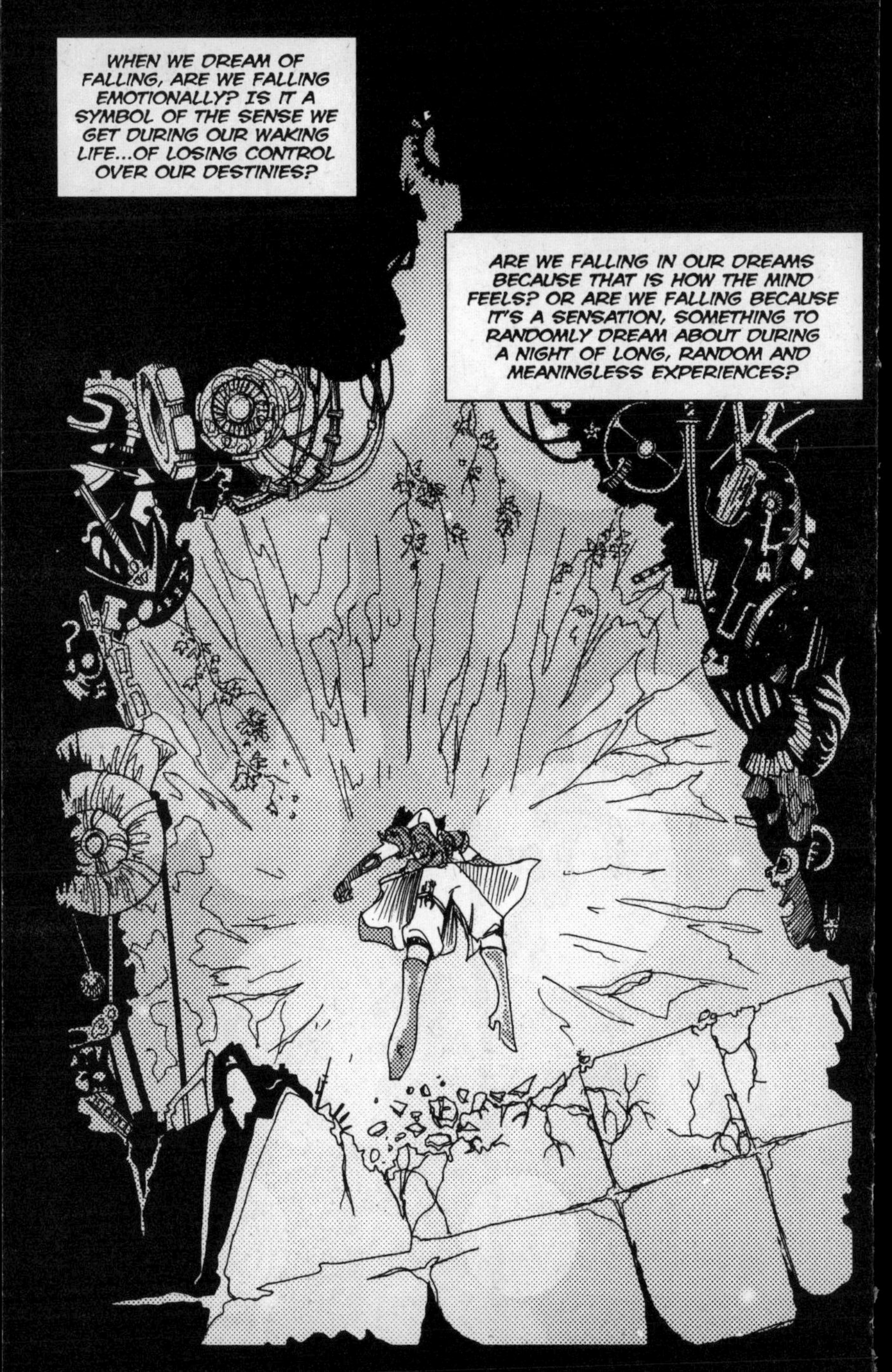
WHEN WE DREAM OF FALLING, ARE WE FALLING EMOTIONALLY? IS IT A SYMBOL OF THE SENSE WE GET DURING OUR WAKING LIFE...OF LOSING CONTROL OVER OUR DESTINIES?
ARE WE FALLING IN OUR DREAMS BECAUSE THAT IS HOW THE MIND FEELS? OR ARE WE FALLING BECAUSE IT'S A SENSATION, SOMETHING TO RANDOMLY DREAM ABOUT DURING A NIGHT OF LONG, RANDOM AND MEANINGLESS EXPERIENCES?

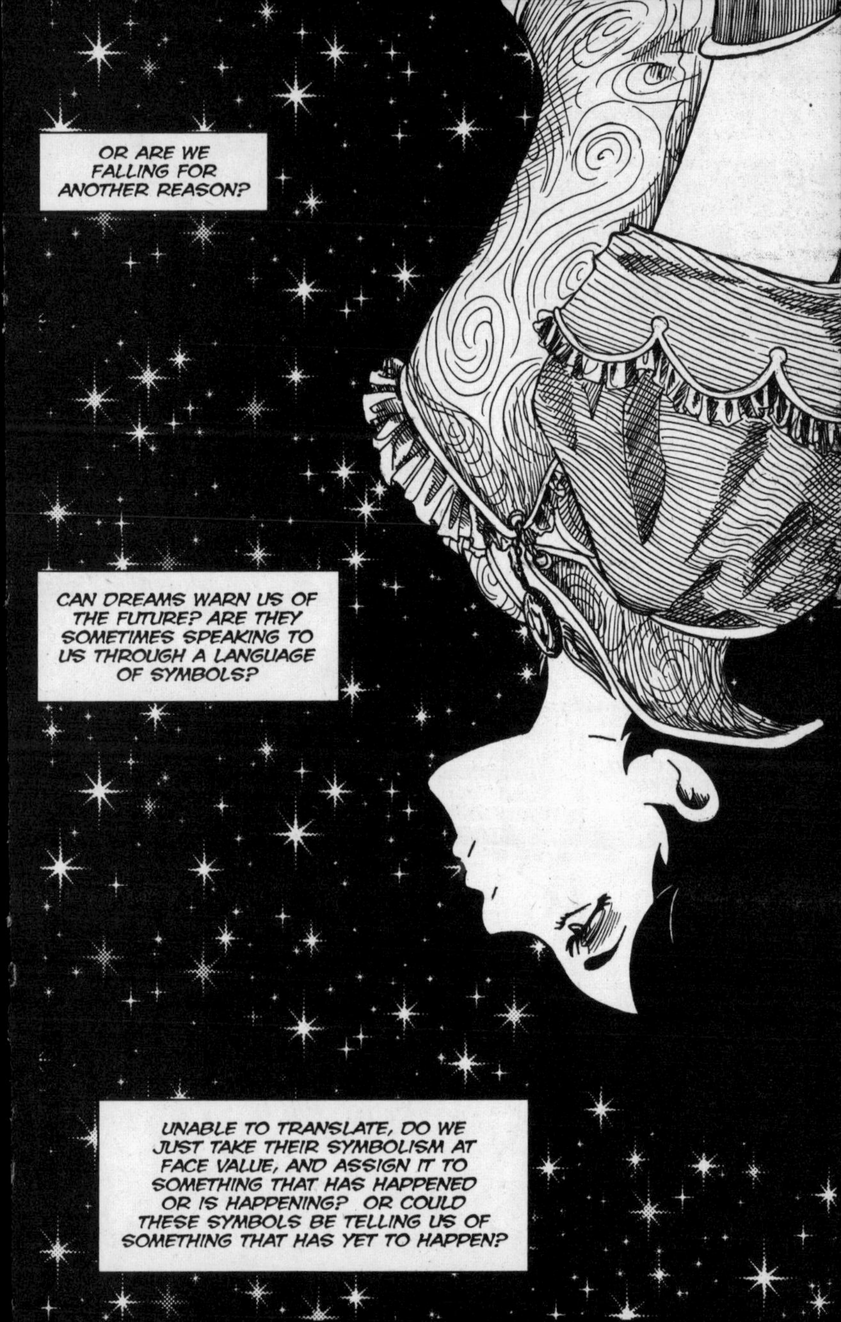
OR ARE WE FALLING FOR ANOTHER REASON?
CAN DREAMS WARN US OF THE FUTURE? ARE THEY SOMETIMES SPEAKING TO US THROUGH A LANGUAGE OF SYMBOLS?
UNABLE TO TRANSLATE, DO WE JUST TAKE THEIR SYMBOLISM AT FACE VALUE, AND ASSIGN IT TO SOMETHING THAT HAS HAPPENED OR IS HAPPENING? OR COULD THESE SYMBOLS BE TELLING US OF SOMETHING THAT HAS YET TO HAPPEN?

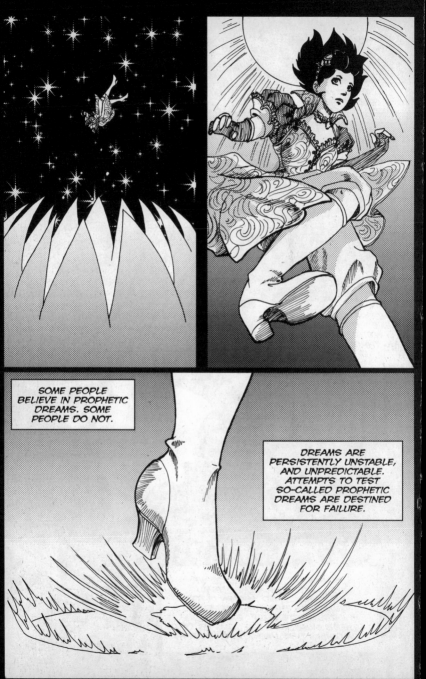

SOME PEOPLE BELIEVE IN PROPHETIC DREAMS. SOME PEOPLE DO NOT.

DREAMS ARE PERSISTENTLY UNSTABLE, AND UNPREDICTABLE. ATTEMPTS TO TEST SO-CALLED PROPHETIC DREAMS ARE DESTINED FOR FAILURE.

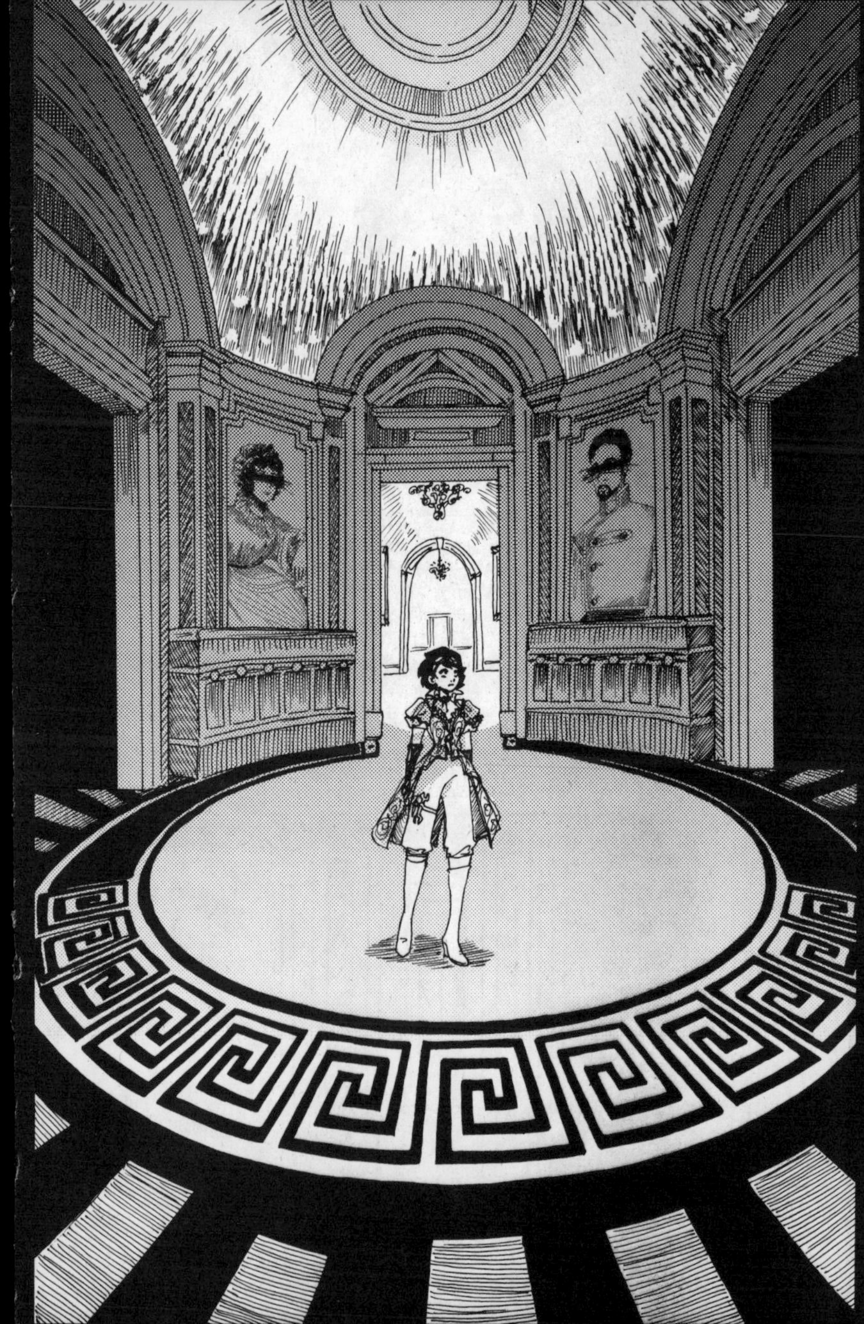

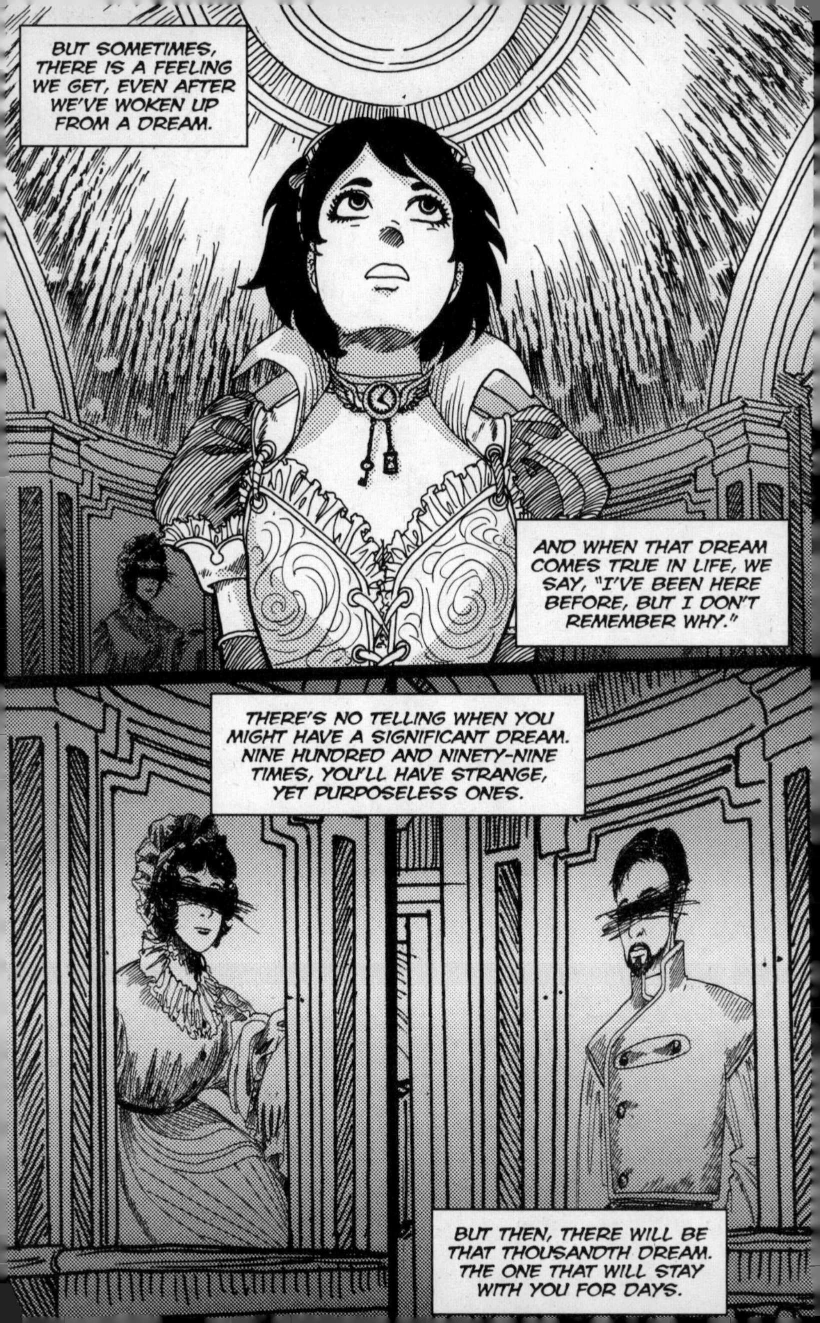
BUT SOMETIMES, THERE IS A FEELING WE GET, EVEN AFTER WE'VE WOKEN UP FROM A DREAM.
AND WHEN THAT DREAM COMES TRUE IN LIFE, WE SAY, "I'VE BEEN HERE BEFORE, BUT I DON'T REMEMBER WHY."
THERE'S NO TELLING WHEN YOU MIGHT HAVE A SIGNIFICANT DREAM. NINE HUNDRED AND NINETY-NINE TIMES, YOU'LL HAVE STRANGE, YET PURPOSELESS ONES.
BUT THEN, THERE WILL BE THAT THOUSANDTH DREAM. THE ONE THAT WILL STAY WITH YOU FOR DAYS.

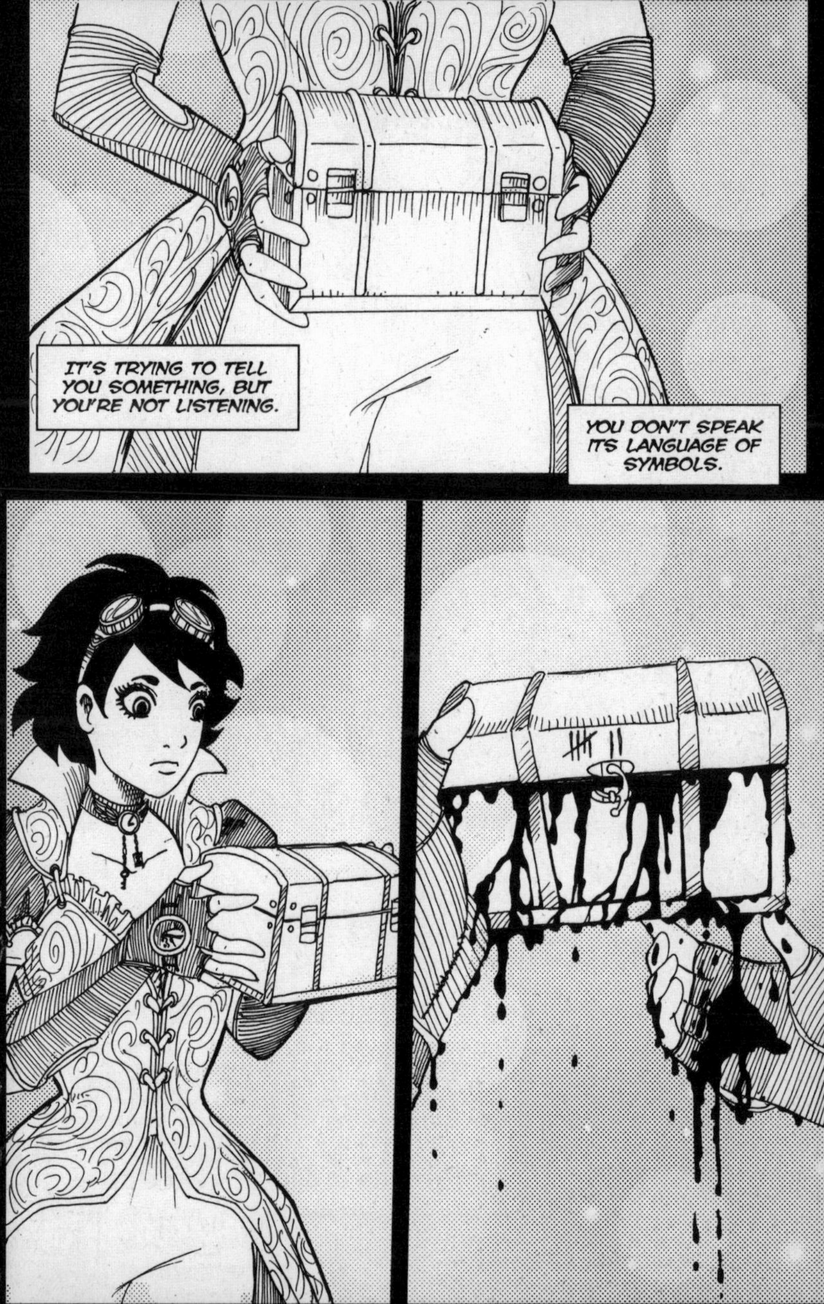
IT'S TRYING TO TELL YOU SOMETHING, BUT YOU'RE NOT LISTENING.
YOU DON'T SPEAK ITS LANGUAGE OF SYMBOLS.

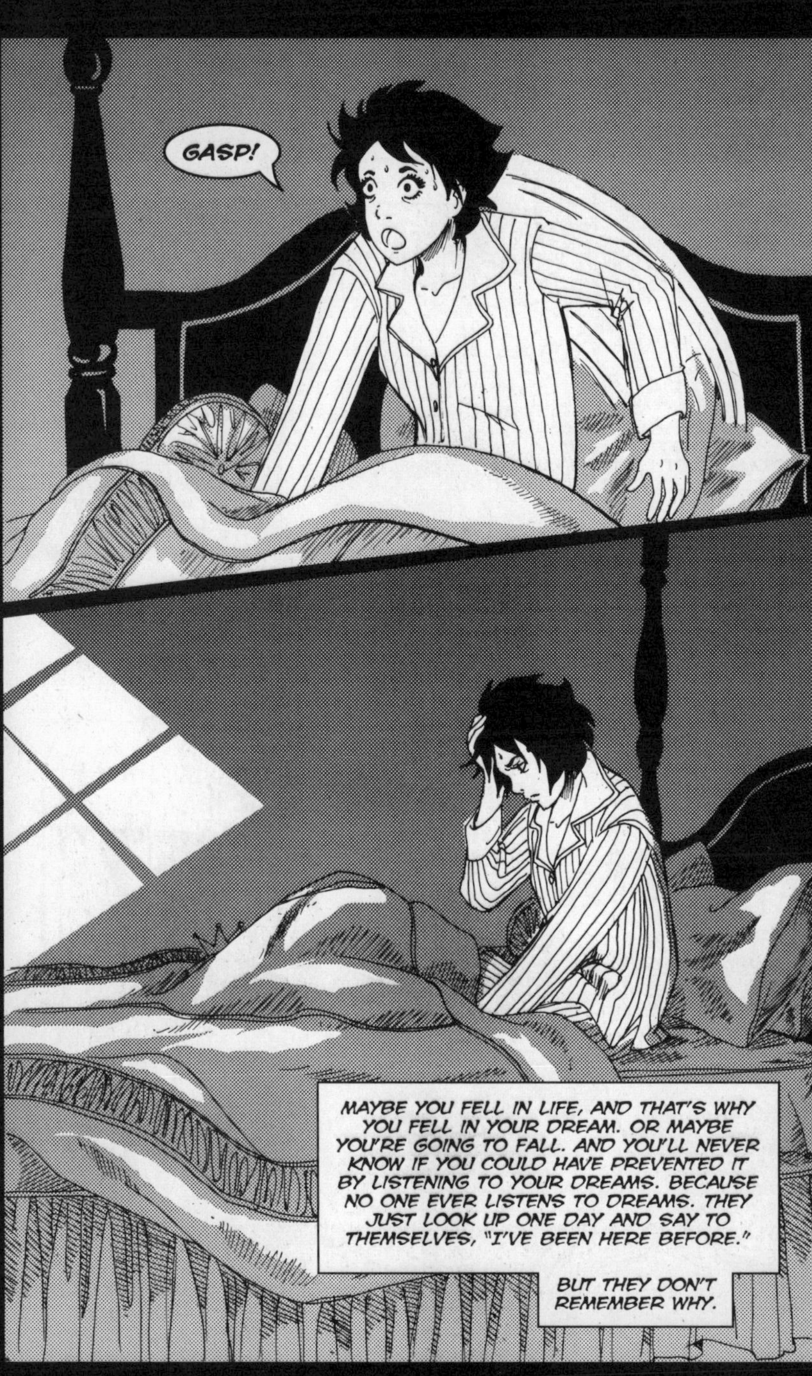
GASP!
MAYBE YOU FELL IN LIFE, AND THAT'S WHY YOU FELL IN YOUR DREAM. OR MAYBE YOU'RE GOING TO FALL. AND YOU'LL NEVER KNOW IF YOU COULD HAVE PREVENTED IT BY LISTENING TO YOUR DREAMS. BECAUSE NO ONE EVER LISTENS TO DREAMS. THEY JUST LOOK UP ONE DAY AND SAY TO THEMSELVES, "I'VE BEEN HERE BEFORE."
BUT THEY DON'T REMEMBER WHY.

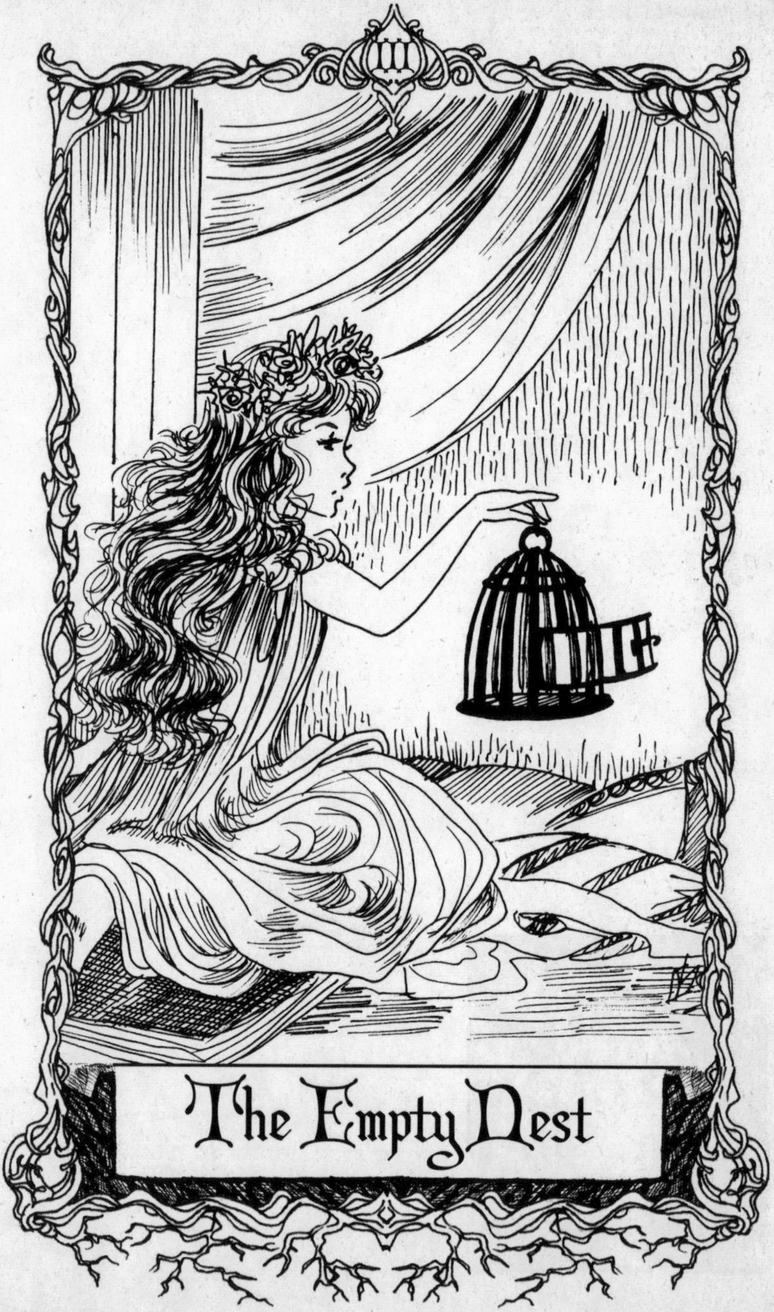

III
The Empty Nest

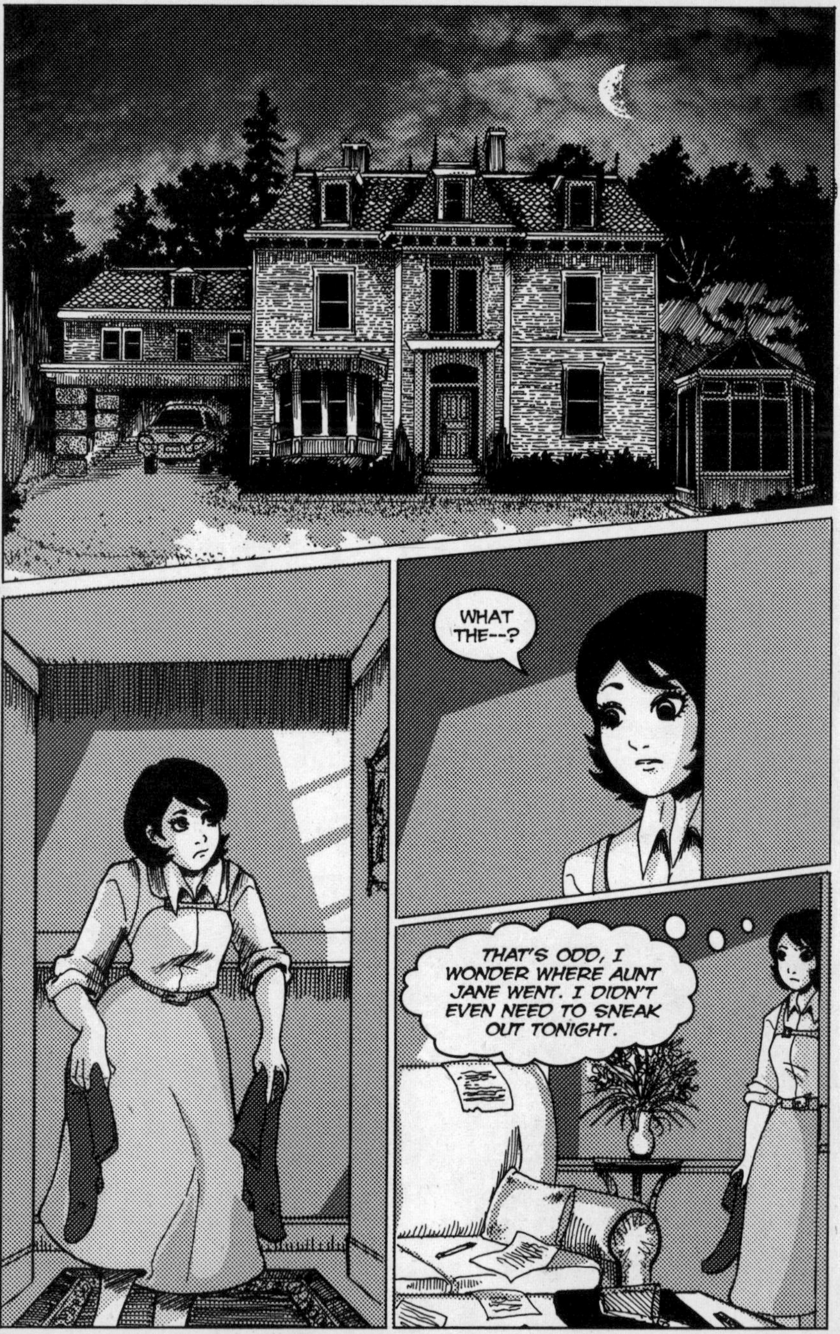
WHAT THE--?
THAT'S ODD, I WONDER WHERE AUNT JANE WENT. I DIDN'T EVEN NEED TO SNEAK OUT TONIGHT.

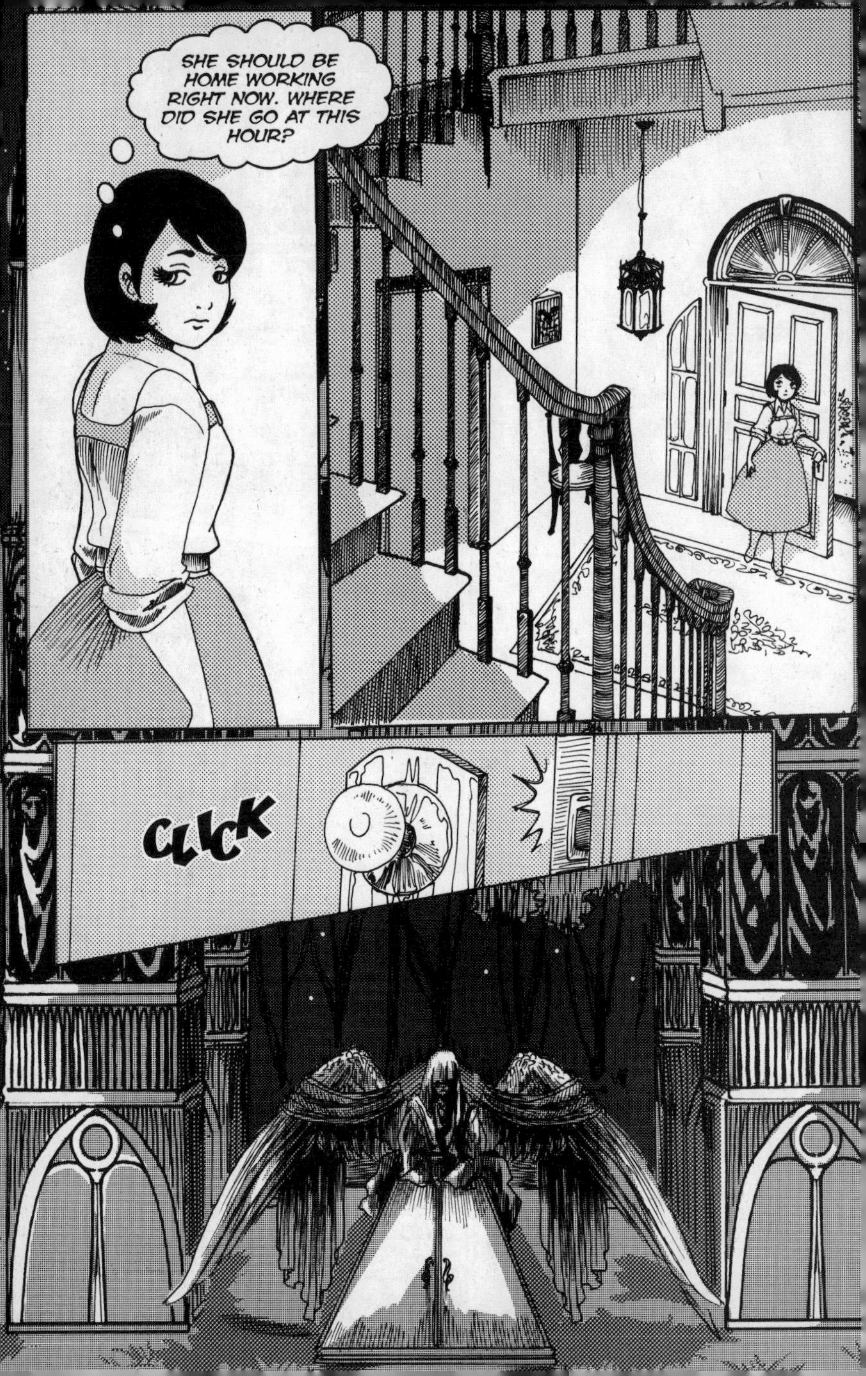
SHE SHOULD BE HOME WORKING RIGHT NOW. WHERE DID SHE GO AT THIS HOUR?
CLICK

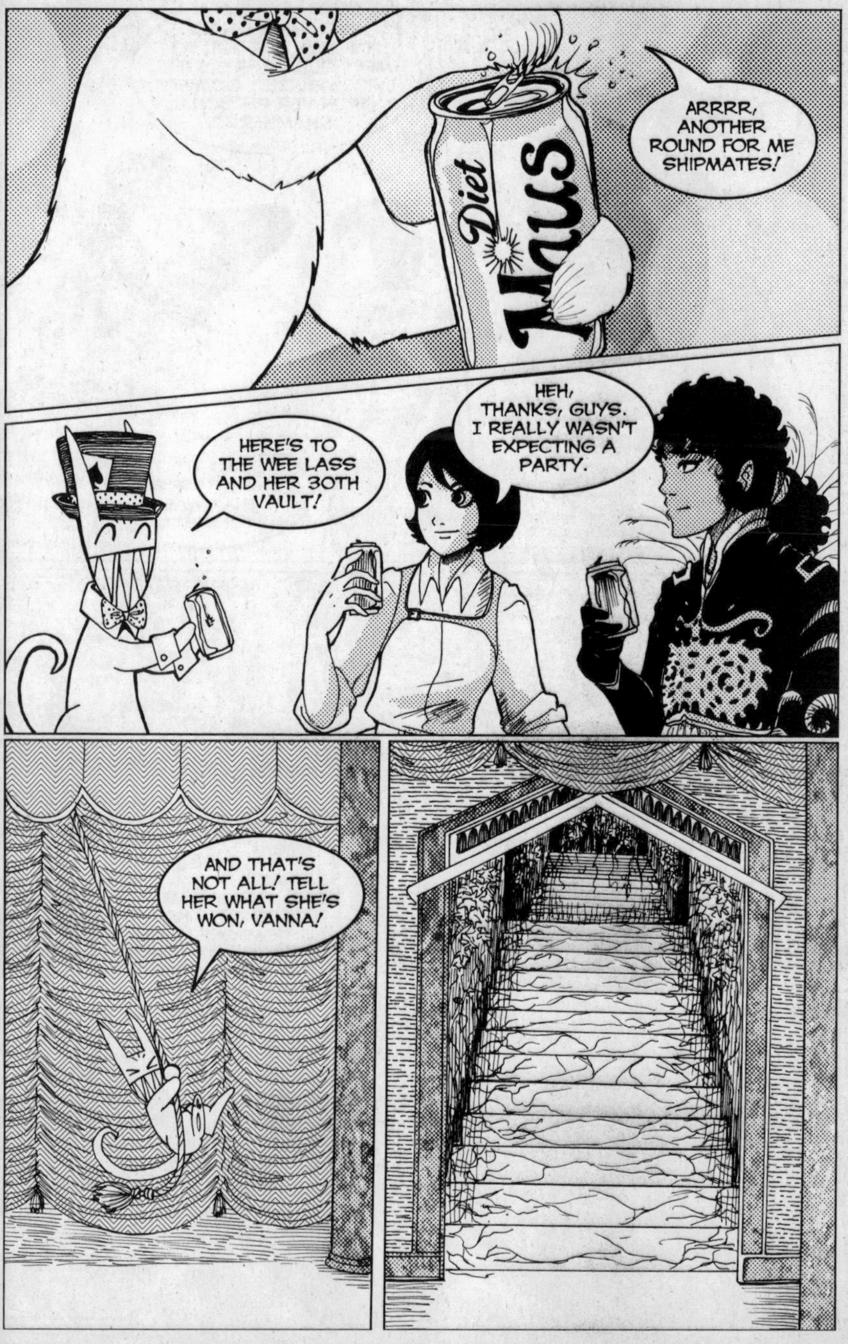
Diet Maus
ARRRR, ANOTHER ROUND FOR ME SHIPMATES!
HERE'S TO THE WEE LASS AND HER 30TH VAULT!
HEH, THANKS, GUYS. I REALLY WASN'T EXPECTING A PARTY.
AND THAT'S NOT ALL! TELL HER WHAT SHE'S WON, VANNA!

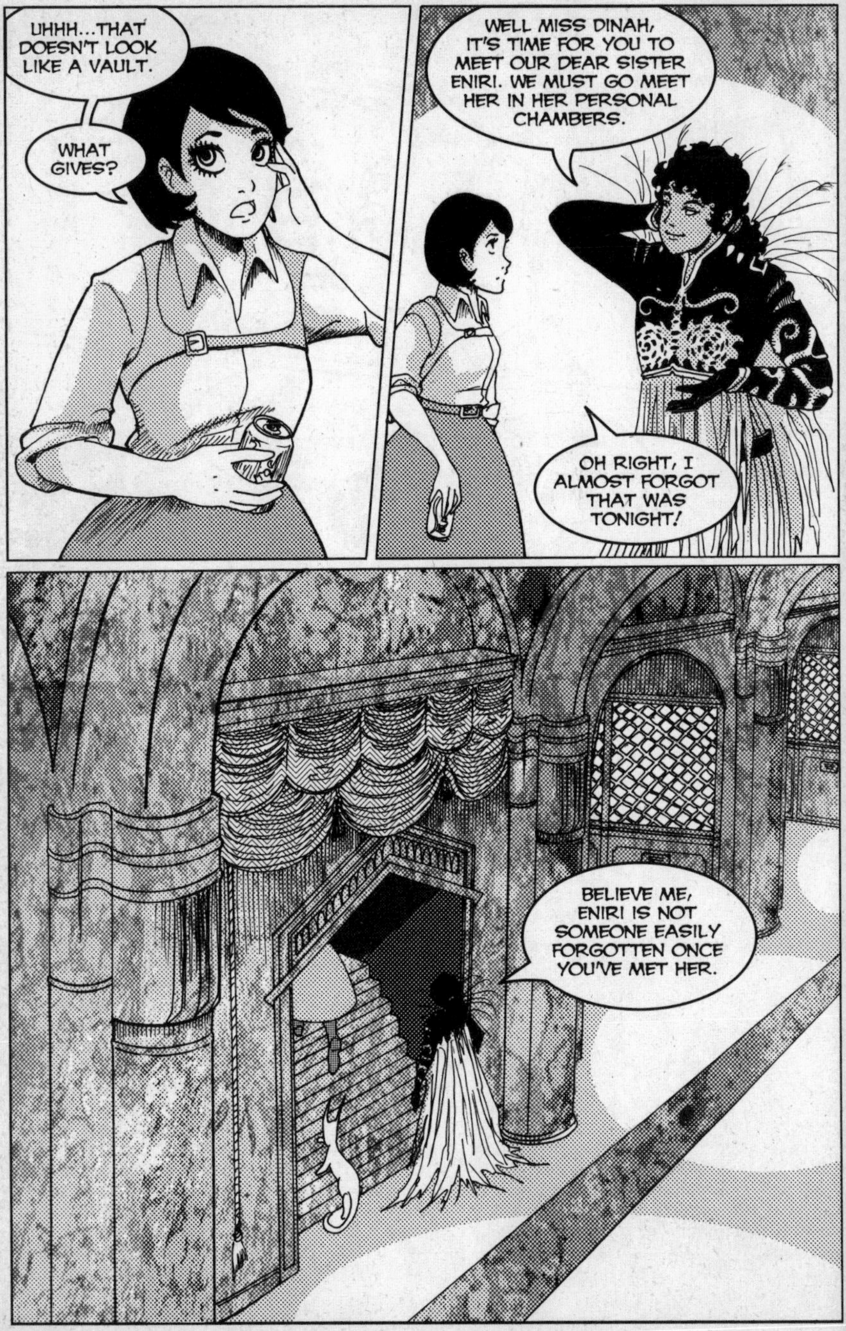
UHHH...THAT DOESN'T LOOK LIKE A VAULT.
WHAT GIVES?
WELL MISS DINAH, IT'S TIME FOR YOU TO MEET OUR DEAR SISTER ENIRI. WE MUST GO MEET HER IN HER PERSONAL CHAMBERS.
OH RIGHT, I ALMOST FORGOT THAT WAS TONIGHT!
BELIEVE ME, ENIRI IS NOT SOMEONE EASILY FORGOTTEN ONCE YOU'VE MET HER.

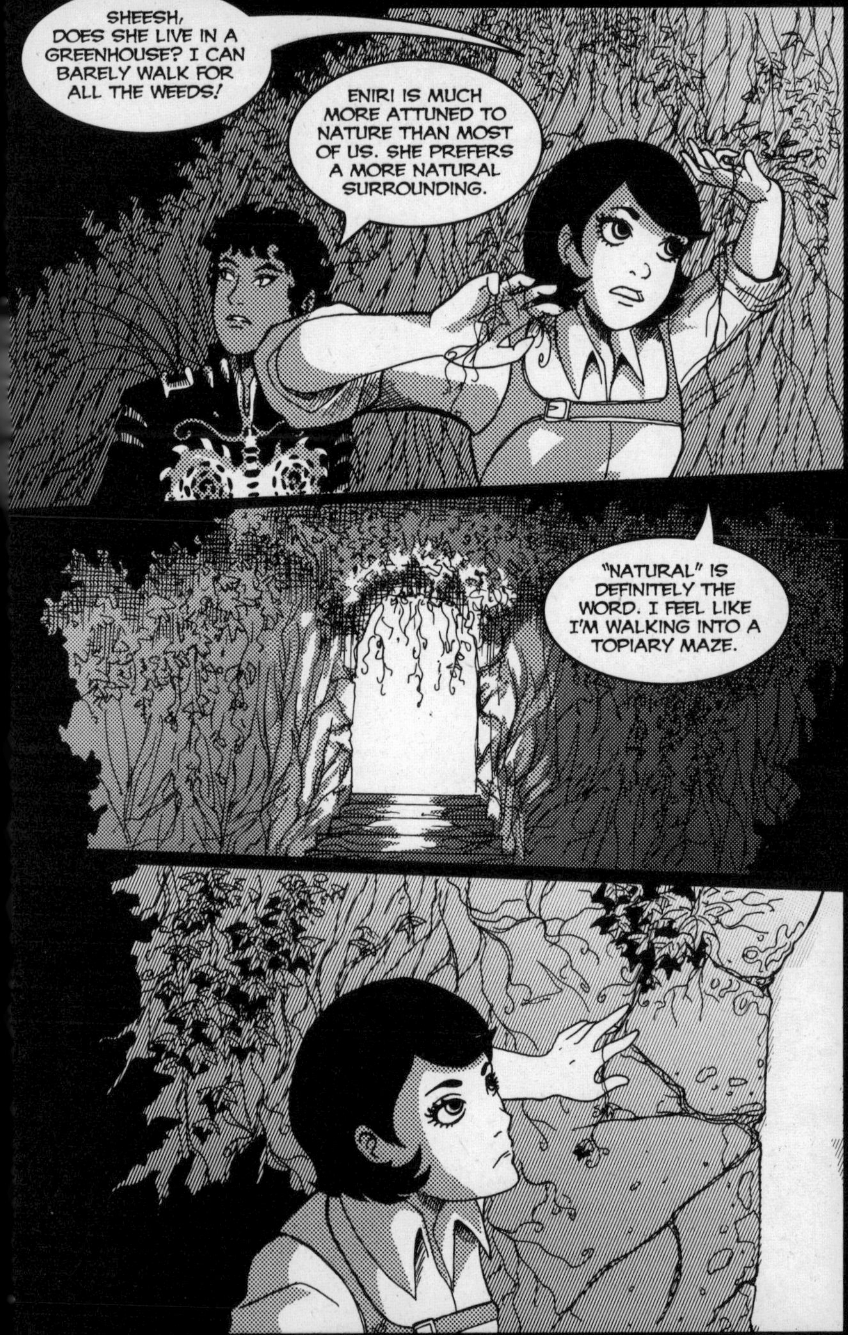
SHEESH, DOES SHE LIVE IN A GREENHOUSE? I CAN BARELY WALK FOR ALL THE WEEDS!
ENIRI IS MUCH MORE ATTUNED TO NATURE THAN MOST OF US. SHE PREFERS A MORE NATURAL SURROUNDING.
"NATURAL" IS DEFINITELY THE WORD. I FEEL LIKE I'M WALKING INTO A TOPIARY MAZE.

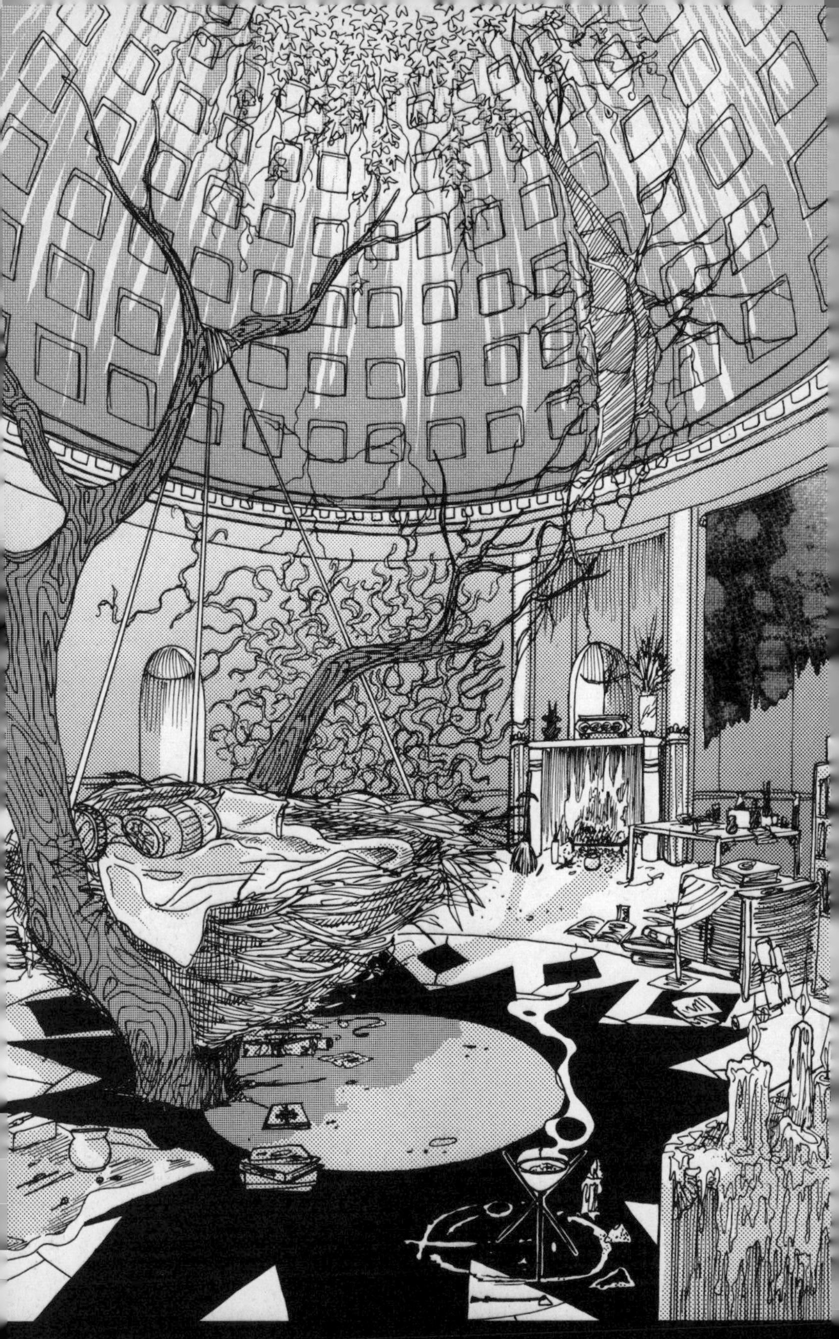

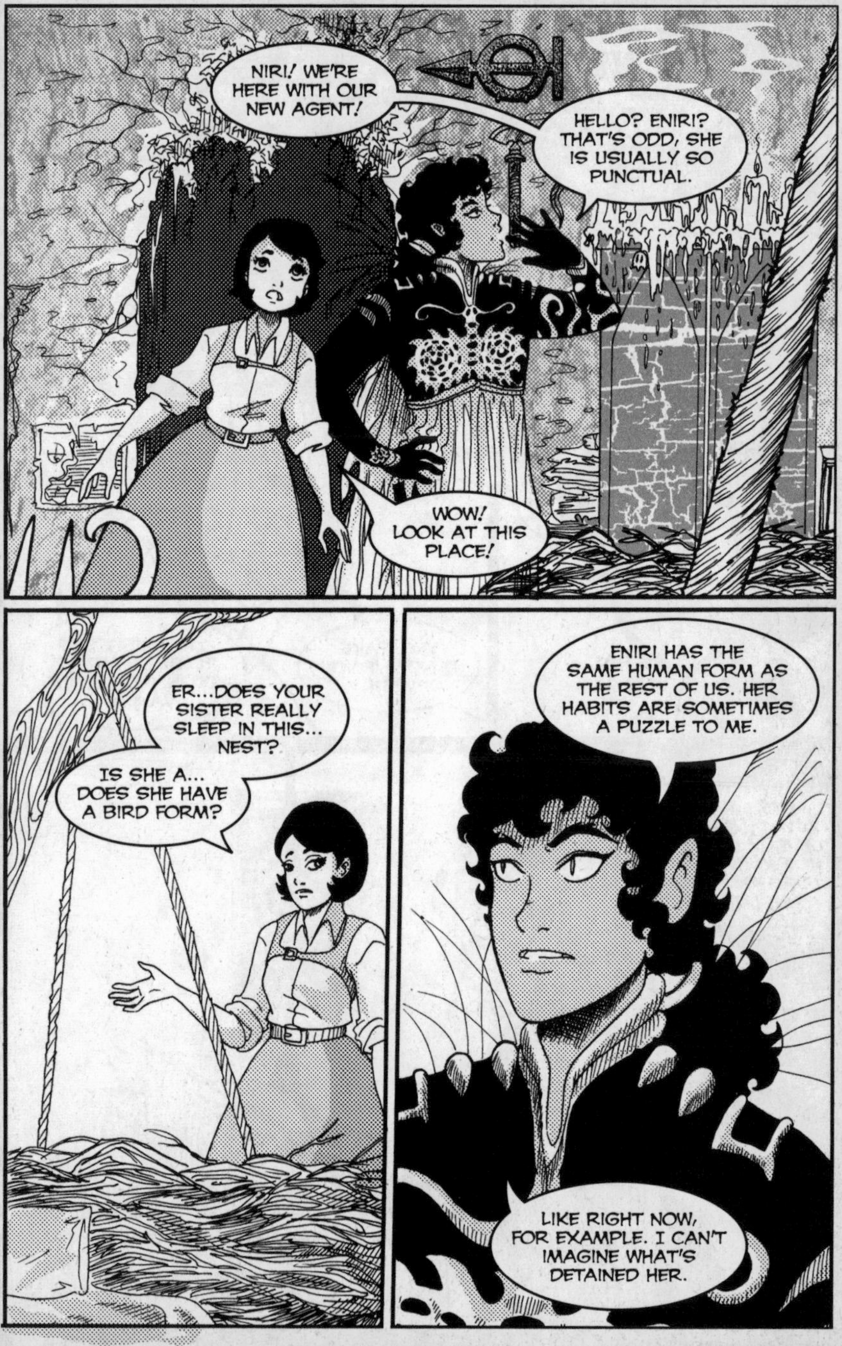
NIRI! WE'RE HERE WITH OUR NEW AGENT!
HELLO? ENIRI? THAT'S ODD, SHE IS USUALLY SO PUNCTUAL.
WOW! LOOK AT THIS PLACE!
ER...DOES YOUR SISTER REALLY SLEEP IN THIS... NEST?
IS SHE A... DOES SHE HAVE A BIRD FORM?
ENIRI HAS THE SAME HUMAN FORM AS THE REST OF US. HER HABITS ARE SOMETIMES A PUZZLE TO ME.
LIKE RIGHT NOW, FOR EXAMPLE. I CAN'T IMAGINE WHAT'S DETAINED HER.

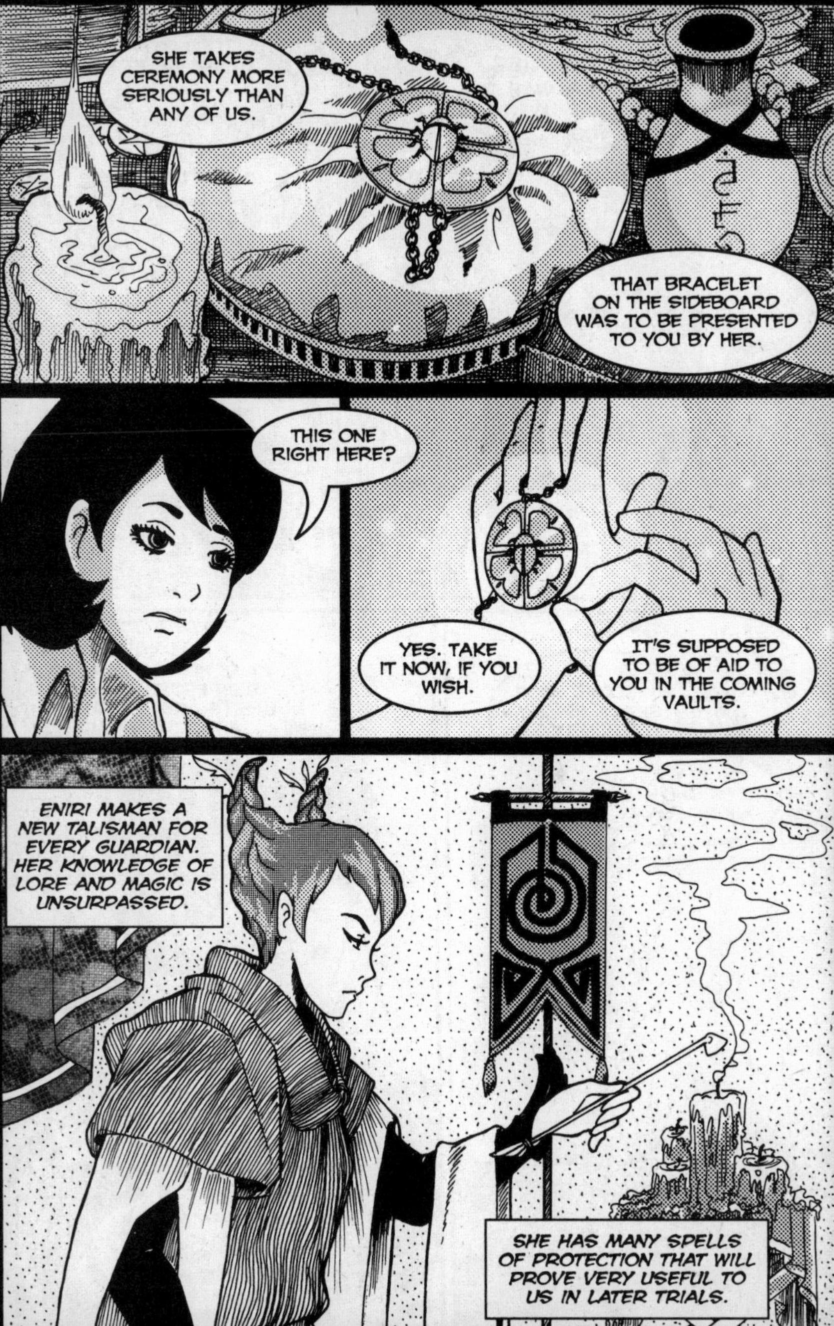
SHE TAKES CEREMONY MORE SERIOUSLY THAN ANY OF US.
THAT BRACELET ON THE SIDEBOARD WAS TO BE PRESENTED TO YOU BY HER.
THIS ONE RIGHT HERE?
YES. TAKE IT NOW, IF YOU WISH.
IT'S SUPPOSED TO BE OF AID TO YOU IN THE COMING VAULTS.
ENIRI MAKES A NEW TALISMAN FOR EVERY GUARDIAN. HER KNOWLEDGE OF LORE AND MAGIC IS UNSURPASSED.
SHE HAS MANY SPELLS OF PROTECTION THAT WILL PROVE VERY USEFUL TO US IN LATER TRIALS.

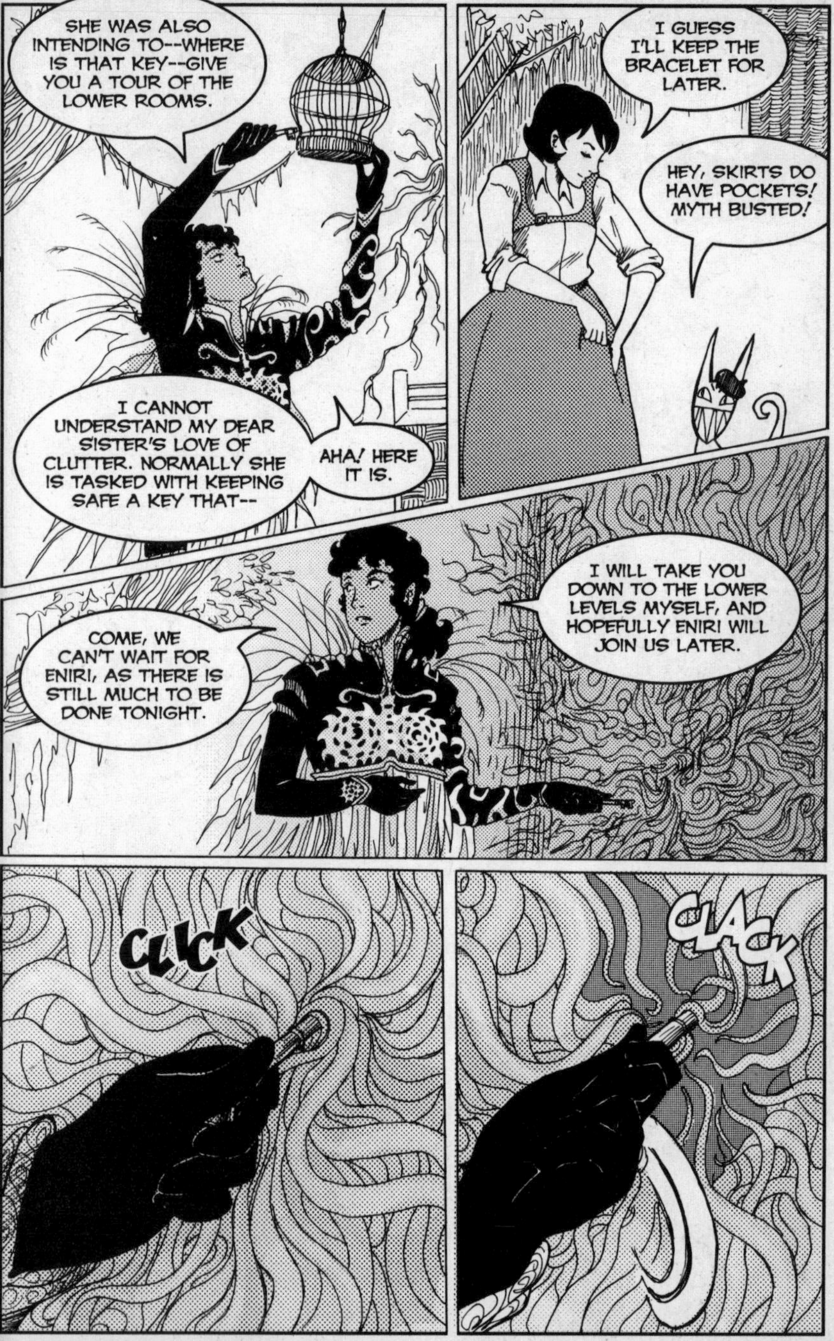
SHE WAS ALSO INTENDING TO--WHERE IS THAT KEY--GIVE YOU A TOUR OF THE LOWER ROOMS.
I CANNOT UNDERSTAND MY DEAR SISTER'S LOVE OF CLUTTER. NORMALLY SHE IS TASKED WITH KEEPING SAFE A KEY THAT--
AHA! HERE IT IS.
I GUESS I'LL KEEP THE BRACELET FOR LATER.
HEY, SKIRTS DO HAVE POCKETS! MYTH BUSTED!
COME, WE CAN'T WAIT FOR ENIRI, AS THERE IS STILL MUCH TO BE DONE TONIGHT.
I WILL TAKE YOU DOWN TO THE LOWER LEVELS MYSELF, AND HOPEFULLY ENIRI WILL JOIN US LATER.
CLICK
CLACK

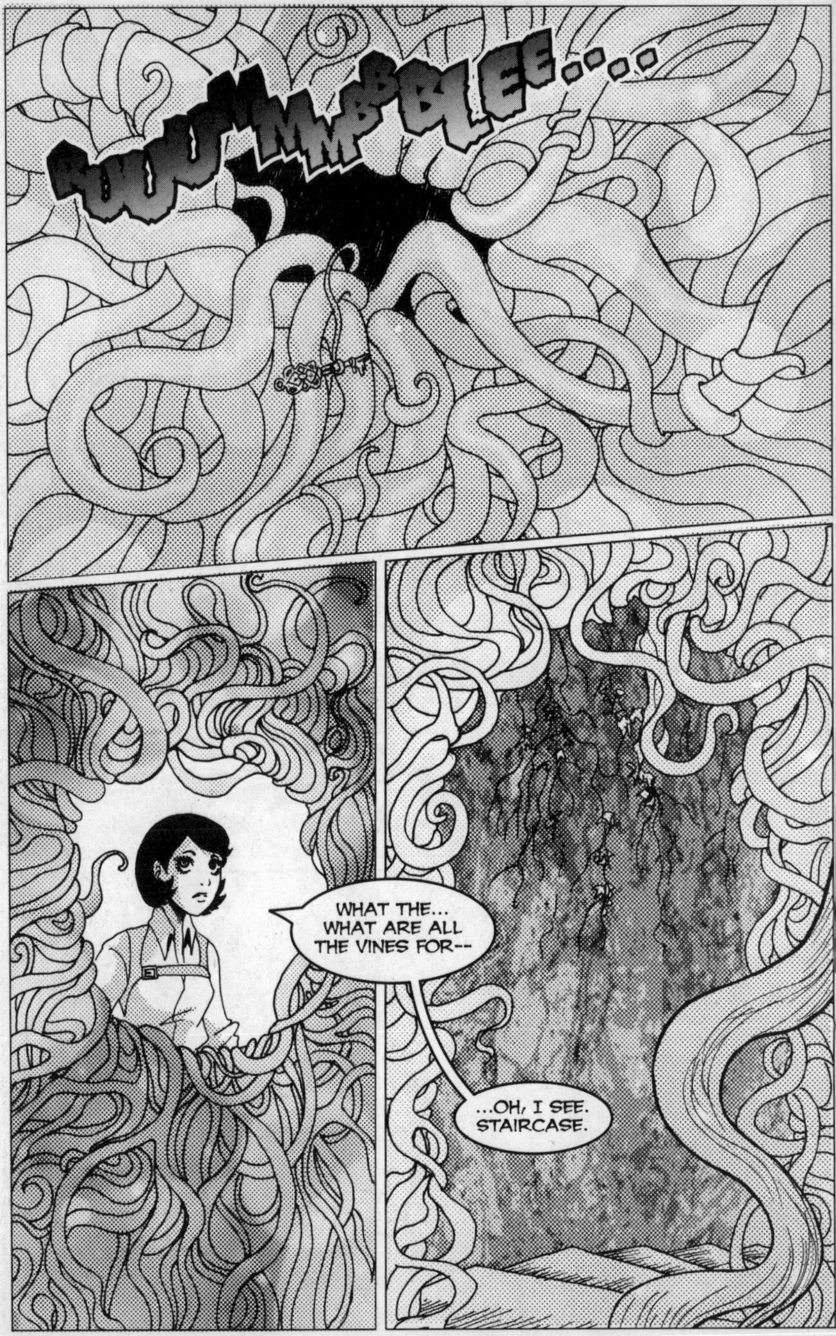
RUUUMMMBBLEE....
WHAT THE... WHAT ARE ALL THE VINES FOR--
...OH, I SEE. STAIRCASE.

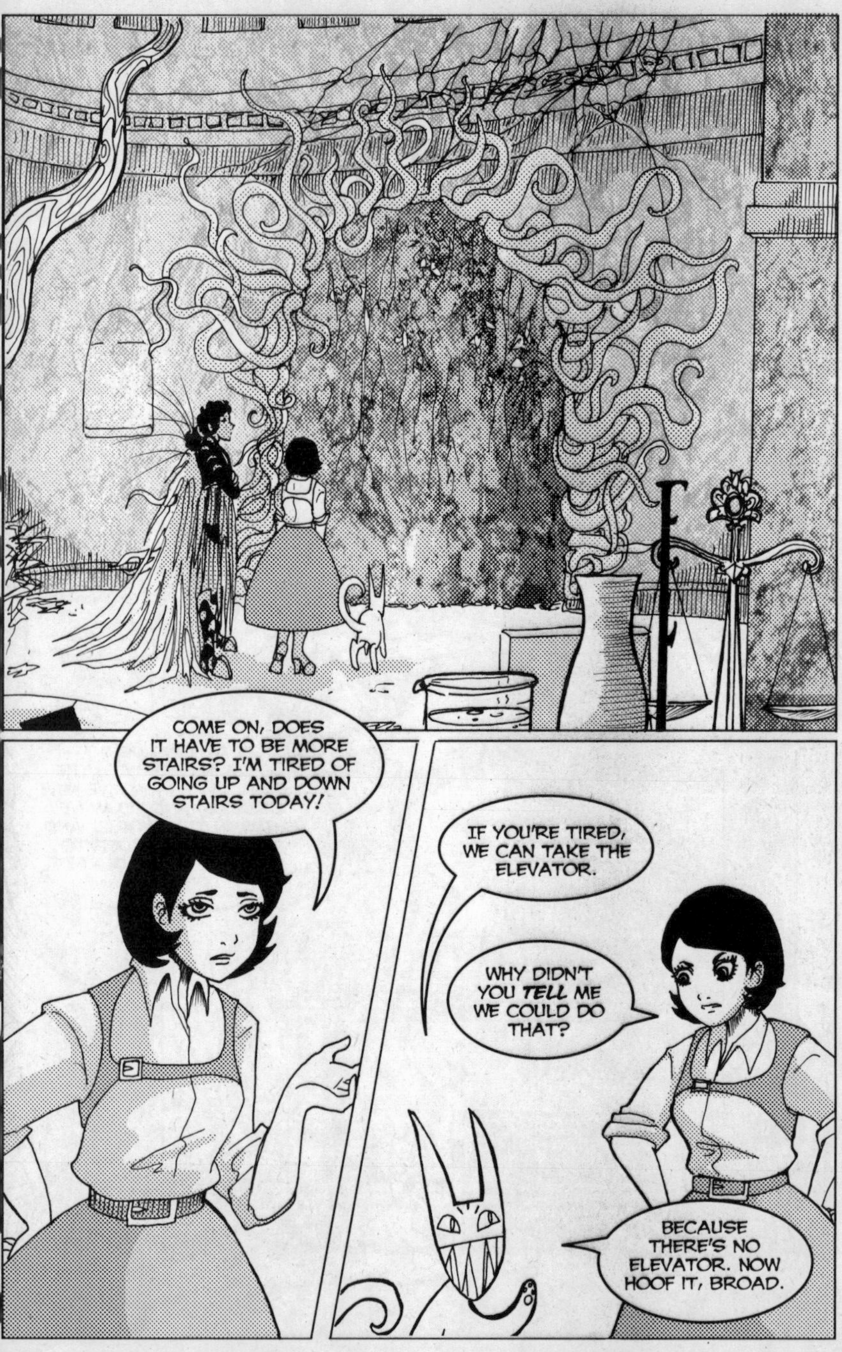
COME ON, DOES IT HAVE TO BE MORE STAIRS? I'M TIRED OF GOING UP AND DOWN STAIRS TODAY!
IF YOU'RE TIRED, WE CAN TAKE THE ELEVATOR.
WHY DIDN'T YOU **TELL** ME WE COULD DO THAT?
BECAUSE THERE'S NO ELEVATOR. NOW HOOF IT, BROAD.

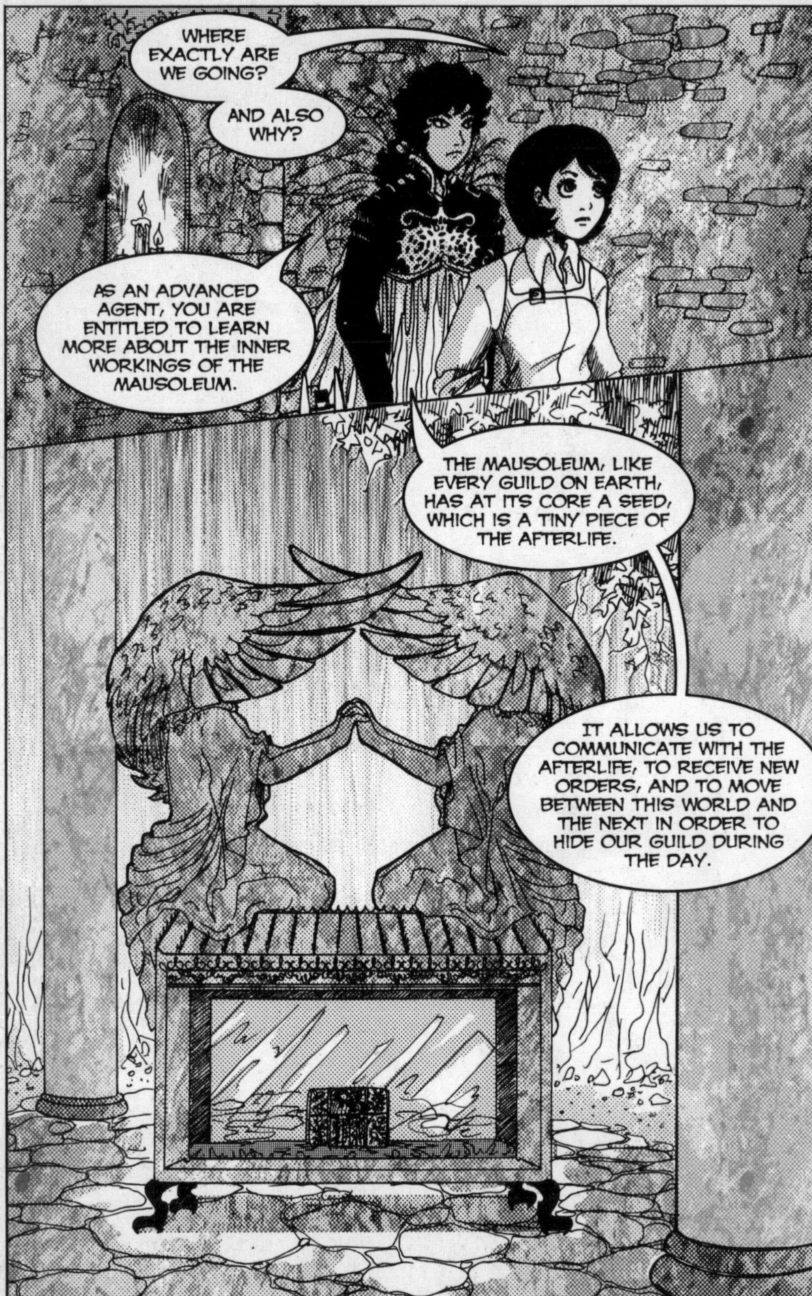
WHERE EXACTLY ARE WE GOING?
AND ALSO WHY?
AS AN ADVANCED AGENT, YOU ARE ENTITLED TO LEARN MORE ABOUT THE INNER WORKINGS OF THE MAUSOLEUM.
THE MAUSOLEUM, LIKE EVERY GUILD ON EARTH, HAS AT ITS CORE A SEED, WHICH IS A TINY PIECE OF THE AFTERLIFE.
IT ALLOWS US TO COMMUNICATE WITH THE AFTERLIFE, TO RECEIVE NEW ORDERS, AND TO MOVE BETWEEN THIS WORLD AND THE NEXT IN ORDER TO HIDE OUR GUILD DURING THE DAY.

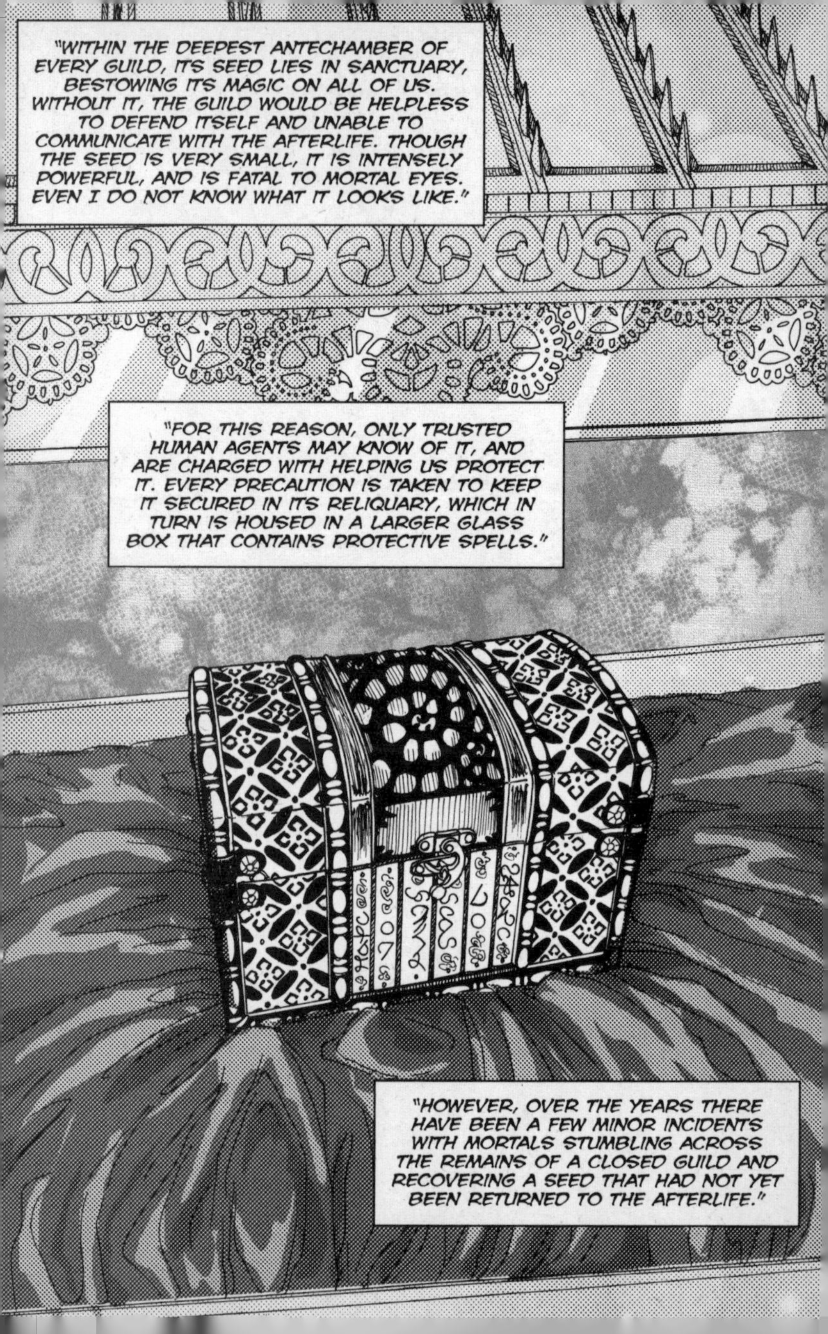
"WITHIN THE DEEPEST ANTECHAMBER OF EVERY GUILD, ITS SEED LIES IN SANCTUARY, BESTOWING ITS MAGIC ON ALL OF US. WITHOUT IT, THE GUILD WOULD BE HELPLESS TO DEFEND ITSELF AND UNABLE TO COMMUNICATE WITH THE AFTERLIFE. THOUGH THE SEED IS VERY SMALL, IT IS INTENSELY POWERFUL, AND IS FATAL TO MORTAL EYES. EVEN I DO NOT KNOW WHAT IT LOOKS LIKE."
"FOR THIS REASON, ONLY TRUSTED HUMAN AGENTS MAY KNOW OF IT, AND ARE CHARGED WITH HELPING US PROTECT IT. EVERY PRECAUTION IS TAKEN TO KEEP IT SECURED IN ITS RELIQUARY, WHICH IN TURN IS HOUSED IN A LARGER GLASS BOX THAT CONTAINS PROTECTIVE SPELLS."
"HOWEVER, OVER THE YEARS THERE HAVE BEEN A FEW MINOR INCIDENTS WITH MORTALS STUMBLING ACROSS THE REMAINS OF A CLOSED GUILD AND RECOVERING A SEED THAT HAD NOT YET BEEN RETURNED TO THE AFTERLIFE."

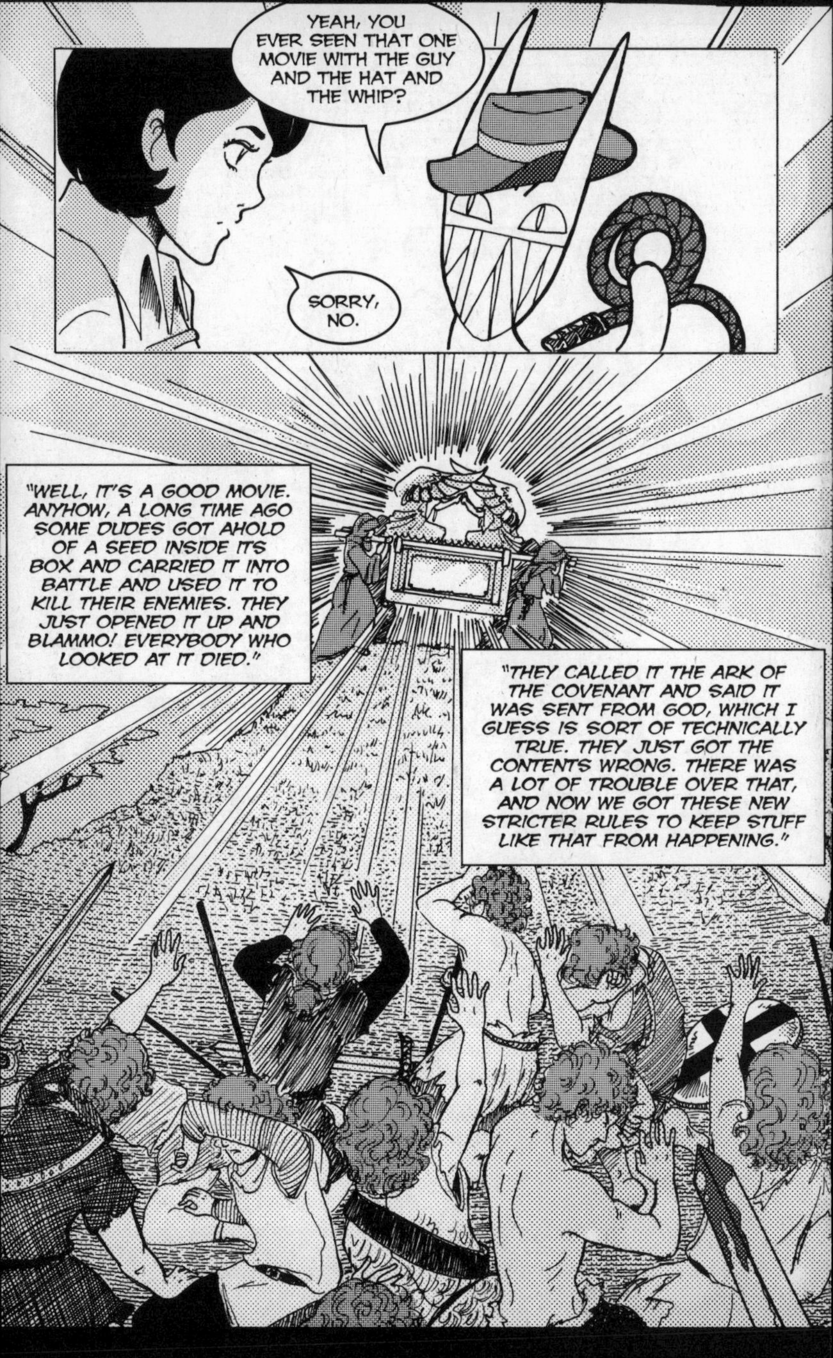
YEAH, YOU EVER SEEN THAT ONE MOVIE WITH THE GUY AND THE HAT AND THE WHIP?
SORRY, NO.
"WELL, IT'S A GOOD MOVIE. ANYHOW, A LONG TIME AGO SOME DUDES GOT AHOLD OF A SEED INSIDE ITS BOX AND CARRIED IT INTO BATTLE AND USED IT TO KILL THEIR ENEMIES. THEY JUST OPENED IT UP AND BLAMMO! EVERYBODY WHO LOOKED AT IT DIED."
"THEY CALLED IT THE ARK OF THE COVENANT AND SAID IT WAS SENT FROM GOD, WHICH I GUESS IS SORT OF TECHNICALLY TRUE. THEY JUST GOT THE CONTENTS WRONG. THERE WAS A LOT OF TROUBLE OVER THAT, AND NOW WE GOT THESE NEW STRICTER RULES TO KEEP STUFF LIKE THAT FROM HAPPENING."

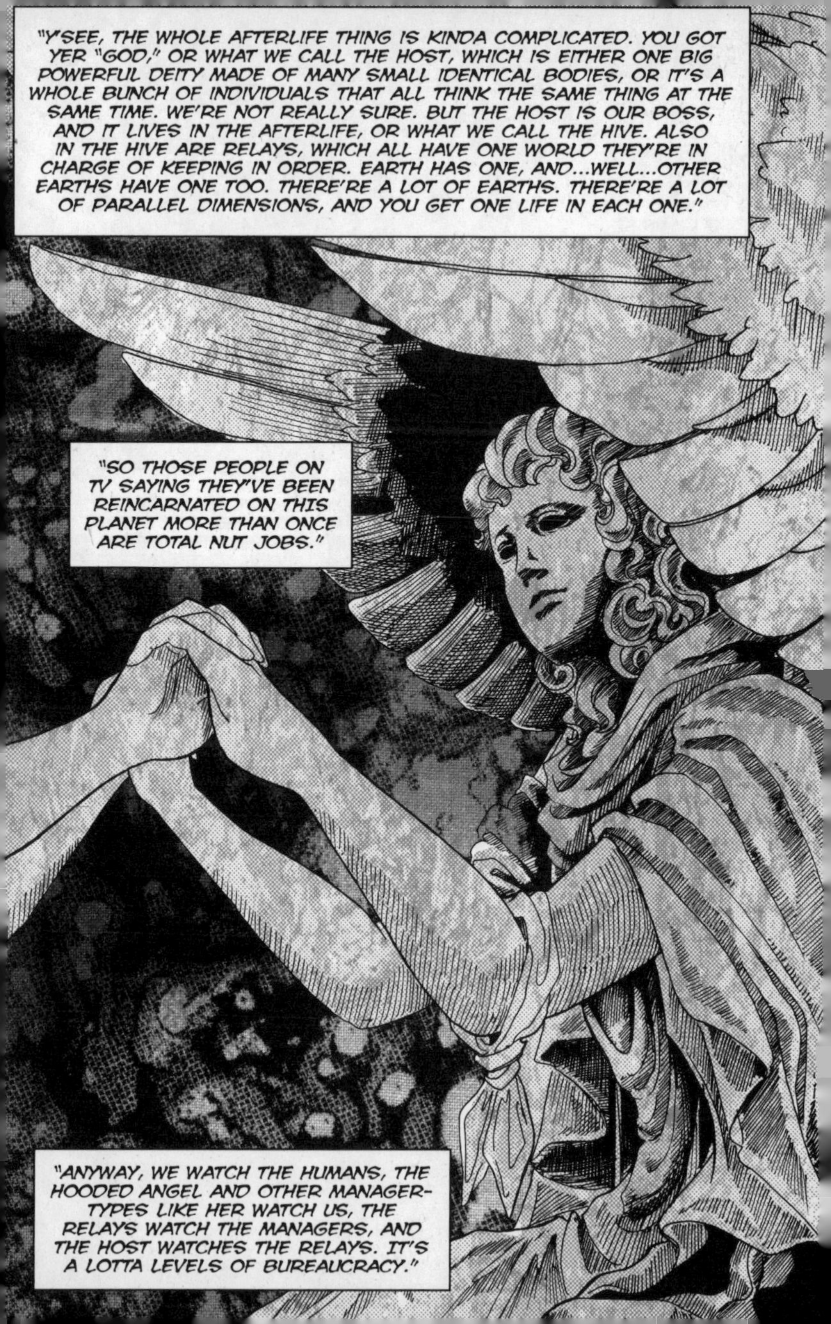
"Y'SEE, THE WHOLE AFTERLIFE THING IS KINDA COMPLICATED. YOU GOT YER "GOD," OR WHAT WE CALL THE HOST, WHICH IS EITHER ONE BIG POWERFUL DEITY MADE OF MANY SMALL IDENTICAL BODIES, OR IT'S A WHOLE BUNCH OF INDIVIDUALS THAT ALL THINK THE SAME THING AT THE SAME TIME. WE'RE NOT REALLY SURE. BUT THE HOST IS OUR BOSS, AND IT LIVES IN THE AFTERLIFE, OR WHAT WE CALL THE HIVE. ALSO IN THE HIVE ARE RELAYS, WHICH ALL HAVE ONE WORLD THEY'RE IN CHARGE OF KEEPING IN ORDER. EARTH HAS ONE, AND...WELL...OTHER EARTHS HAVE ONE TOO. THERE'RE A LOT OF EARTHS. THERE'RE A LOT OF PARALLEL DIMENSIONS, AND YOU GET ONE LIFE IN EACH ONE."
"SO THOSE PEOPLE ON TV SAYING THEY'VE BEEN REINCARNATED ON THIS PLANET MORE THAN ONCE ARE TOTAL NUT JOBS."
"ANYWAY, WE WATCH THE HUMANS, THE HOODED ANGEL AND OTHER MANAGER-TYPES LIKE HER WATCH US, THE RELAYS WATCH THE MANAGERS, AND THE HOST WATCHES THE RELAYS. IT'S A LOTTA LEVELS OF BUREAUCRACY."

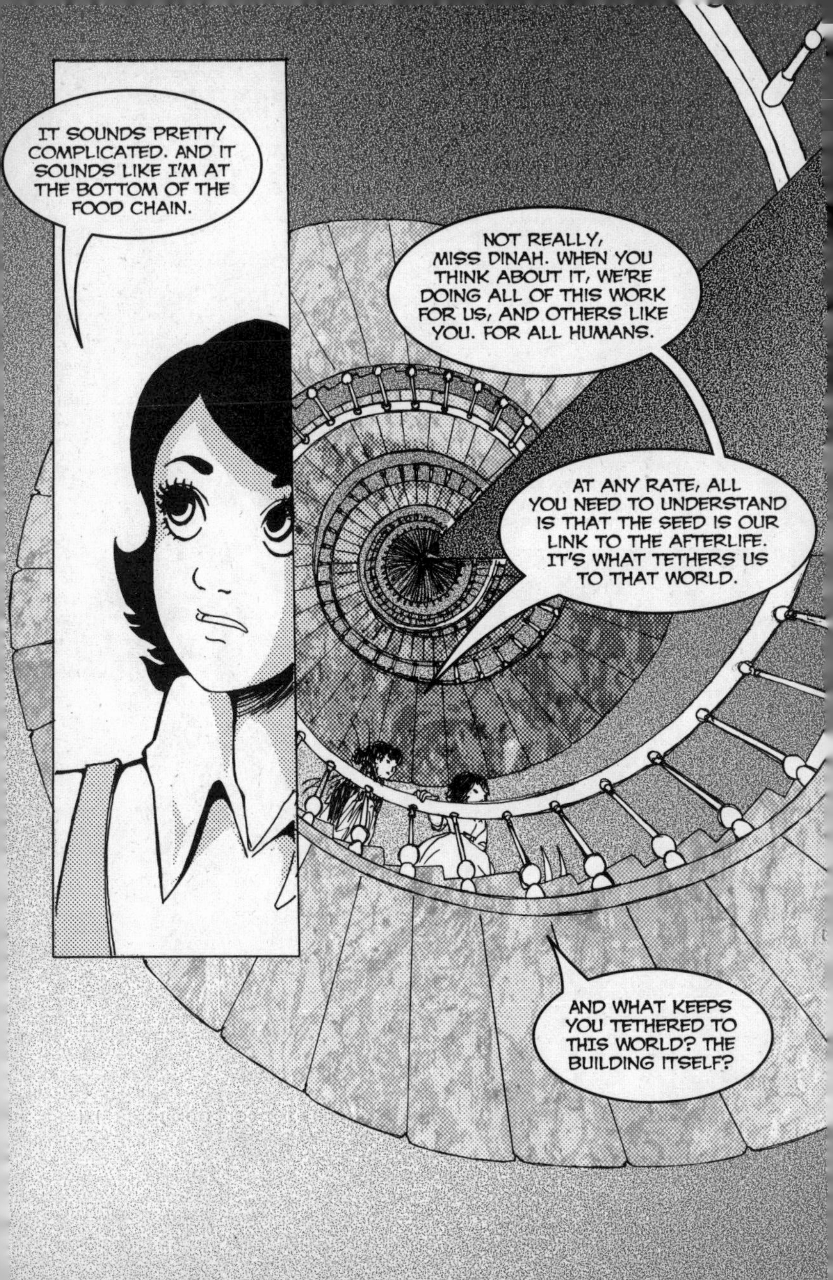
IT SOUNDS PRETTY COMPLICATED. AND IT SOUNDS LIKE I'M AT THE BOTTOM OF THE FOOD CHAIN.
NOT REALLY, MISS DINAH. WHEN YOU THINK ABOUT IT, WE'RE DOING ALL OF THIS WORK FOR US, AND OTHERS LIKE YOU. FOR ALL HUMANS.
AT ANY RATE, ALL YOU NEED TO UNDERSTAND IS THAT THE SEED IS OUR LINK TO THE AFTERLIFE. IT'S WHAT TETHERS US TO THAT WORLD.
AND WHAT KEEPS YOU TETHERED TO THIS WORLD? THE BUILDING ITSELF?

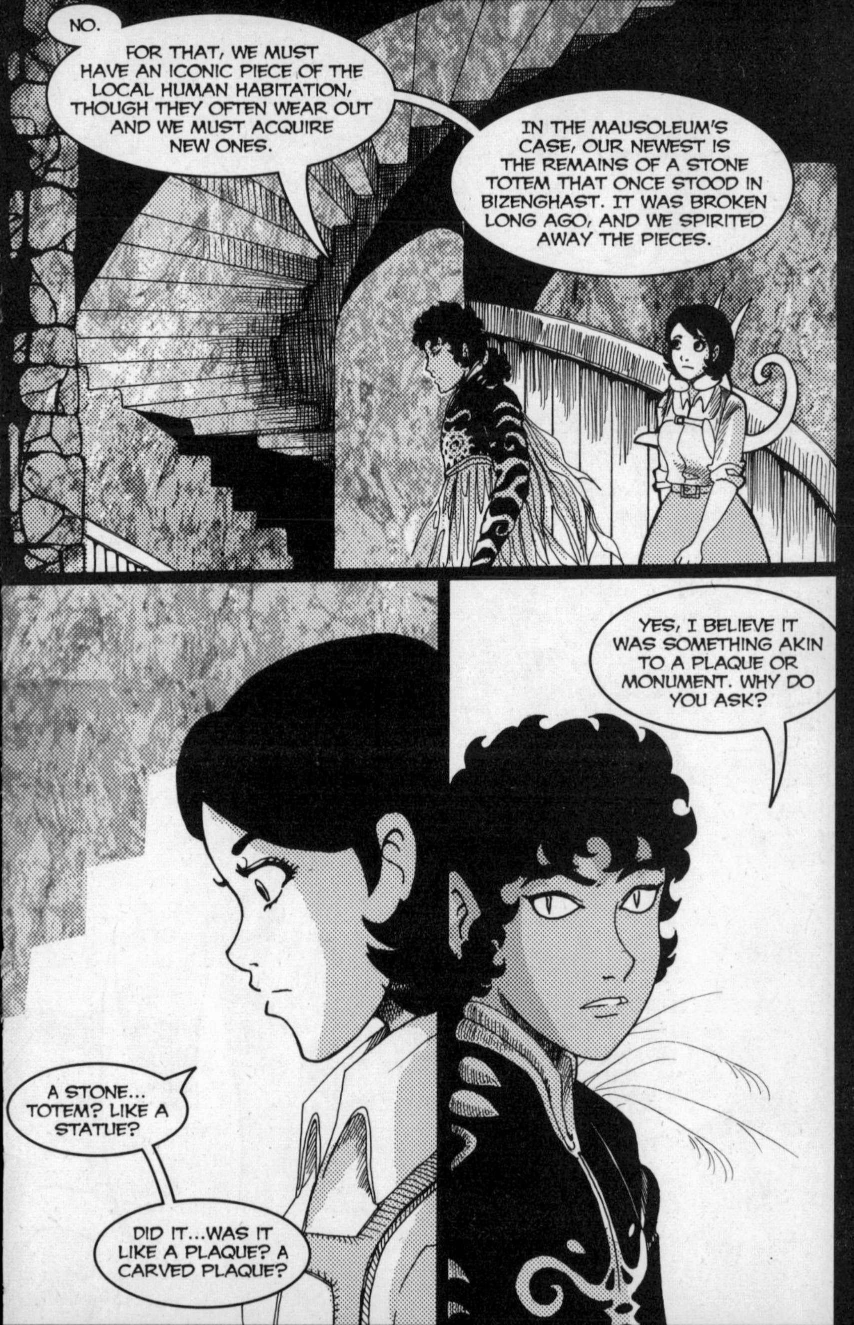
NO.
FOR THAT, WE MUST HAVE AN ICONIC PIECE OF THE LOCAL HUMAN HABITATION, THOUGH THEY OFTEN WEAR OUT AND WE MUST ACQUIRE NEW ONES.
IN THE MAUSOLEUM'S CASE, OUR NEWEST IS THE REMAINS OF A STONE TOTEM THAT ONCE STOOD IN BIZENGHAST. IT WAS BROKEN LONG AGO, AND WE SPIRITED AWAY THE PIECES.
A STONE... TOTEM? LIKE A STATUE?
DID IT...WAS IT LIKE A PLAQUE? A CARVED PLAQUE?
YES, I BELIEVE IT WAS SOMETHING AKIN TO A PLAQUE OR MONUMENT. WHY DO YOU ASK?

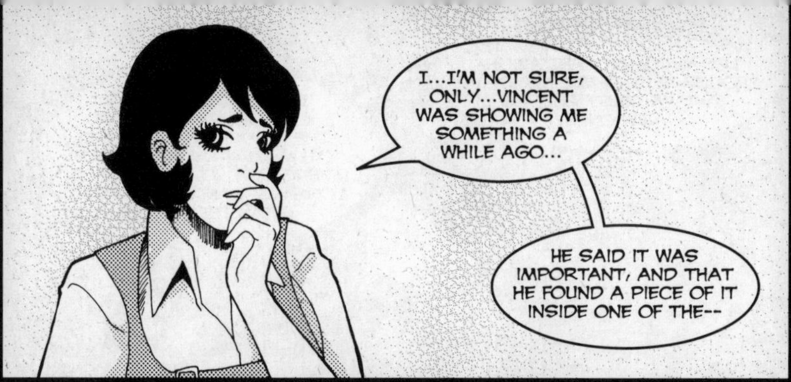
I...I'M NOT SURE, ONLY...VINCENT WAS SHOWING ME SOMETHING A WHILE AGO...
HE SAID IT WAS IMPORTANT, AND THAT HE FOUND A PIECE OF IT INSIDE ONE OF THE--

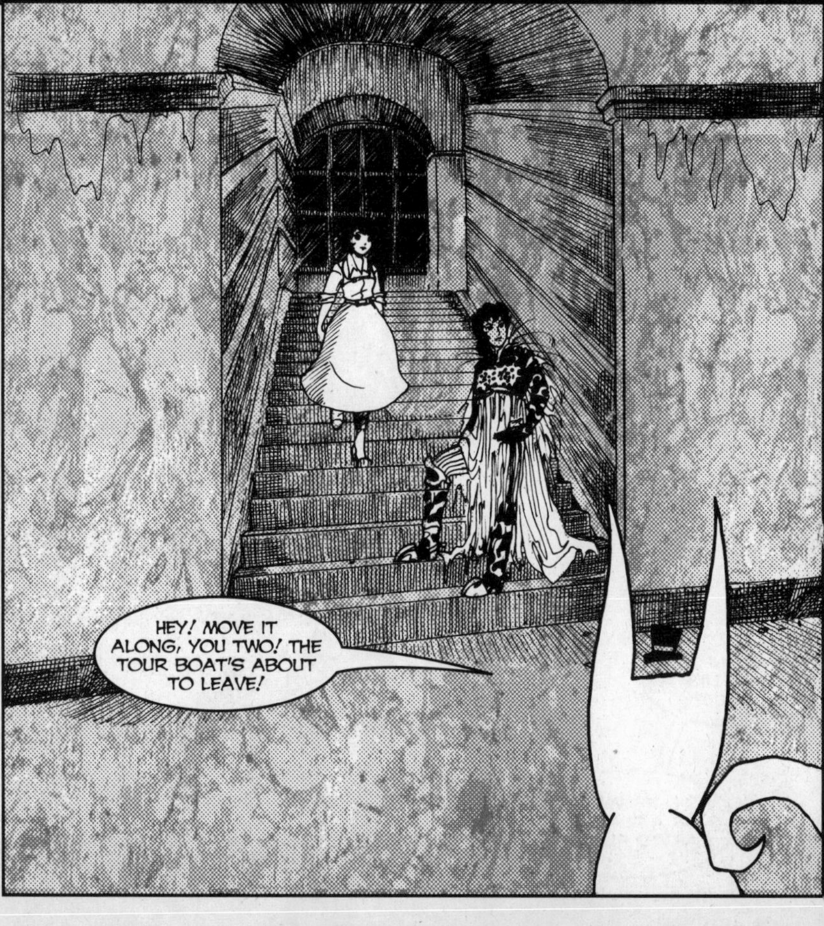
HEY! MOVE IT ALONG, YOU TWO! THE TOUR BOAT'S ABOUT TO LEAVE!

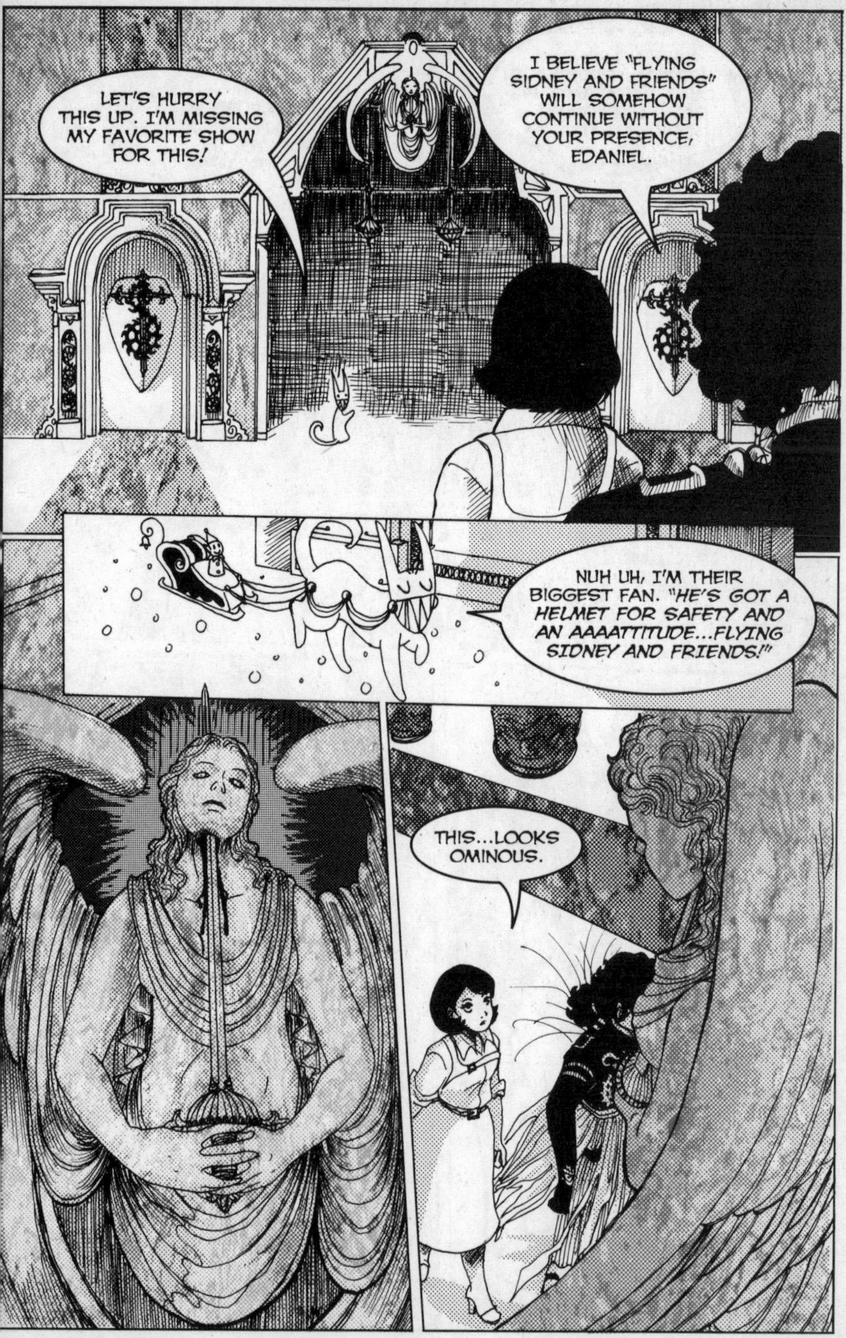
LET'S HURRY THIS UP. I'M MISSING MY FAVORITE SHOW FOR THIS!
I BELIEVE "FLYING SIDNEY AND FRIENDS" WILL SOMEHOW CONTINUE WITHOUT YOUR PRESENCE, EDANIEL.
NUH UH, I'M THEIR BIGGEST FAN. "*HE'S GOT A HELMET FOR SAFETY AND AN AAAATTITUDE...FLYING SIDNEY AND FRIENDS!*"
THIS...LOOKS OMINOUS.

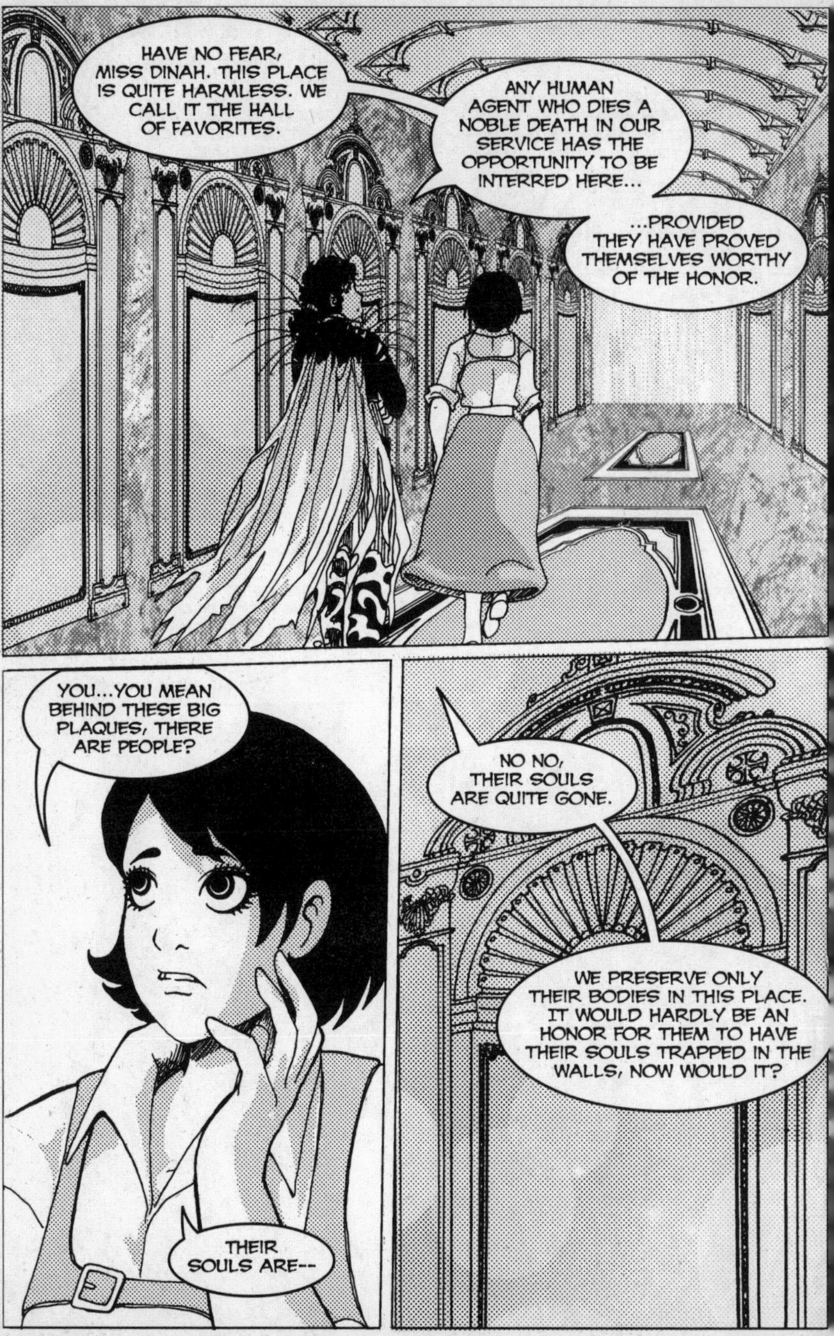
HAVE NO FEAR, MISS DINAH. THIS PLACE IS QUITE HARMLESS. WE CALL IT THE HALL OF FAVORITES.
ANY HUMAN AGENT WHO DIES A NOBLE DEATH IN OUR SERVICE HAS THE OPPORTUNITY TO BE INTERRED HERE...
...PROVIDED THEY HAVE PROVED THEMSELVES WORTHY OF THE HONOR.
YOU...YOU MEAN BEHIND THESE BIG PLAQUES, THERE ARE PEOPLE?
THEIR SOULS ARE--
NO NO, THEIR SOULS ARE QUITE GONE.
WE PRESERVE ONLY THEIR BODIES IN THIS PLACE. IT WOULD HARDLY BE AN HONOR FOR THEM TO HAVE THEIR SOULS TRAPPED IN THE WALLS, NOW WOULD IT?

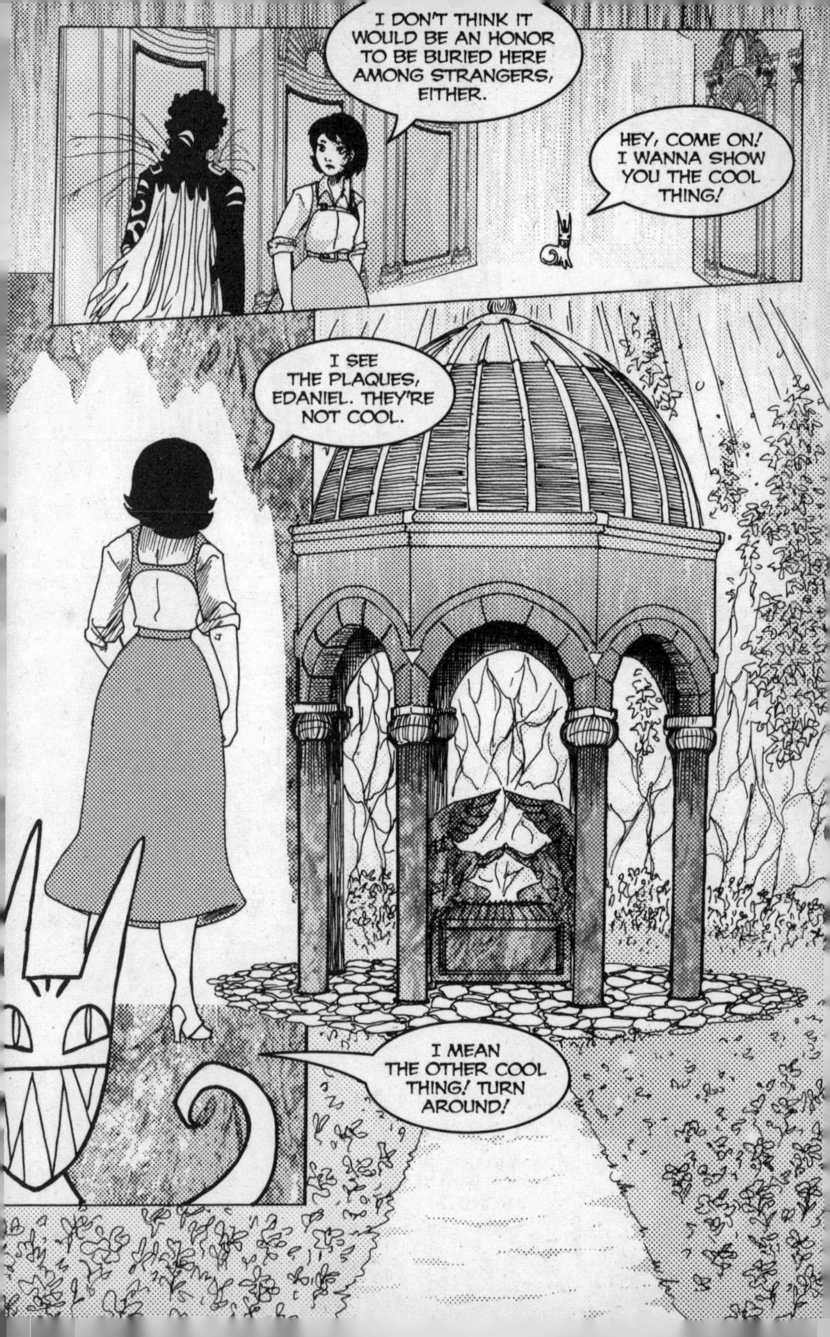
I DON'T THINK IT WOULD BE AN HONOR TO BE BURIED HERE AMONG STRANGERS, EITHER.
HEY, COME ON! I WANNA SHOW YOU THE COOL THING!
I SEE THE PLAQUES, EDANIEL. THEY'RE NOT COOL.
I MEAN THE OTHER COOL THING! TURN AROUND!

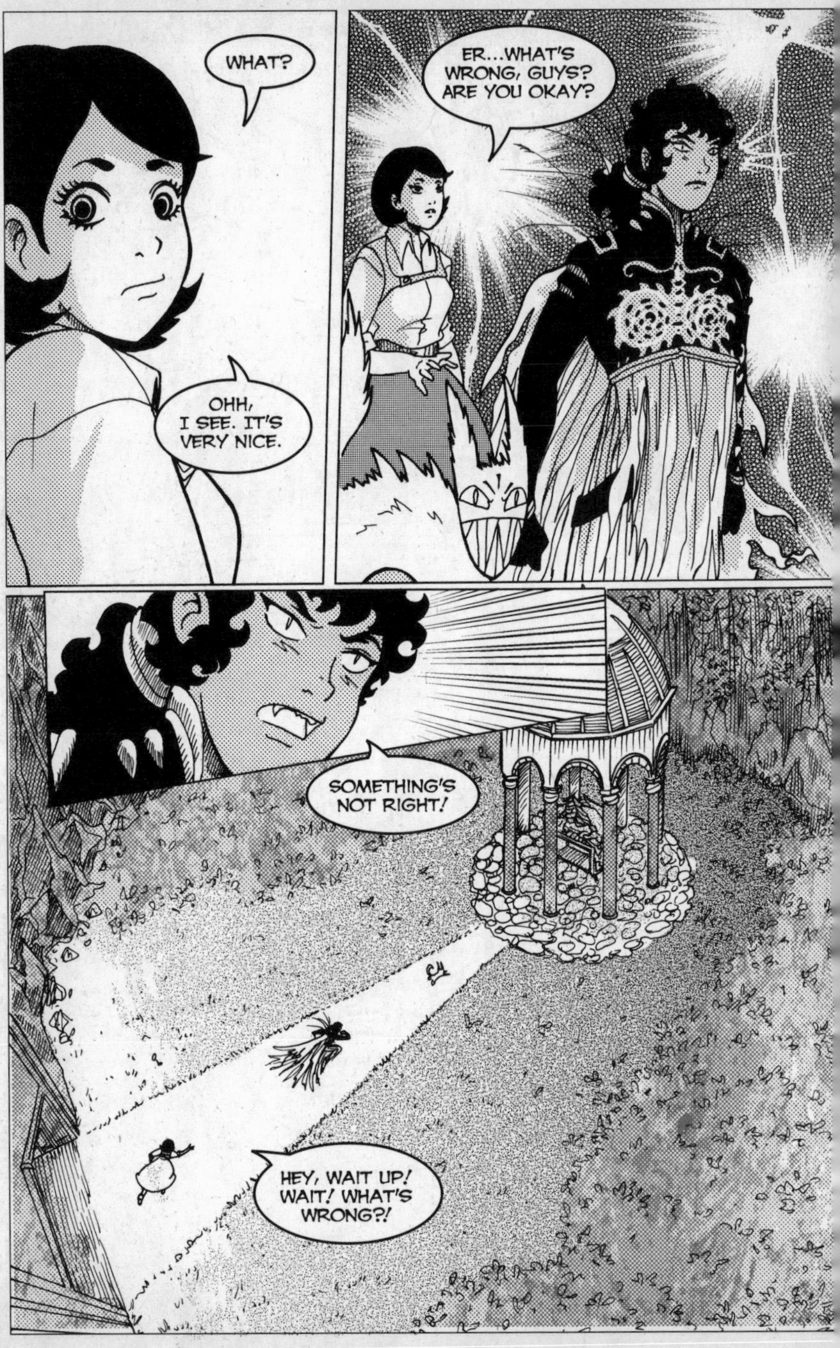
WHAT?
OHH, I SEE. IT'S VERY NICE.
ER...WHAT'S WRONG, GUYS? ARE YOU OKAY?
SOMETHING'S NOT RIGHT!
HEY, WAIT UP! WAIT! WHAT'S WRONG?!

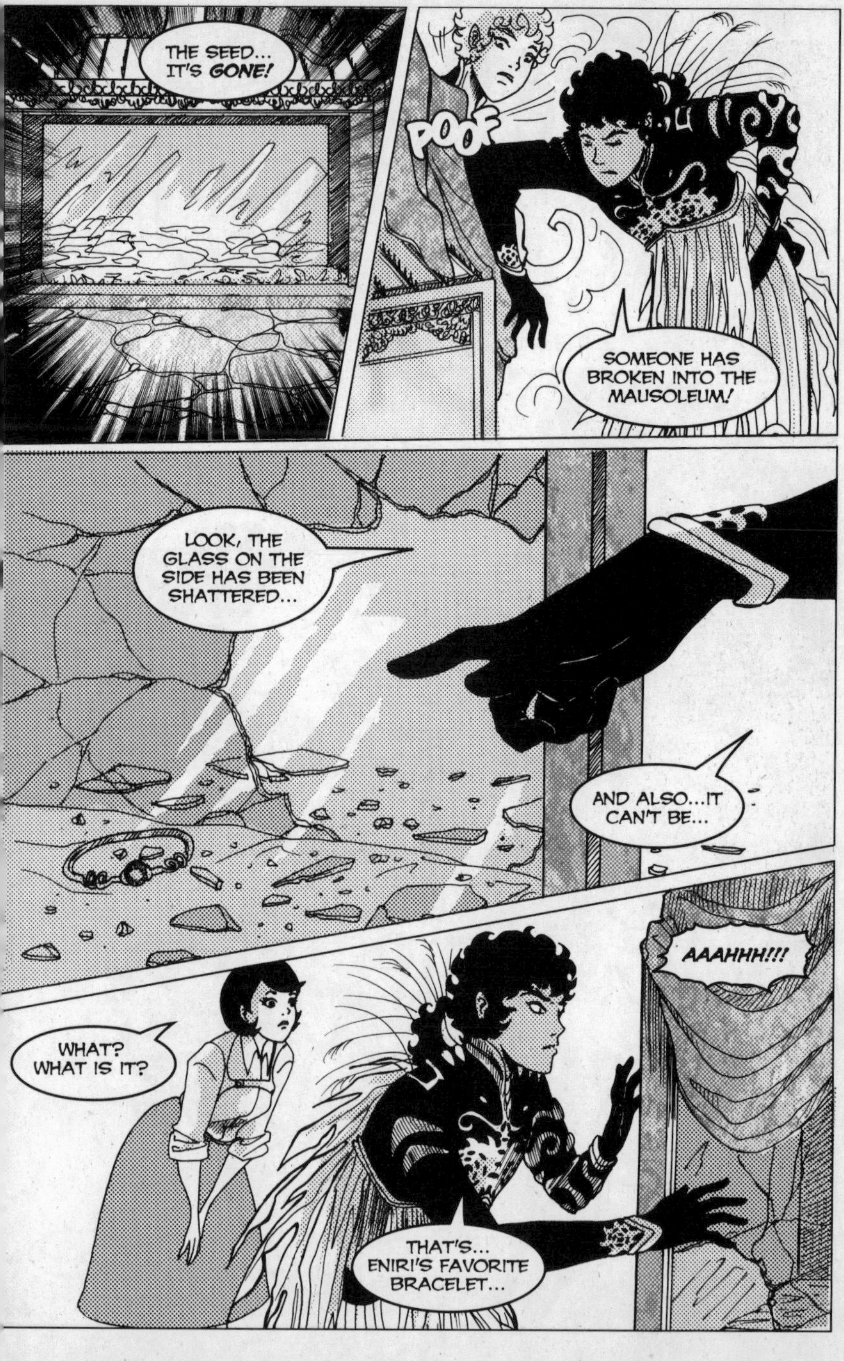
THE SEED... IT'S **GONE!**
POOF
SOMEONE HAS BROKEN INTO THE MAUSOLEUM!
LOOK, THE GLASS ON THE SIDE HAS BEEN SHATTERED...
AND ALSO...IT CAN'T BE...
WHAT? WHAT IS IT?
AAAHHH!!!
THAT'S... ENIRI'S FAVORITE BRACELET...

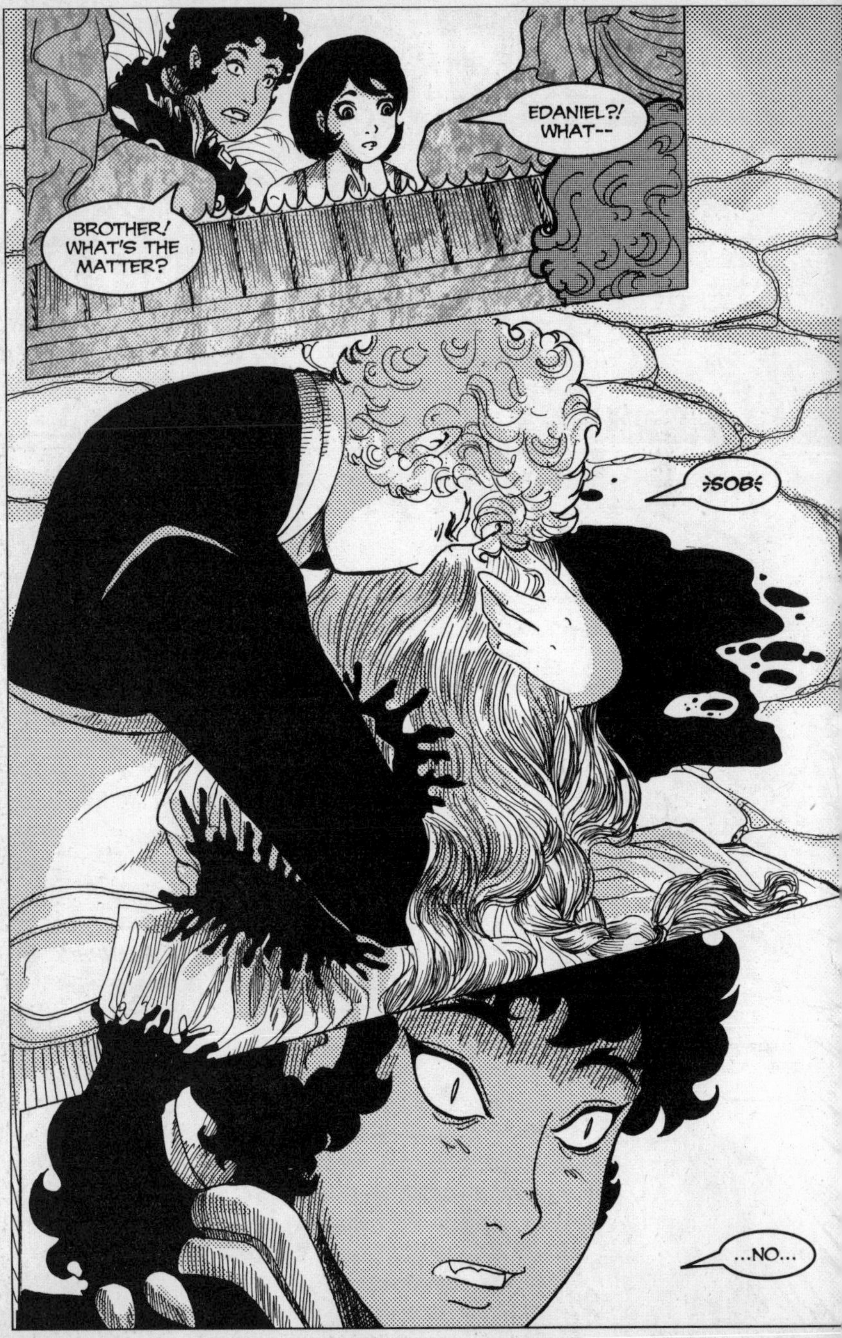
BROTHER! WHAT'S THE MATTER?
EDANIEL?! WHAT--
*SOB*
...NO...

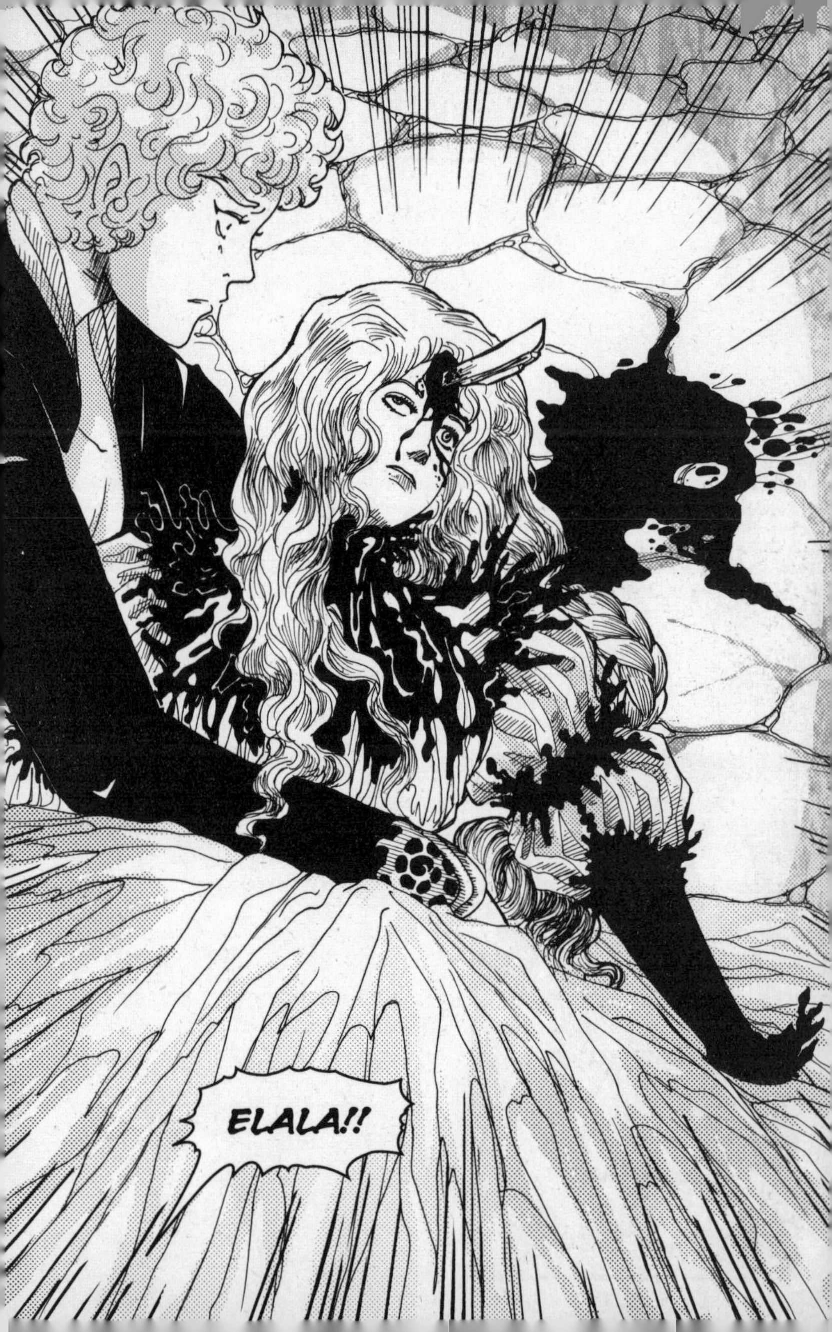
ELALA!!

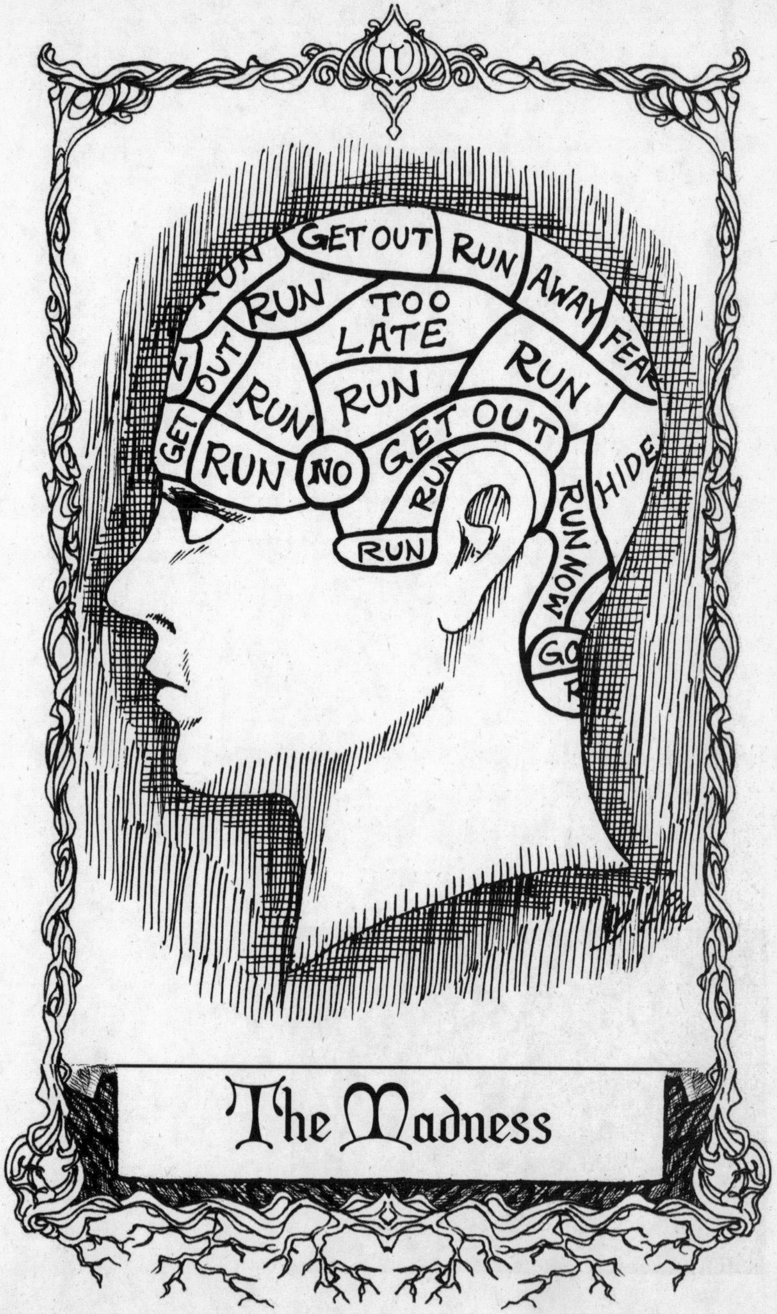
IV
RUN
GET OUT
RUN
AWAY
RUN
TOO LATE
OUT
RUN
RUN
GET
RUN
NO
GET OUT
RUN
HIDE
RUN NOW
RUN
GO

The Madness

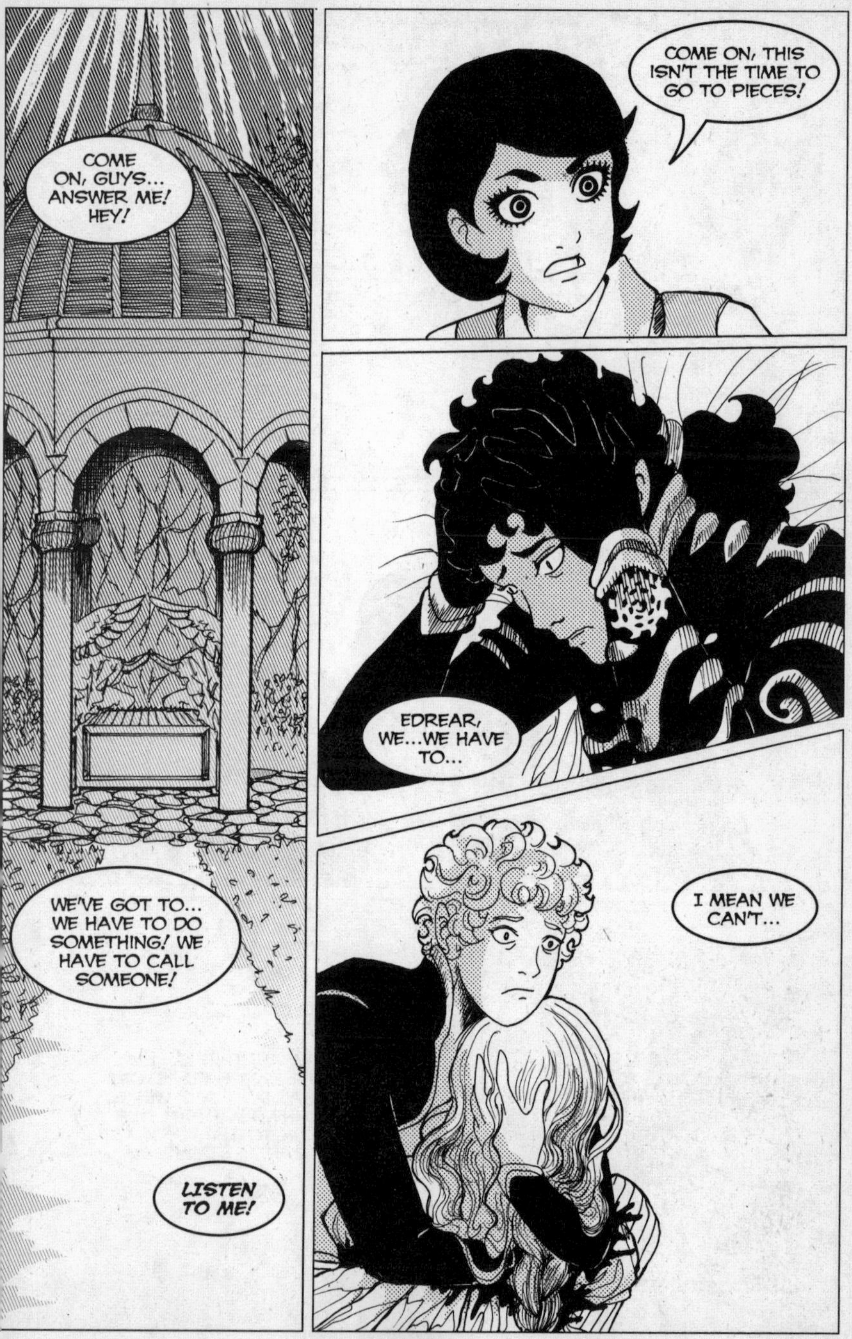
COME ON, GUYS... ANSWER ME! HEY!
WE'VE GOT TO... WE HAVE TO DO SOMETHING! WE HAVE TO CALL SOMEONE!
LISTEN TO ME!
COME ON, THIS ISN'T THE TIME TO GO TO PIECES!
EDREAR, WE...WE HAVE TO...
I MEAN WE CAN'T...

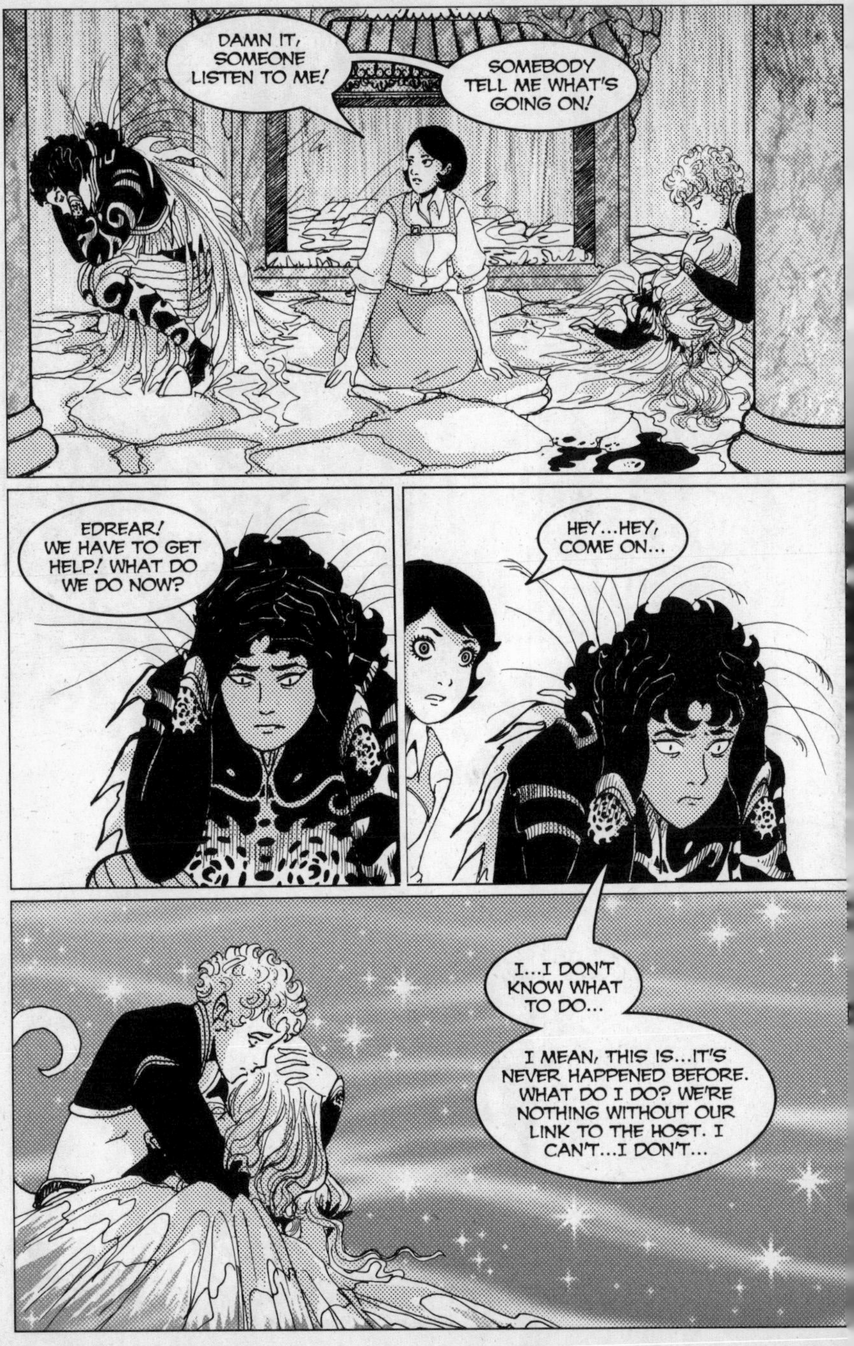
DAMN IT, SOMEONE LISTEN TO ME!
SOMEBODY TELL ME WHAT'S GOING ON!
EDREAR! WE HAVE TO GET HELP! WHAT DO WE DO NOW?
HEY...HEY, COME ON...
I...I DON'T KNOW WHAT TO DO...
I MEAN, THIS IS...IT'S NEVER HAPPENED BEFORE. WHAT DO I DO? WE'RE NOTHING WITHOUT OUR LINK TO THE HOST. I CAN'T...I DON'T...

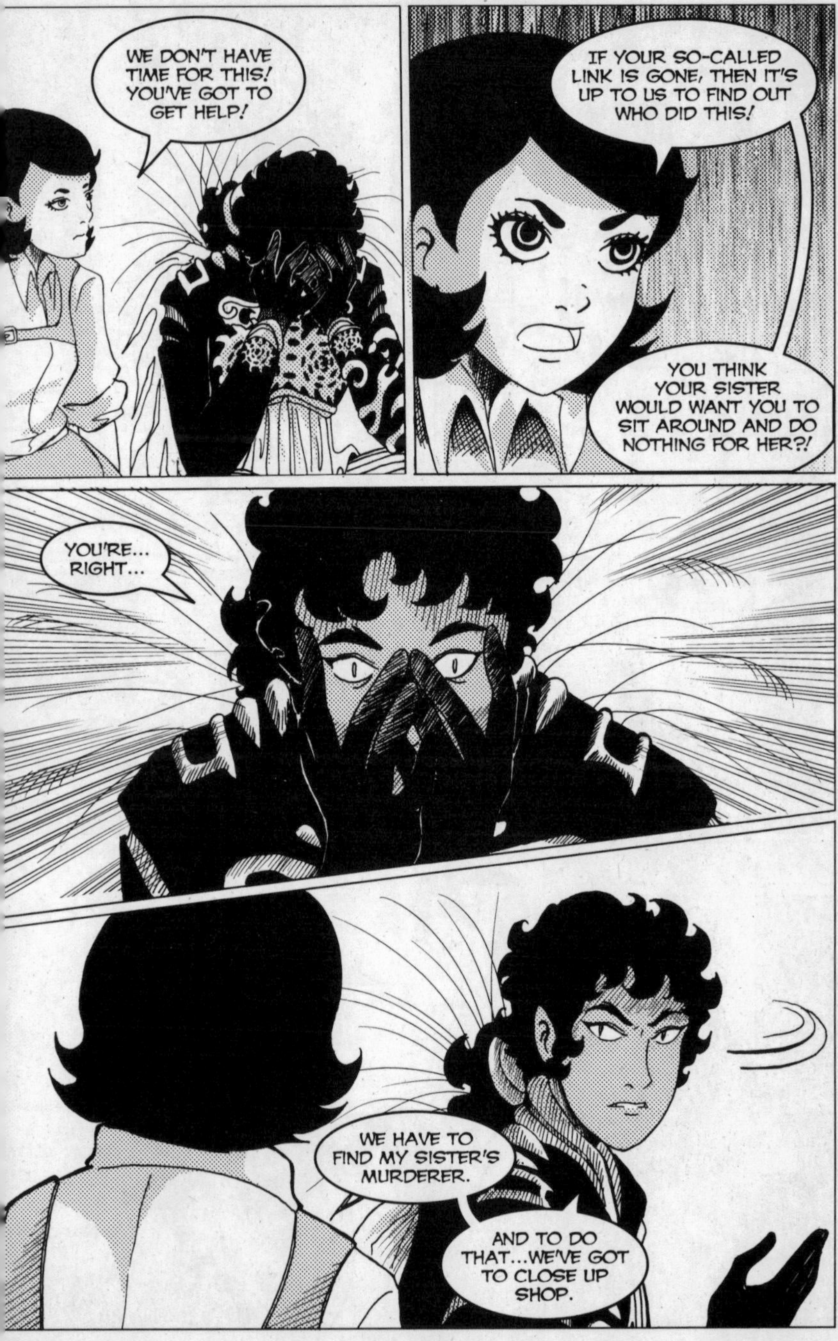
WE DON'T HAVE TIME FOR THIS! YOU'VE GOT TO GET HELP!
IF YOUR SO-CALLED LINK IS GONE, THEN IT'S UP TO US TO FIND OUT WHO DID THIS!
YOU THINK YOUR SISTER WOULD WANT YOU TO SIT AROUND AND DO NOTHING FOR HER?!
YOU'RE... RIGHT...
WE HAVE TO FIND MY SISTER'S MURDERER.
AND TO DO THAT...WE'VE GOT TO CLOSE UP SHOP.

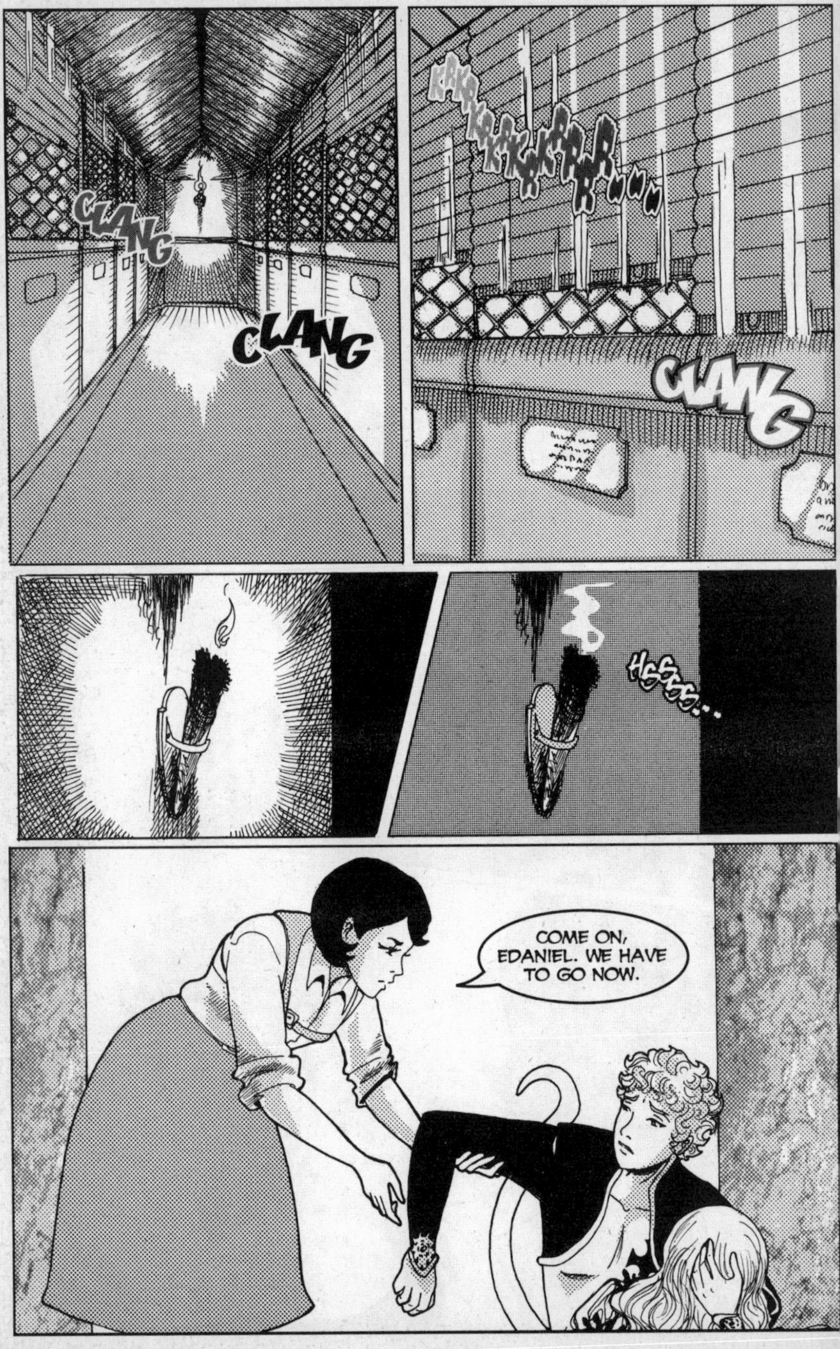

CLANG
CLANG
KRRRRRRRRRRRRR
CLANG
HSSSS...
COME ON, EDANIEL. WE HAVE TO GO NOW.

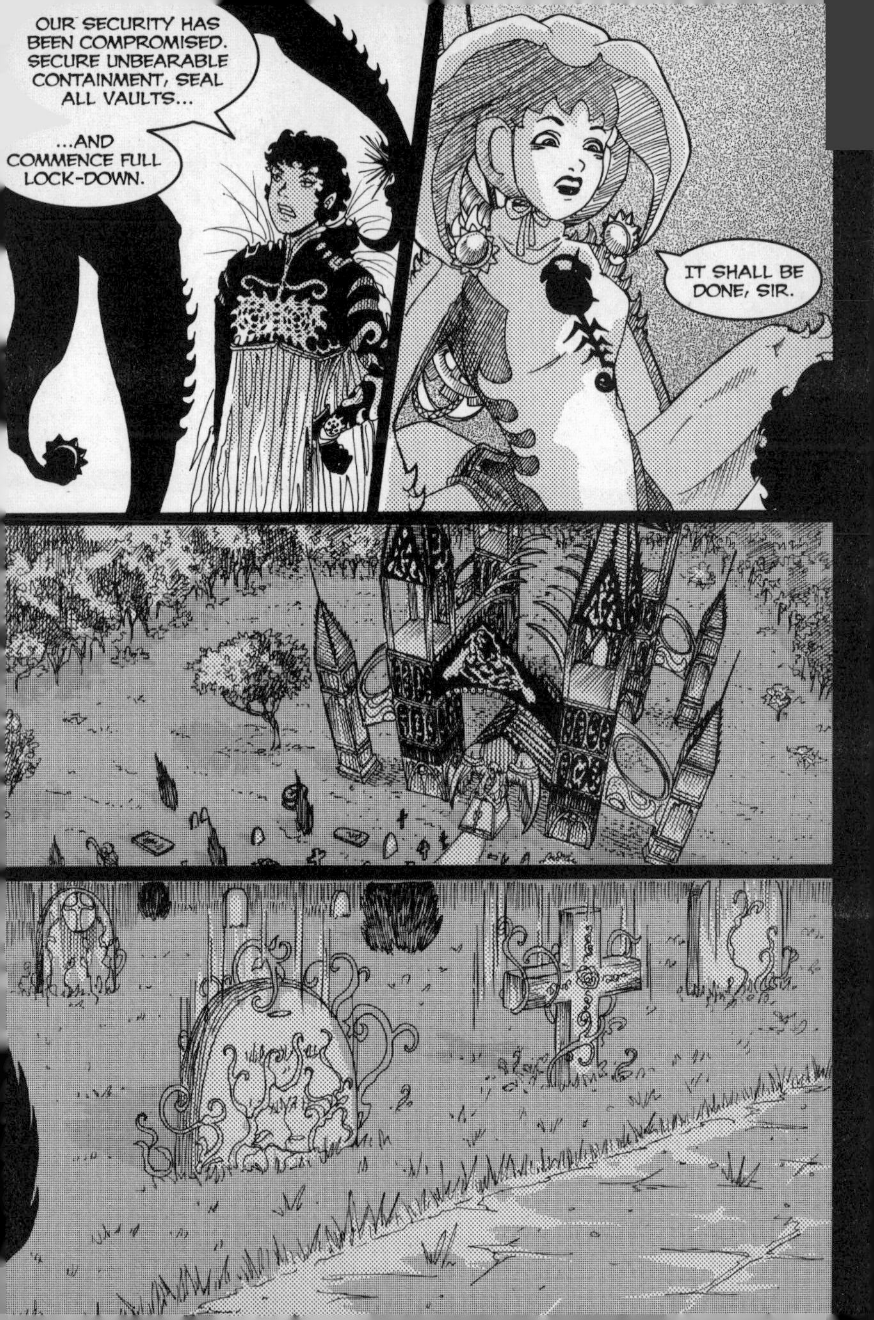
OUR SECURITY HAS BEEN COMPROMISED. SECURE UNBEARABLE CONTAINMENT, SEAL ALL VAULTS...
...AND COMMENCE FULL LOCK-DOWN.
IT SHALL BE DONE, SIR.

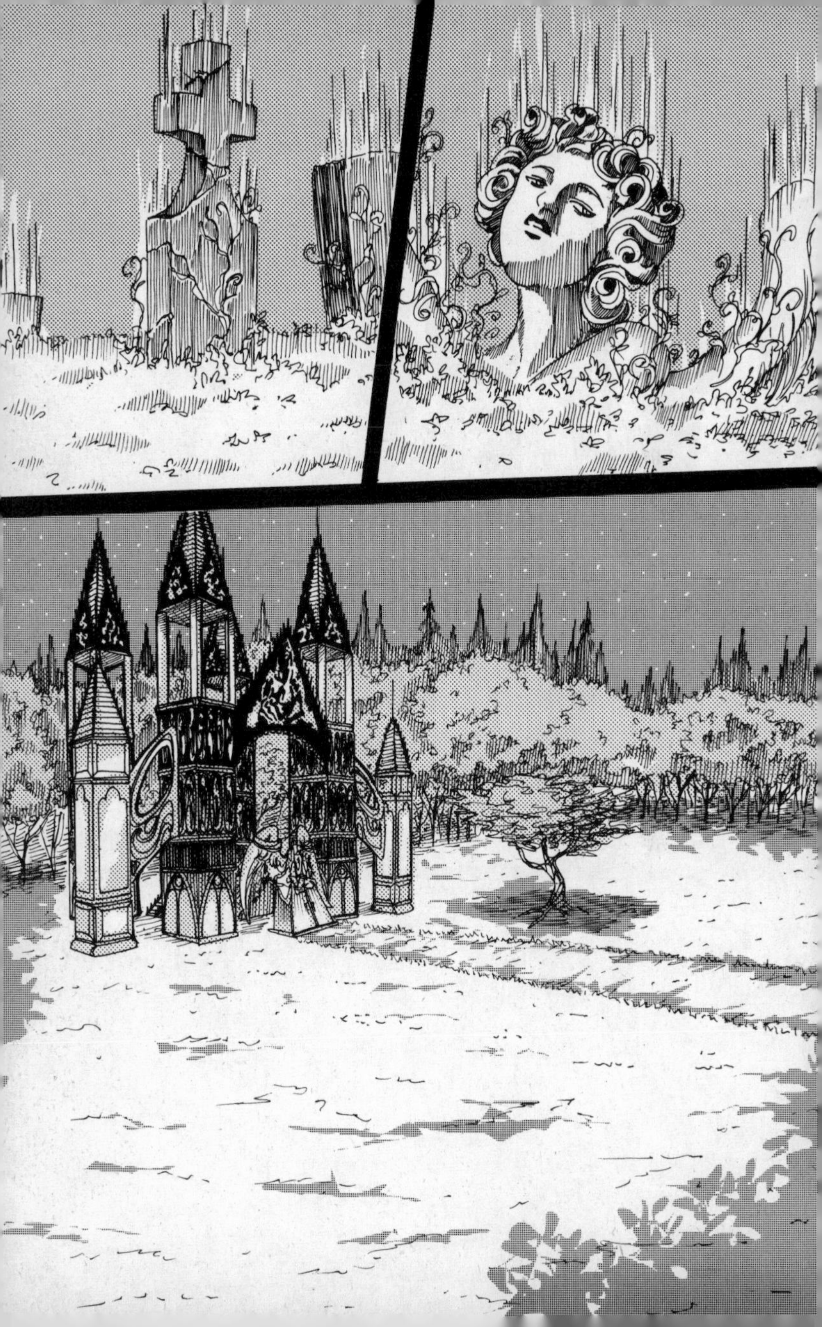

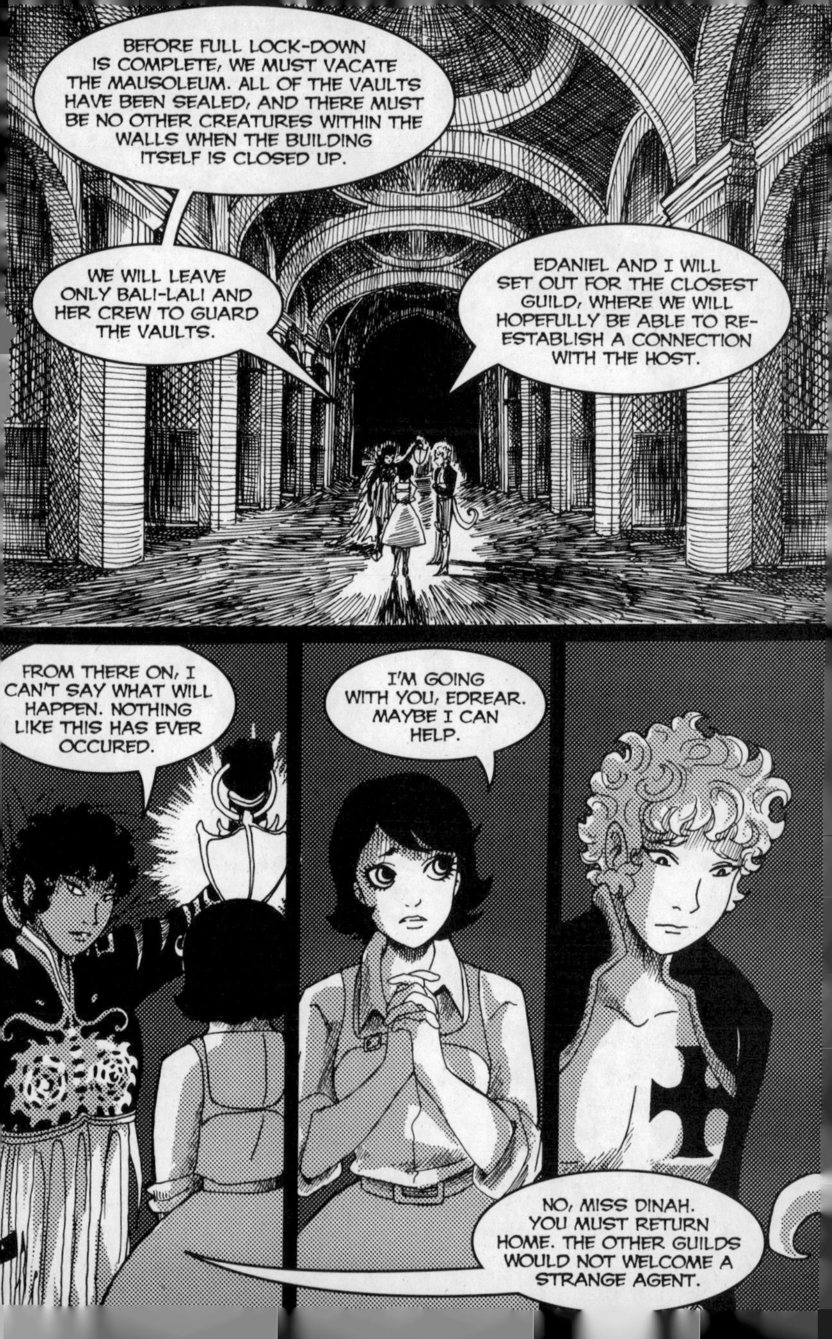
BEFORE FULL LOCK-DOWN IS COMPLETE, WE MUST VACATE THE MAUSOLEUM. ALL OF THE VAULTS HAVE BEEN SEALED, AND THERE MUST BE NO OTHER CREATURES WITHIN THE WALLS WHEN THE BUILDING ITSELF IS CLOSED UP.
WE WILL LEAVE ONLY BALI-LALI AND HER CREW TO GUARD THE VAULTS.
EDANIEL AND I WILL SET OUT FOR THE CLOSEST GUILD, WHERE WE WILL HOPEFULLY BE ABLE TO RE-ESTABLISH A CONNECTION WITH THE HOST.
FROM THERE ON, I CAN'T SAY WHAT WILL HAPPEN. NOTHING LIKE THIS HAS EVER OCCURED.
I'M GOING WITH YOU, EDREAR. MAYBE I CAN HELP.
NO, MISS DINAH. YOU MUST RETURN HOME. THE OTHER GUILDS WOULD NOT WELCOME A STRANGE AGENT.

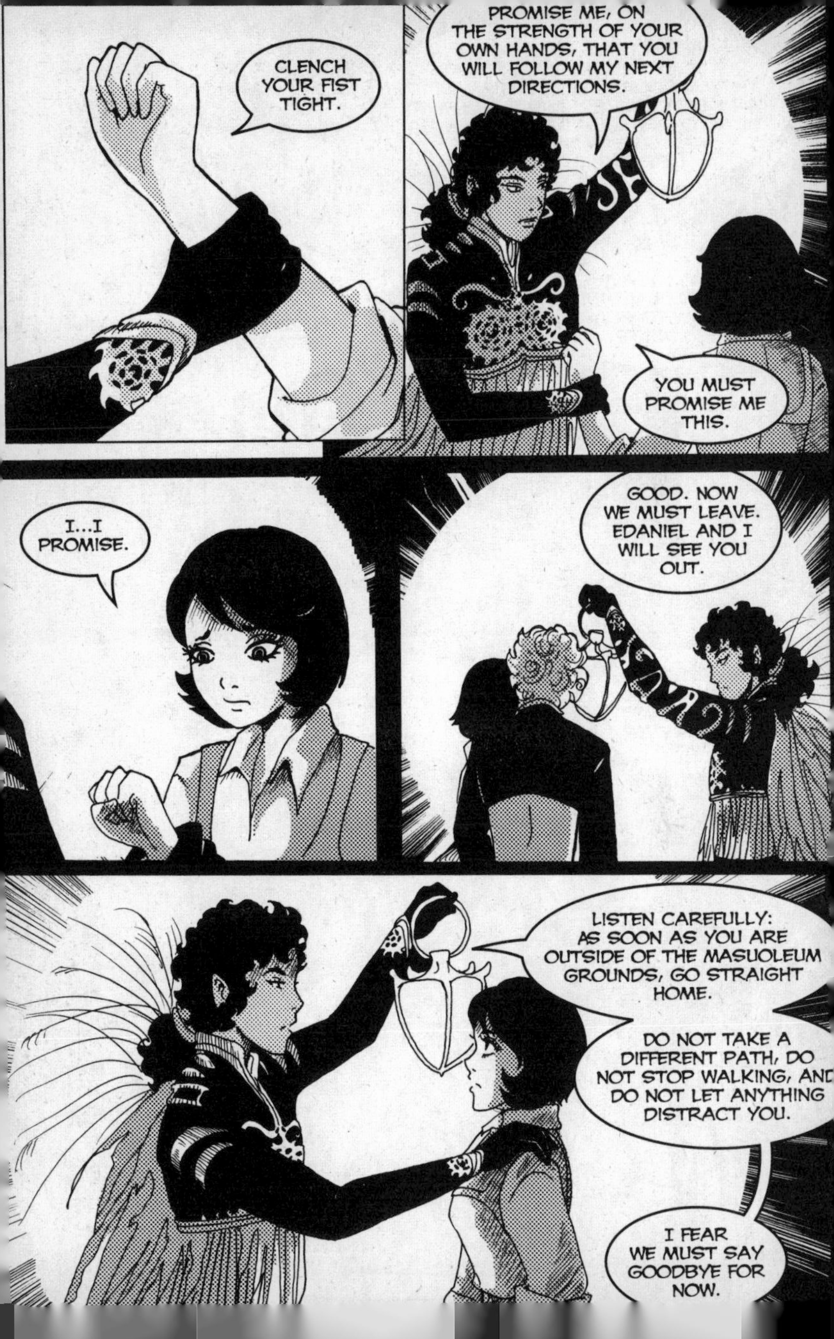
CLENCH YOUR FIST TIGHT.
PROMISE ME, ON THE STRENGTH OF YOUR OWN HANDS, THAT YOU WILL FOLLOW MY NEXT DIRECTIONS.
YOU MUST PROMISE ME THIS.
I...I PROMISE.
GOOD. NOW WE MUST LEAVE. EDANIEL AND I WILL SEE YOU OUT.
LISTEN CAREFULLY: AS SOON AS YOU ARE OUTSIDE OF THE MASUOLEUM GROUNDS, GO STRAIGHT HOME.
DO NOT TAKE A DIFFERENT PATH, DO NOT STOP WALKING, AND DO NOT LET ANYTHING DISTRACT YOU.
I FEAR WE MUST SAY GOODBYE FOR NOW.

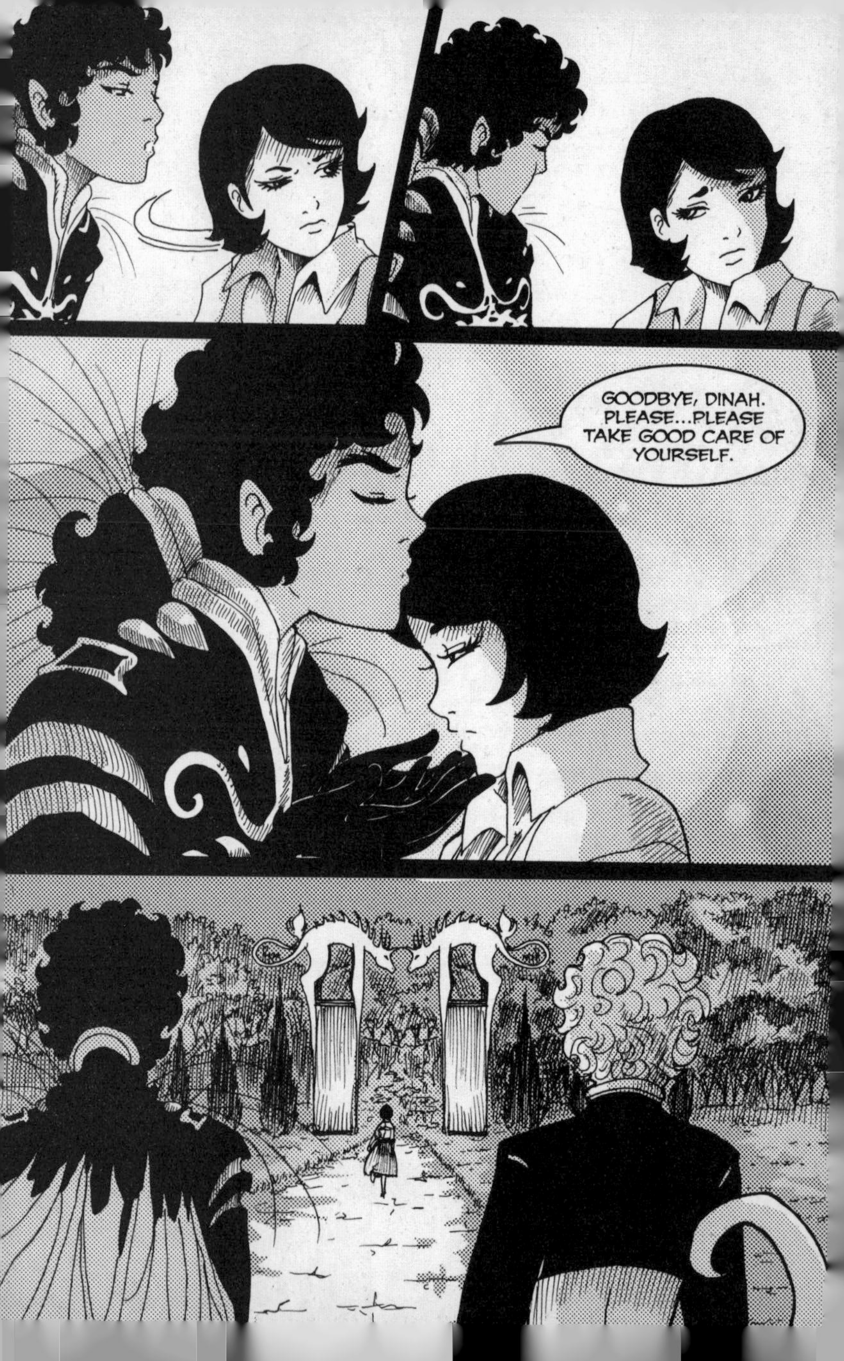
GOODBYE, DINAH. PLEASE...PLEASE TAKE GOOD CARE OF YOURSELF.

DUDE, WHAT THE HELL WAS THAT ALL ABOUT? WHY DO YOU GET SO INVOLVED?
I DO NOT MEAN TO...SOMETIMES IT JUST HAPPENS. I CAN'T EXPLAIN THESE HUMAN FEELINGS I SOME-TIMES HAVE.
YEAH, FOR CHICKS. ALWAYS FOR WOMEN.
I CAN'T HELP IT. THEY'RE SO PRETTY.
YOU'RE SUCH A SUCKER.

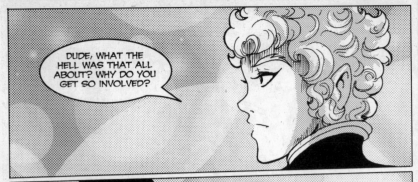

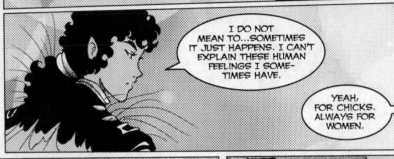

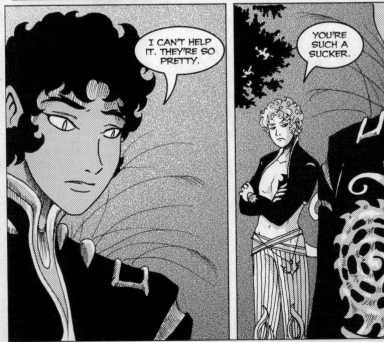

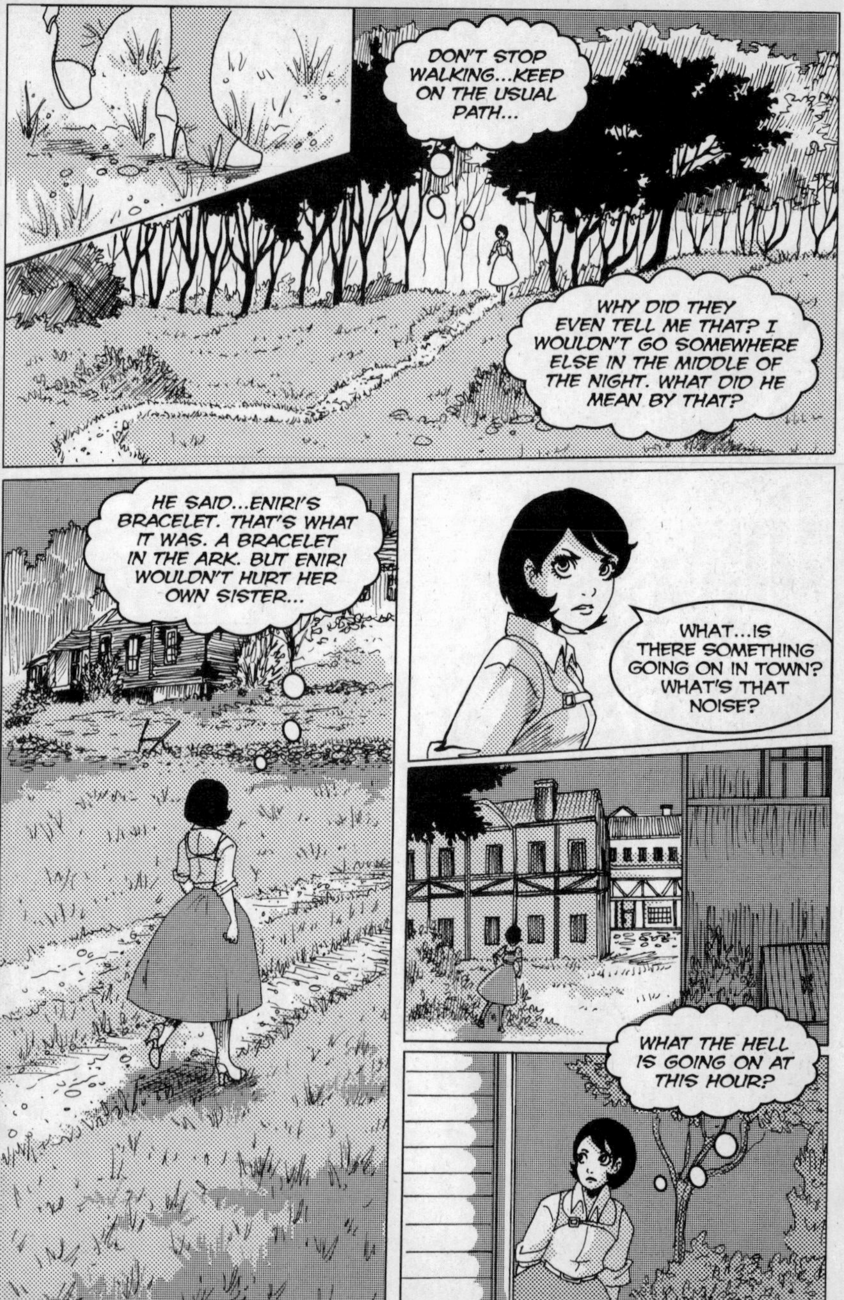
DON'T STOP WALKING...KEEP ON THE USUAL PATH...
WHY DID THEY EVEN TELL ME THAT? I WOULDN'T GO SOMEWHERE ELSE IN THE MIDDLE OF THE NIGHT. WHAT DID HE MEAN BY THAT?
HE SAID...ENIRI'S BRACELET. THAT'S WHAT IT WAS. A BRACELET IN THE ARK. BUT ENIRI WOULDN'T HURT HER OWN SISTER...
WHAT...IS THERE SOMETHING GOING ON IN TOWN? WHAT'S THAT NOISE?
WHAT THE HELL IS GOING ON AT THIS HOUR?

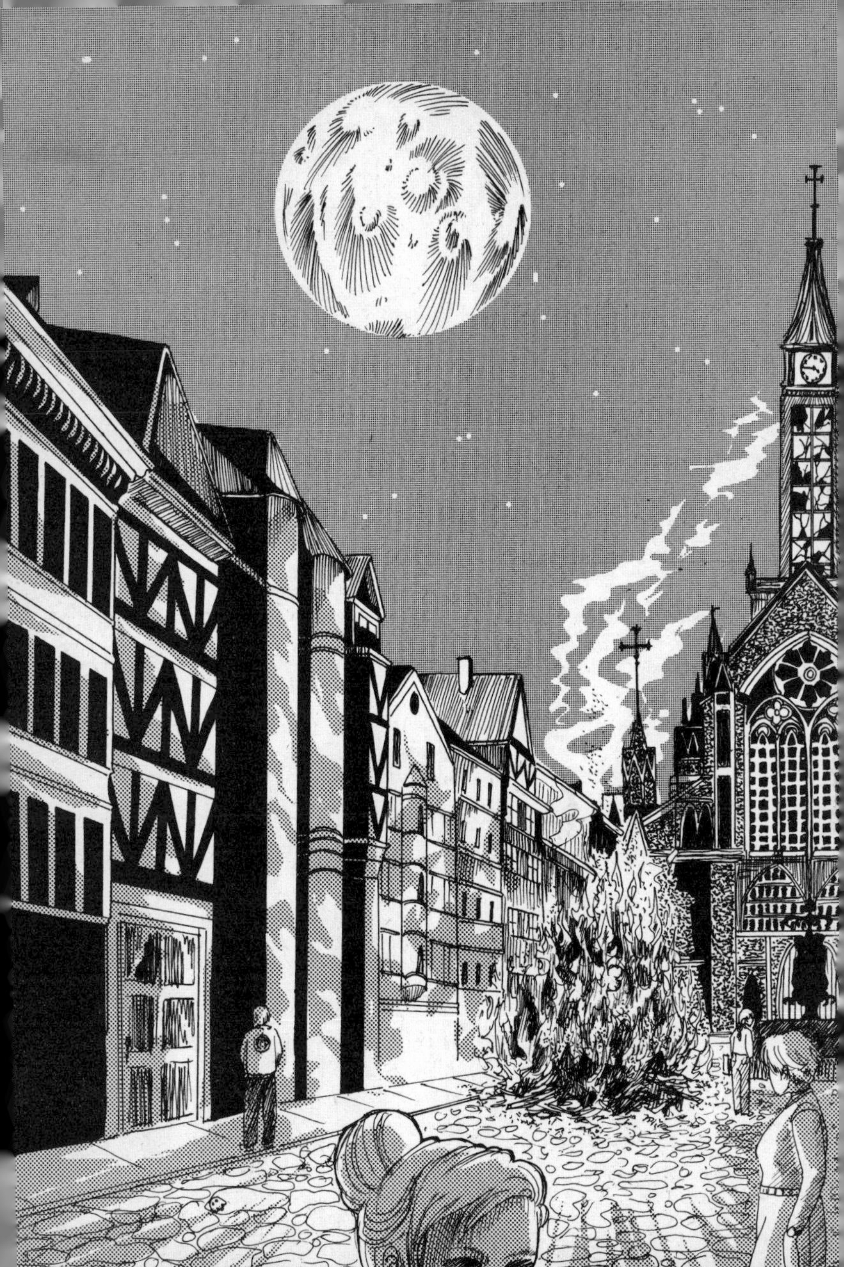

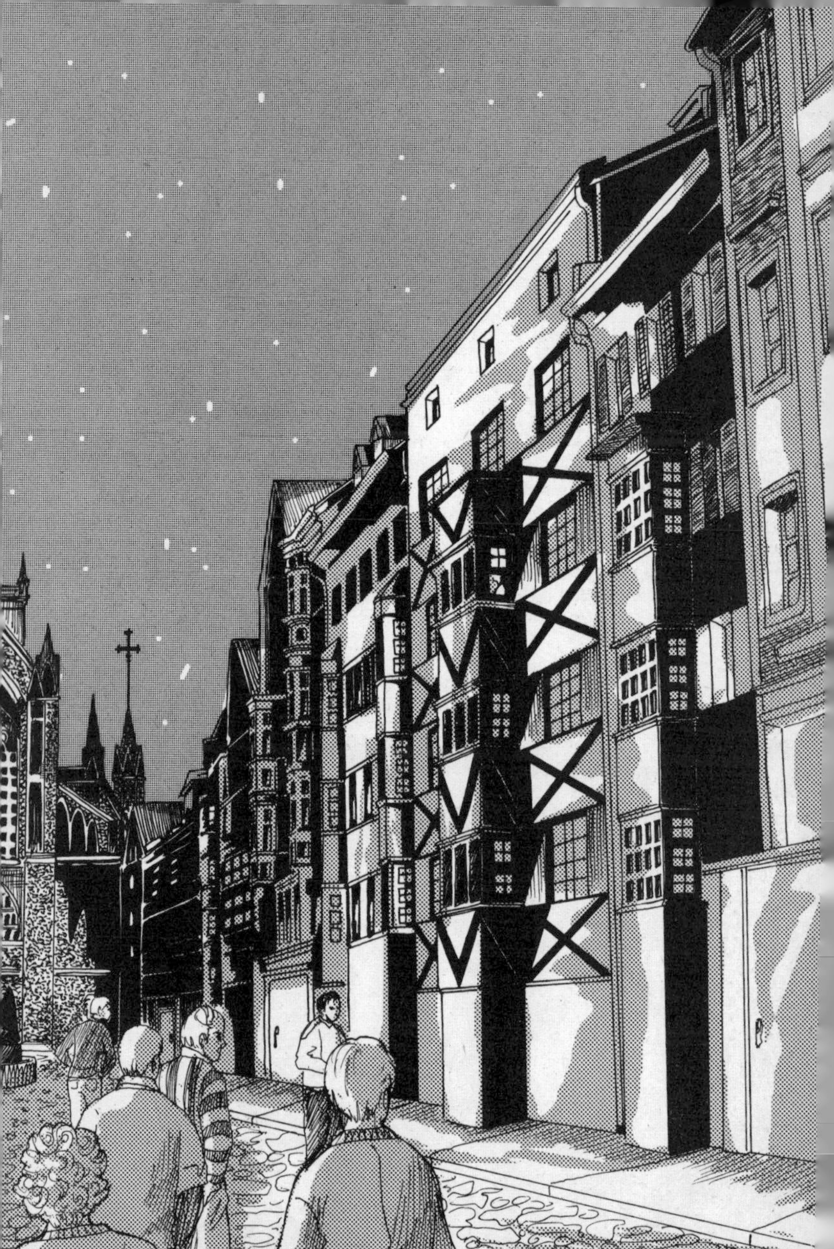

WHAT'S GOING ON?! HAS EVERYBODY LOST THEIR MINDS?

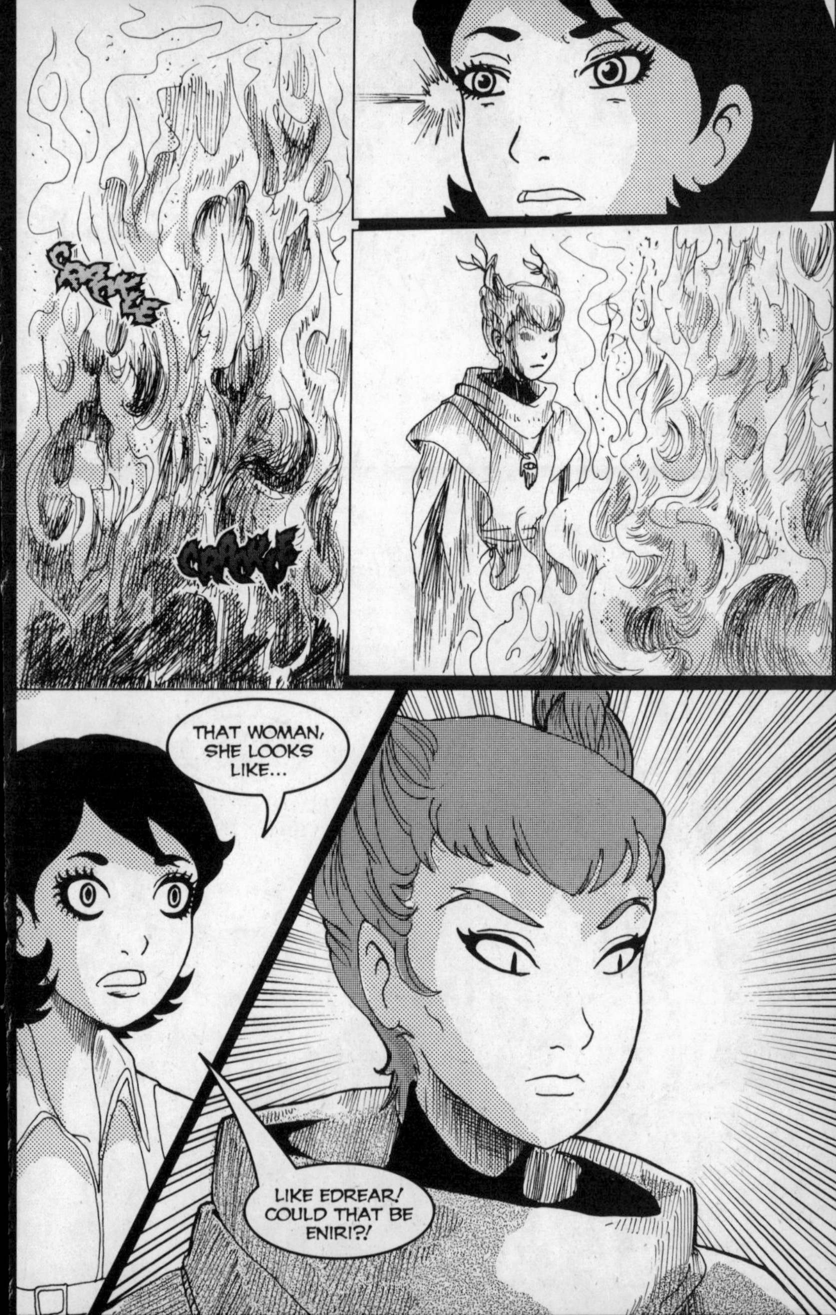
THAT WOMAN, SHE LOOKS LIKE...
LIKE EDREAR! COULD THAT BE ENIRI?!

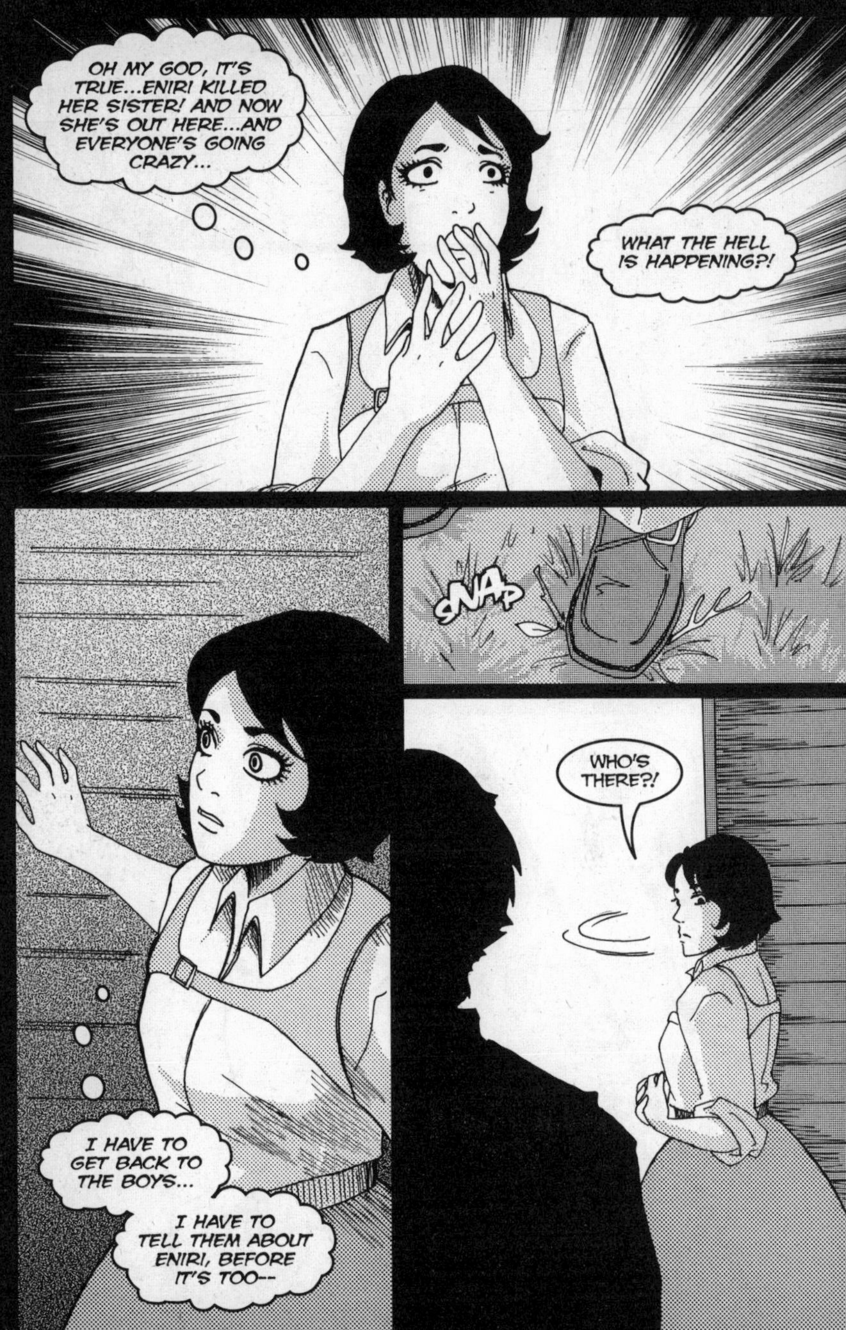
OH MY GOD, IT'S TRUE...ENIRI KILLED HER SISTER! AND NOW SHE'S OUT HERE...AND EVERYONE'S GOING CRAZY...
WHAT THE HELL IS HAPPENING?!
SNAP
I HAVE TO GET BACK TO THE BOYS...
I HAVE TO TELL THEM ABOUT ENIRI, BEFORE IT'S TOO--
WHO'S THERE?!

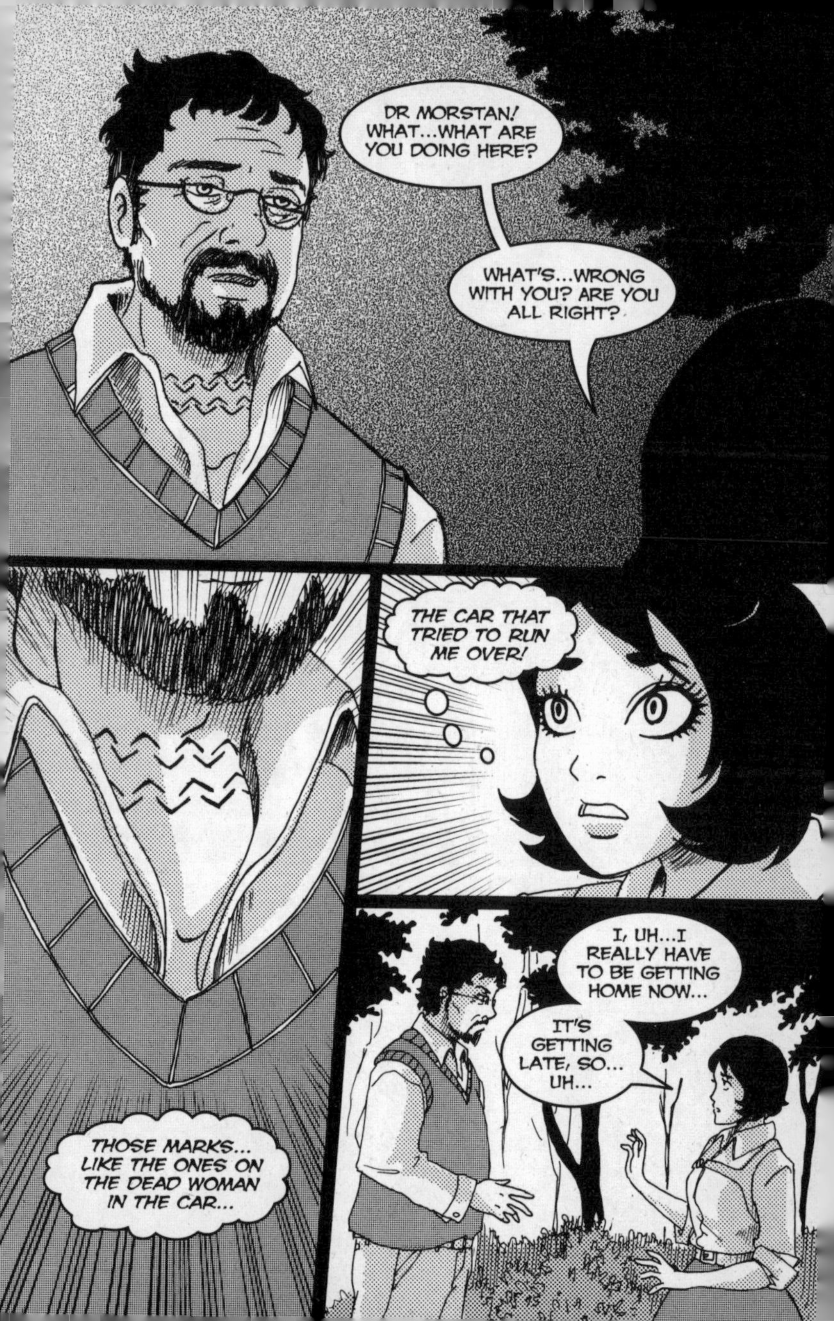
DR MORSTAN! WHAT...WHAT ARE YOU DOING HERE?
WHAT'S...WRONG WITH YOU? ARE YOU ALL RIGHT?
THOSE MARKS... LIKE THE ONES ON THE DEAD WOMAN IN THE CAR...
THE CAR THAT TRIED TO RUN ME OVER!
I, UH...I REALLY HAVE TO BE GETTING HOME NOW...
IT'S GETTING LATE, SO... UH...

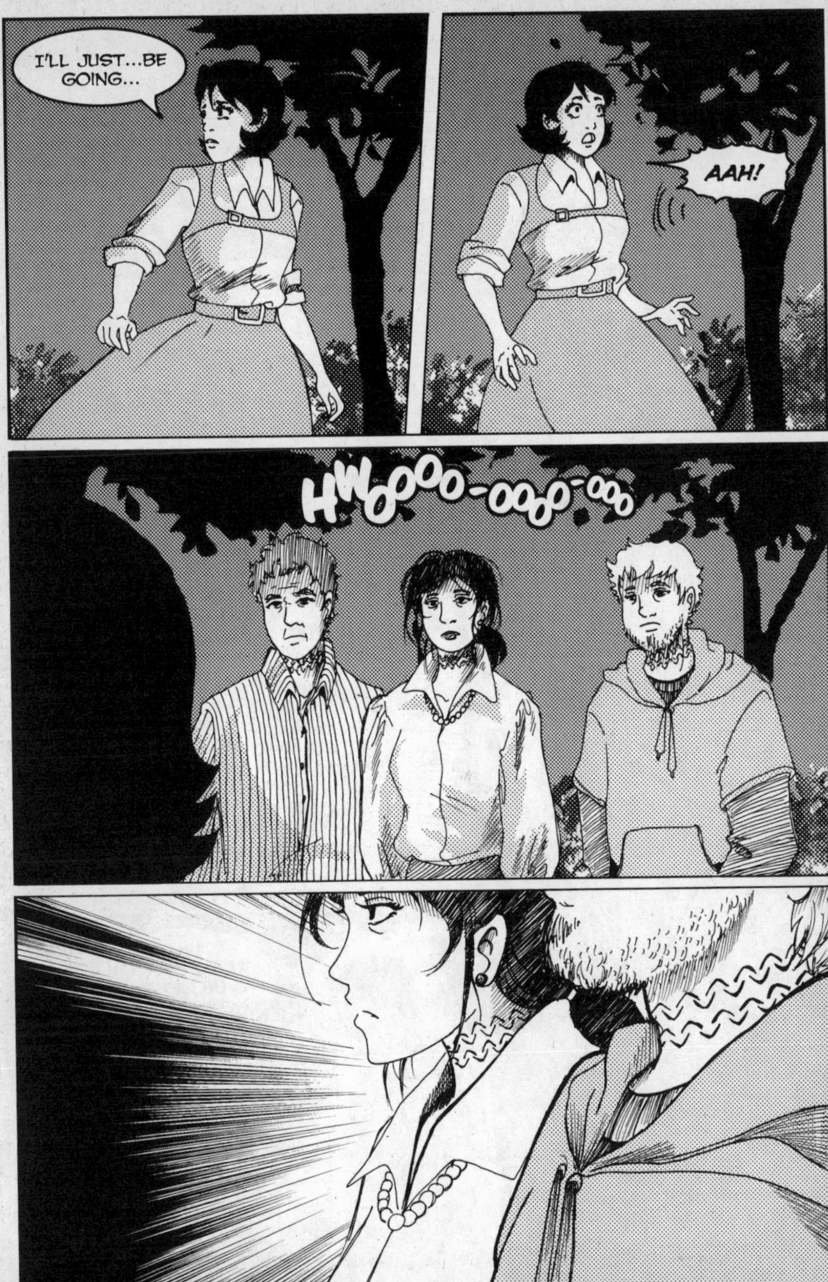
I'LL JUST...BE GOING...
AAH!
HWOOOO-OOOO-OOO

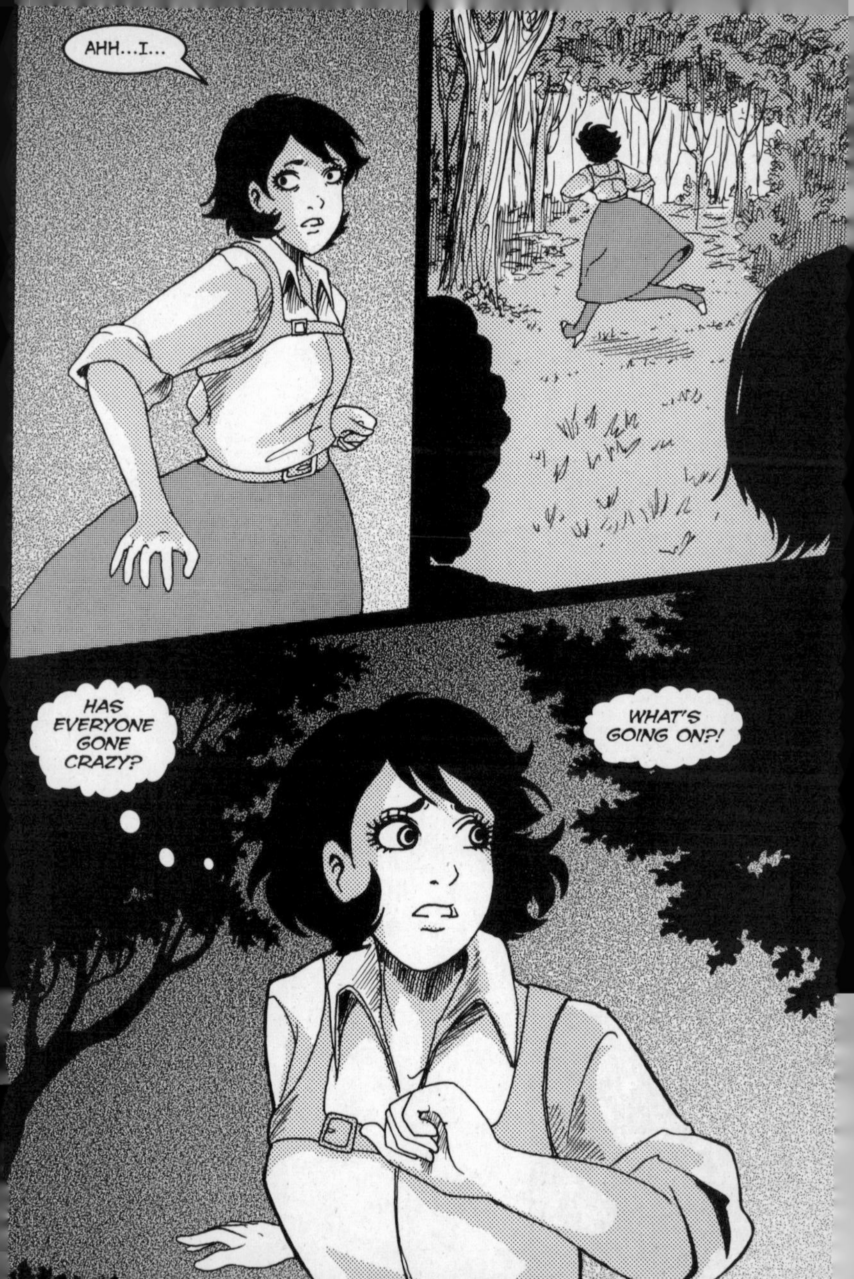
AHH...I...
HAS EVERYONE GONE CRAZY?
WHAT'S GOING ON?!

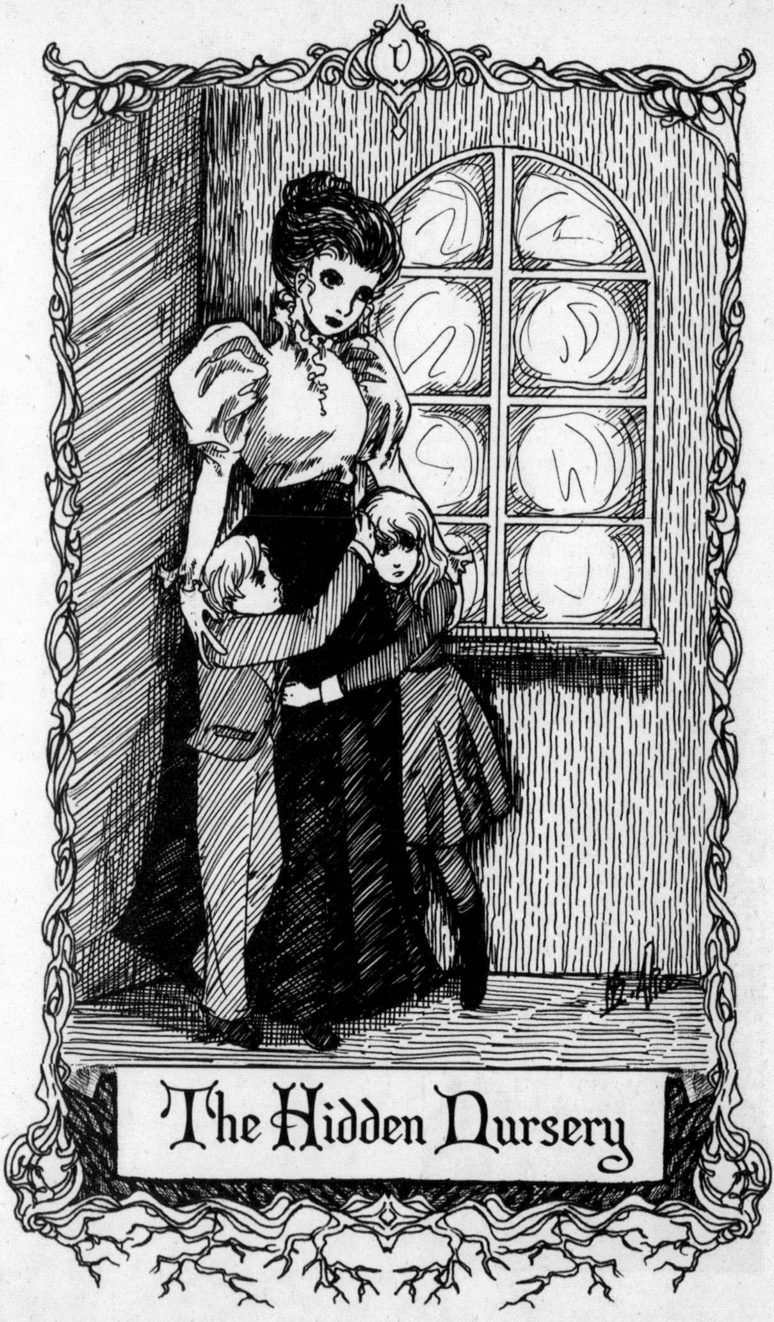
V
The Hidden Nursery

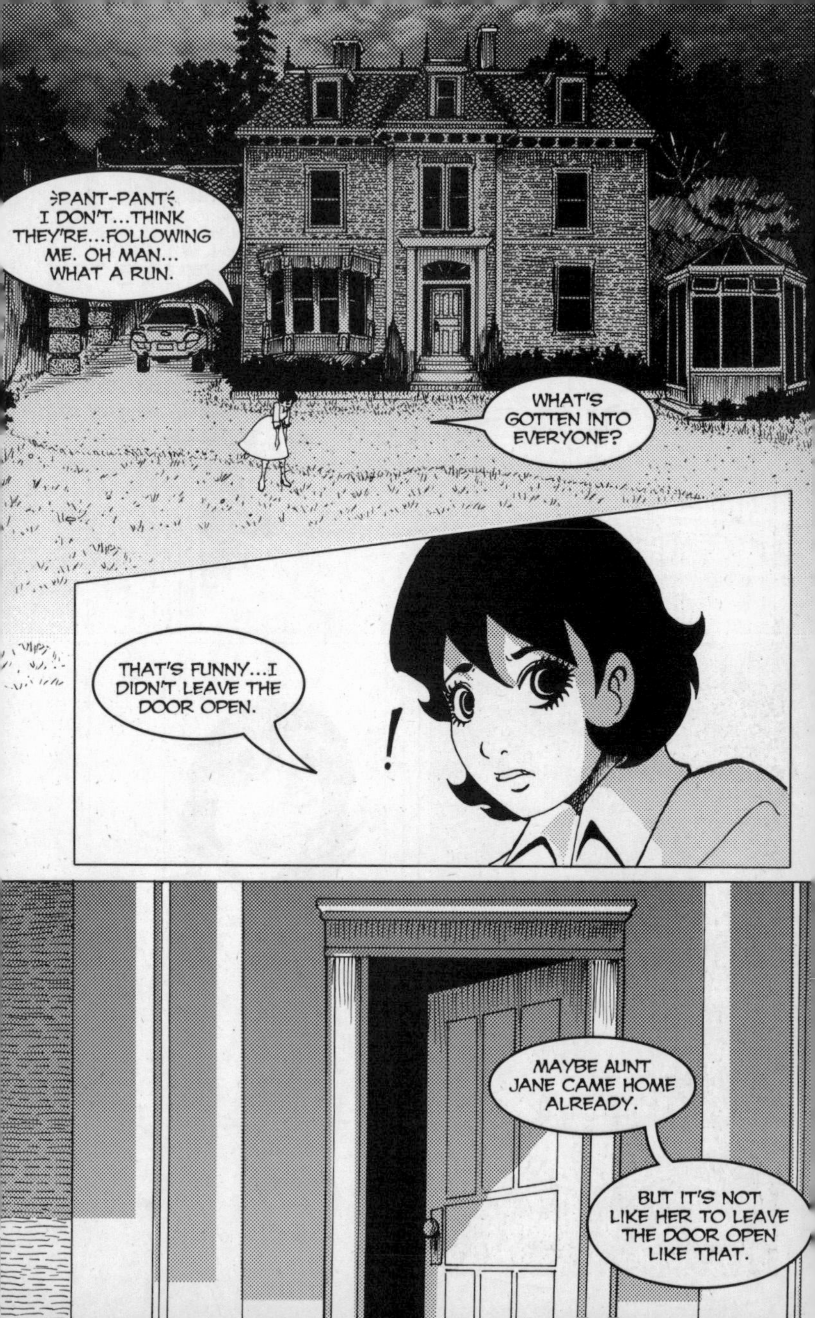

ƎPANT-PANTƐ I DON'T...THINK THEY'RE...FOLLOWING ME. OH MAN... WHAT A RUN.
WHAT'S GOTTEN INTO EVERYONE?
THAT'S FUNNY...I DIDN'T LEAVE THE DOOR OPEN.
!
MAYBE AUNT JANE CAME HOME ALREADY.
BUT IT'S NOT LIKE HER TO LEAVE THE DOOR OPEN LIKE THAT.

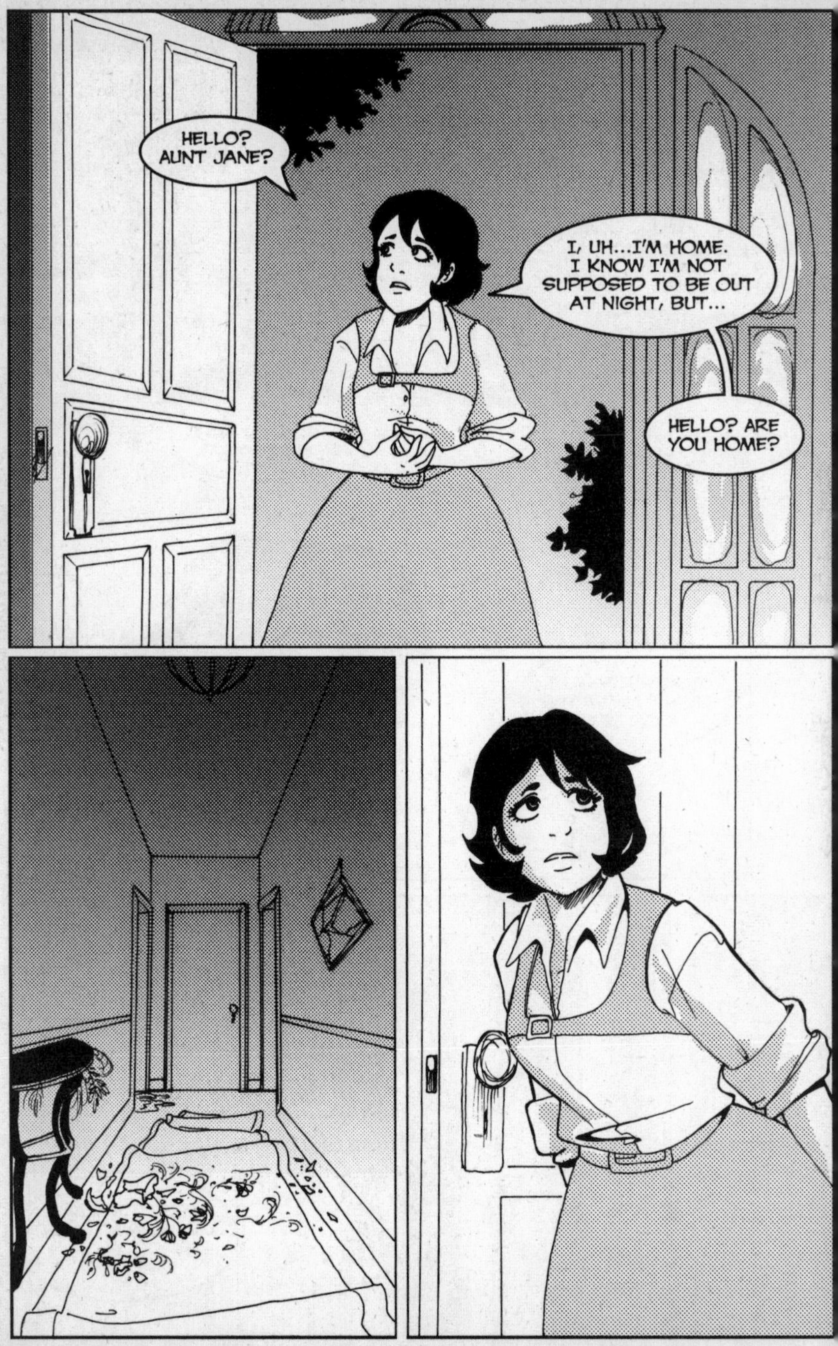
HELLO? AUNT JANE?
I, UH...I'M HOME. I KNOW I'M NOT SUPPOSED TO BE OUT AT NIGHT, BUT...
HELLO? ARE YOU HOME?

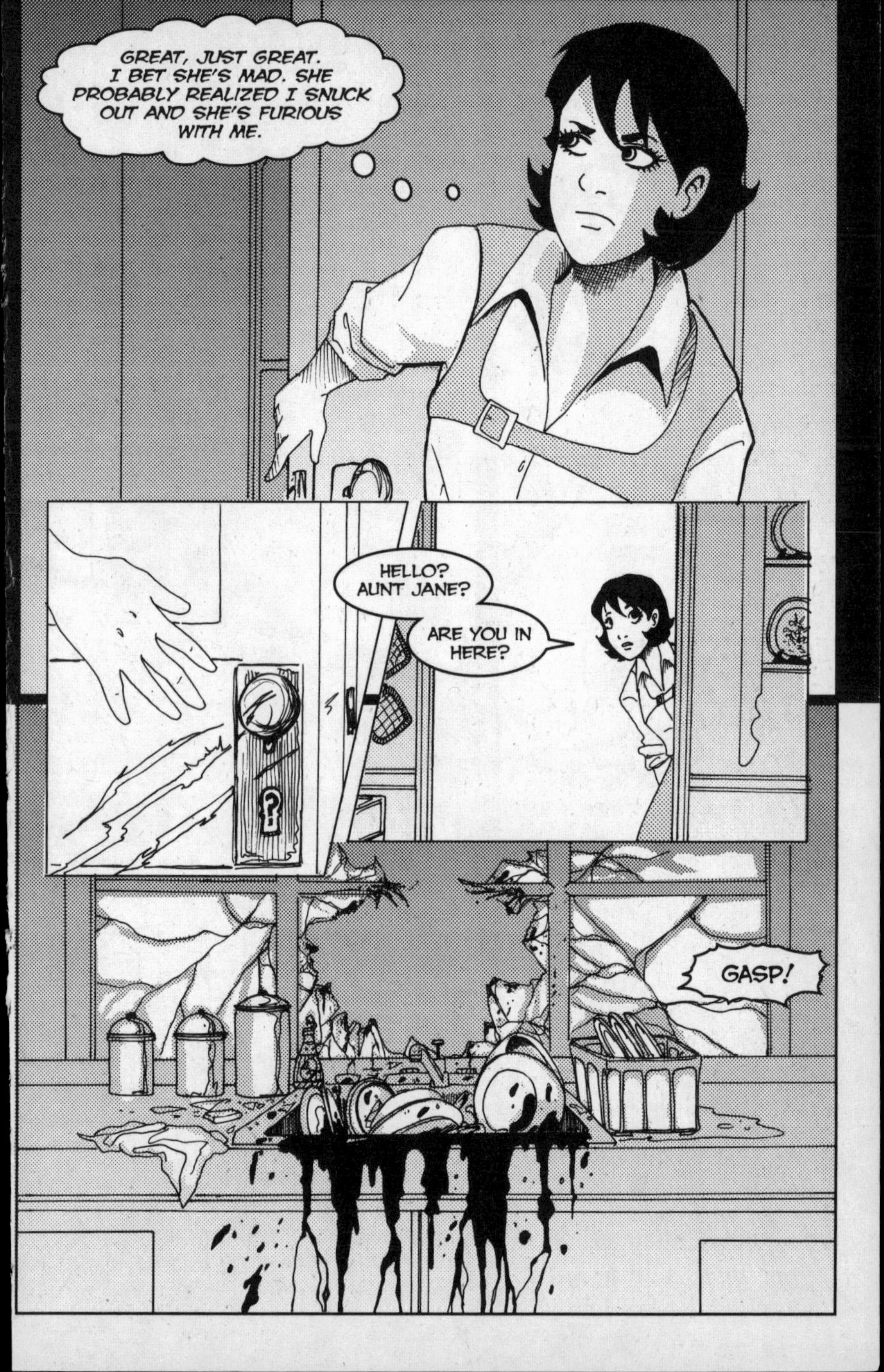
GREAT, JUST GREAT. I BET SHE'S MAD. SHE PROBABLY REALIZED I SNUCK OUT AND SHE'S FURIOUS WITH ME.
HELLO? AUNT JANE?
ARE YOU IN HERE?
GASP!

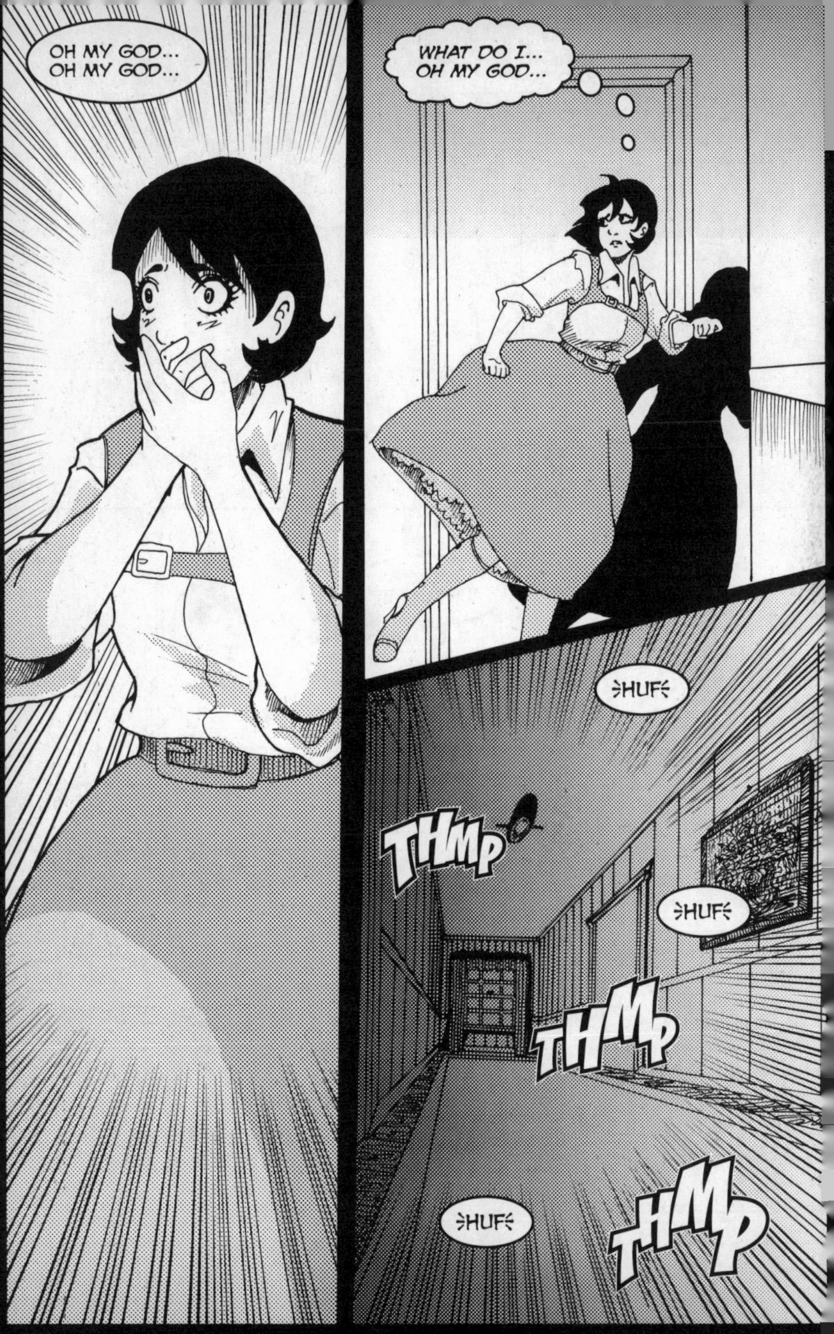
OH MY GOD...
OH MY GOD...
WHAT DO I...
OH MY GOD...
HUF
THMP
HUF
THMP
HUF
THMP

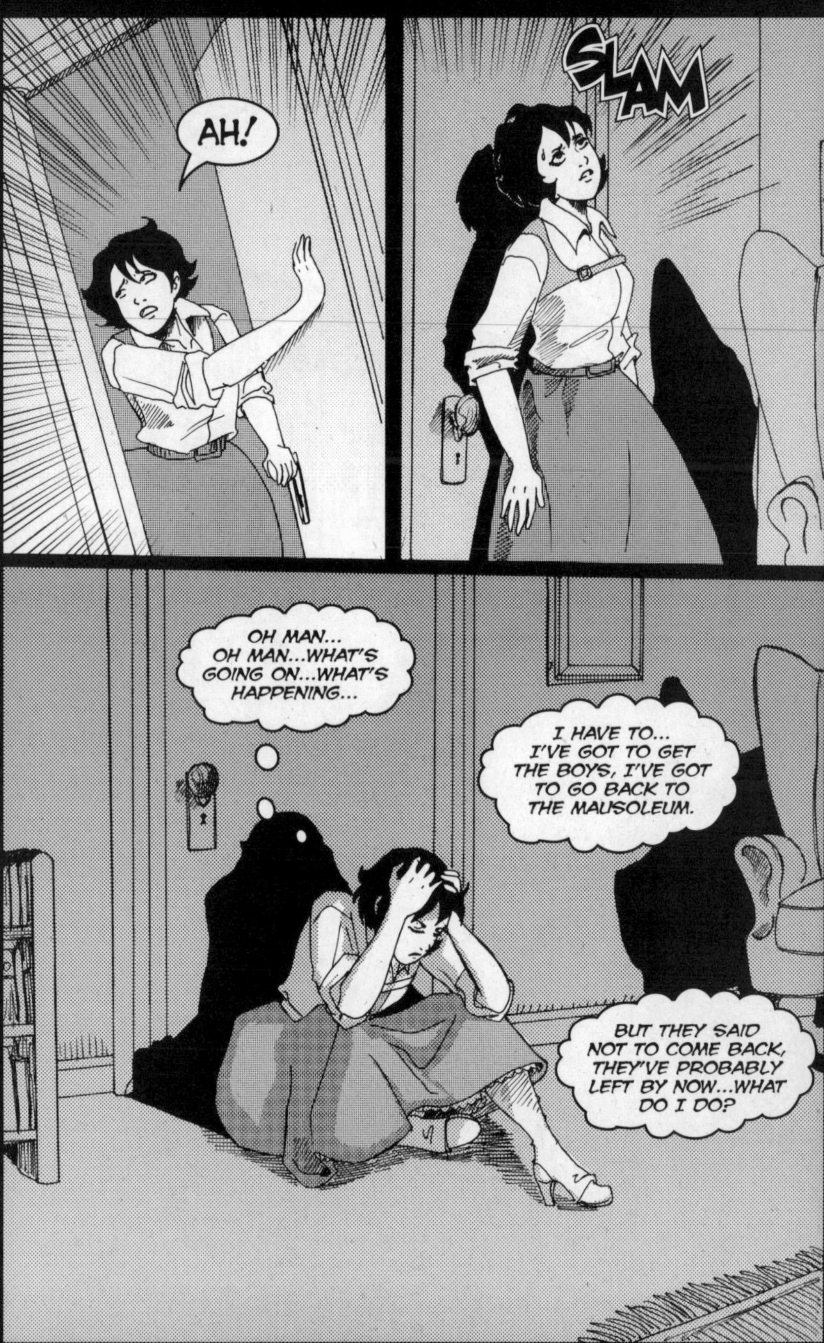
AH!
SLAM
OH MAN... OH MAN...WHAT'S GOING ON...WHAT'S HAPPENING...
I HAVE TO... I'VE GOT TO GET THE BOYS, I'VE GOT TO GO BACK TO THE MAUSOLEUM.
BUT THEY SAID NOT TO COME BACK, THEY"VE PROBABLY LEFT BY NOW...WHAT DO I DO?

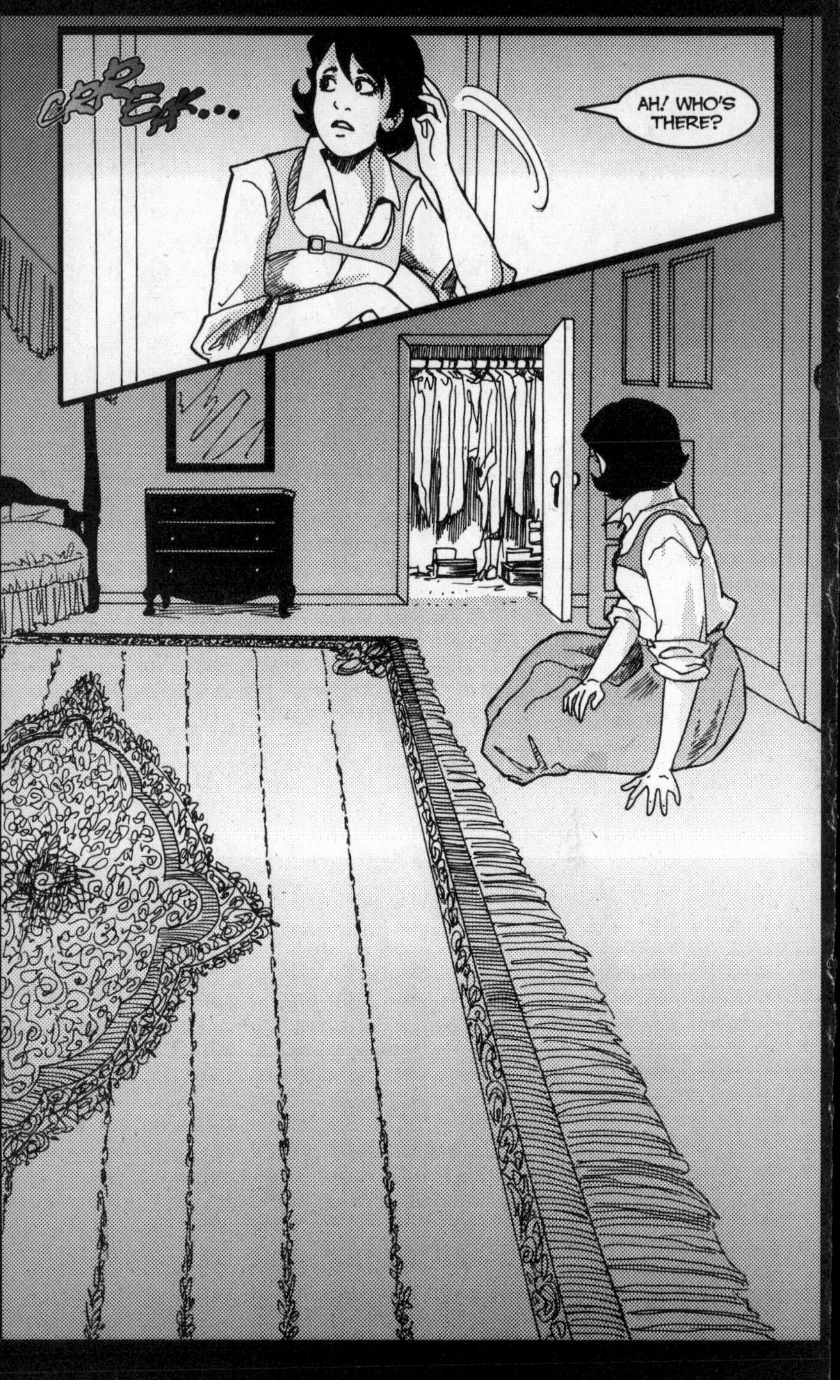
CRREAK...
AH! WHO'S THERE?

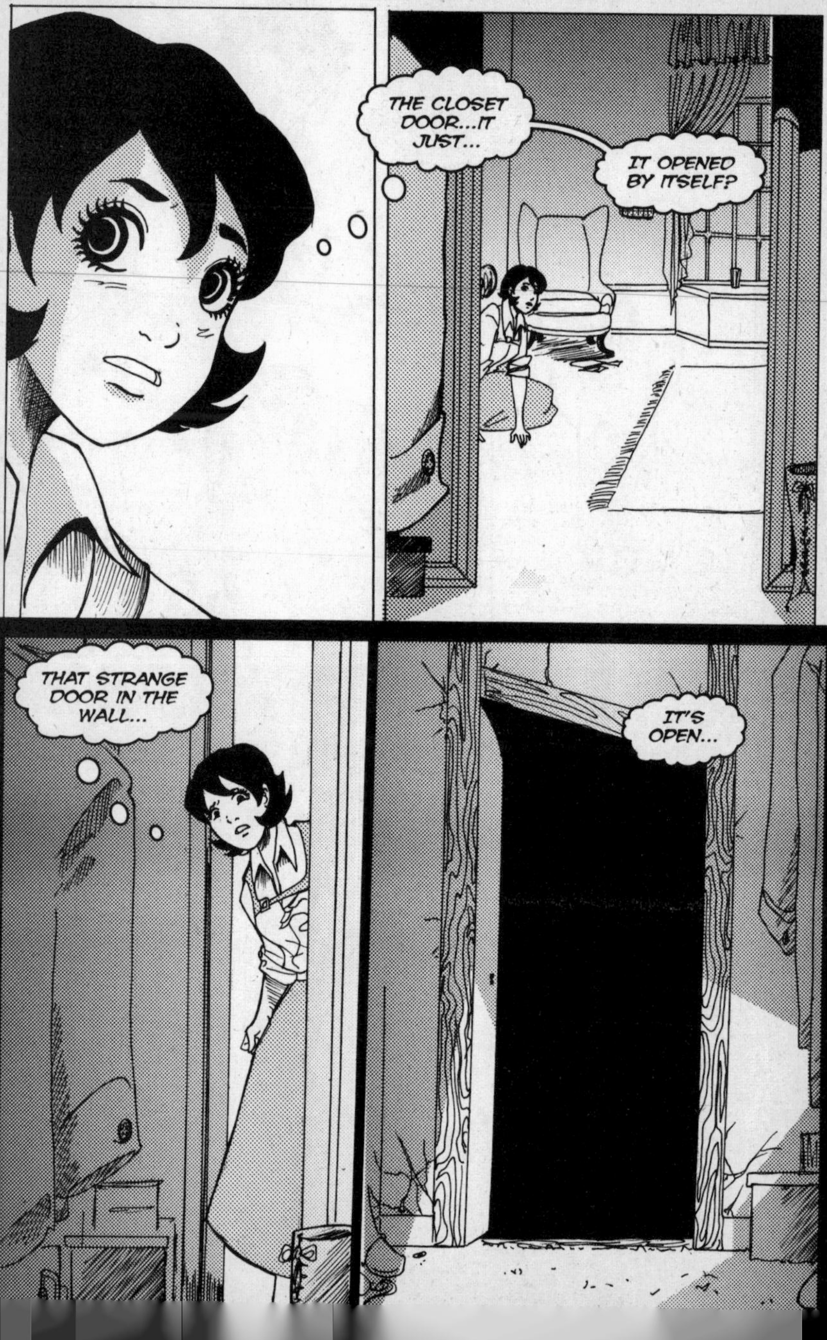
THE CLOSET DOOR...IT JUST...
IT OPENED BY ITSELF?
THAT STRANGE DOOR IN THE WALL...
IT'S OPEN...

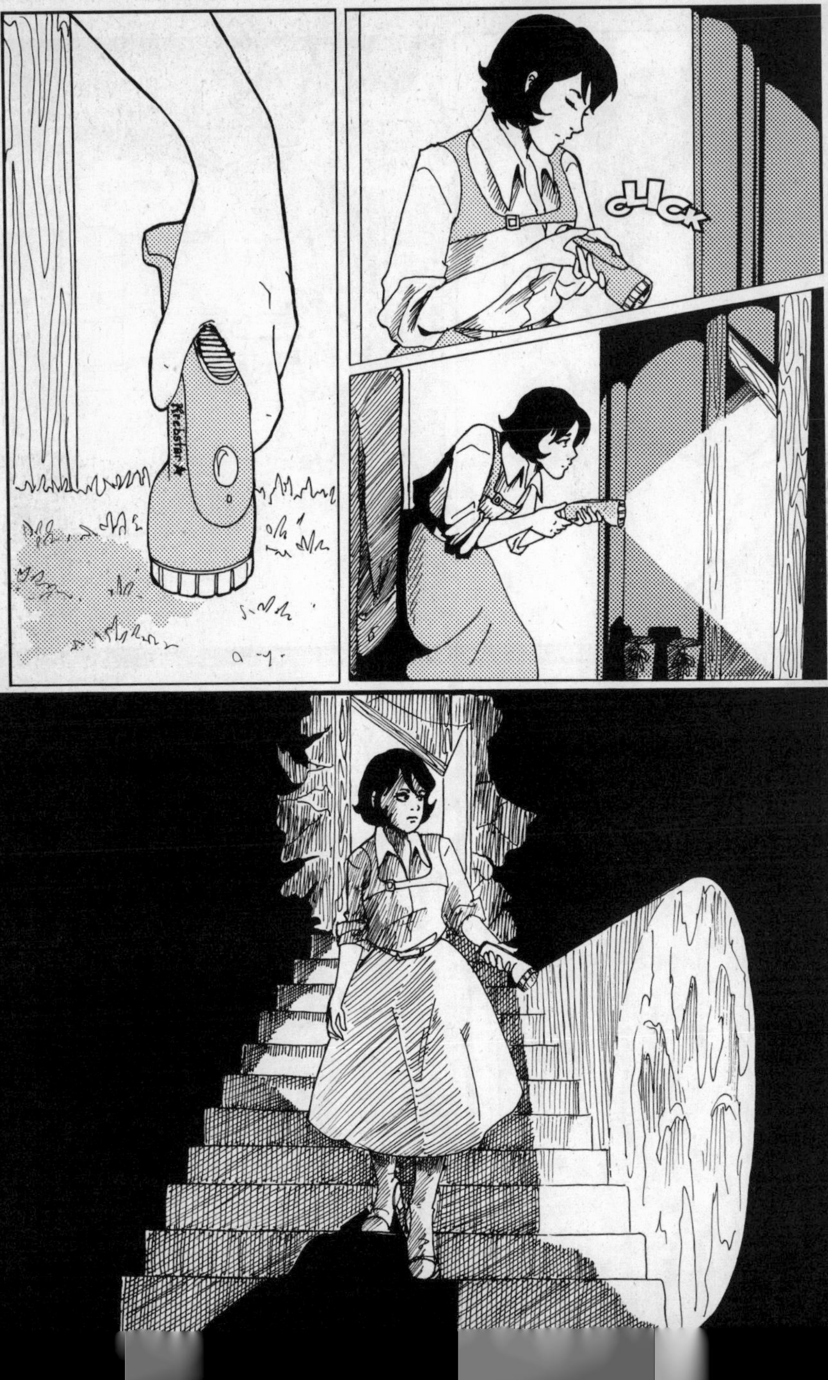
Krebstar★
CLICK

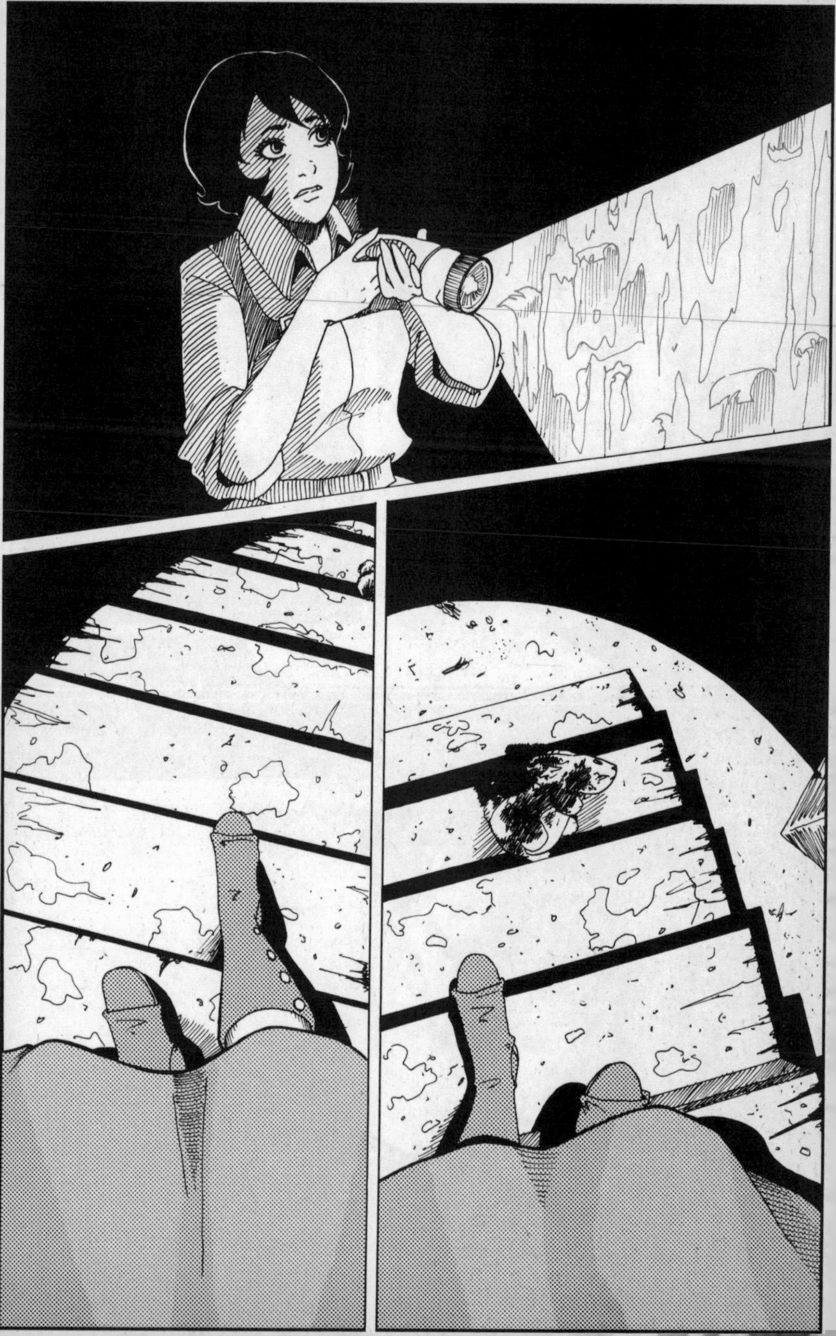

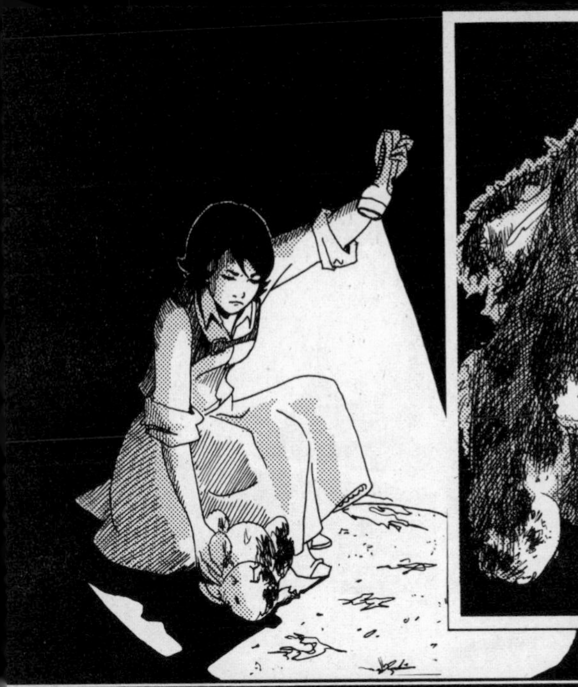
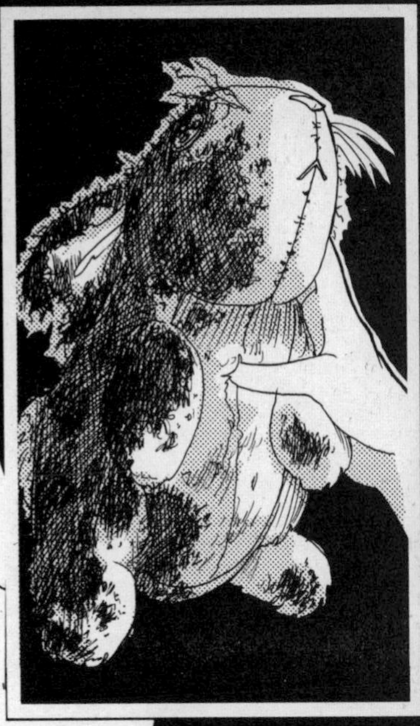
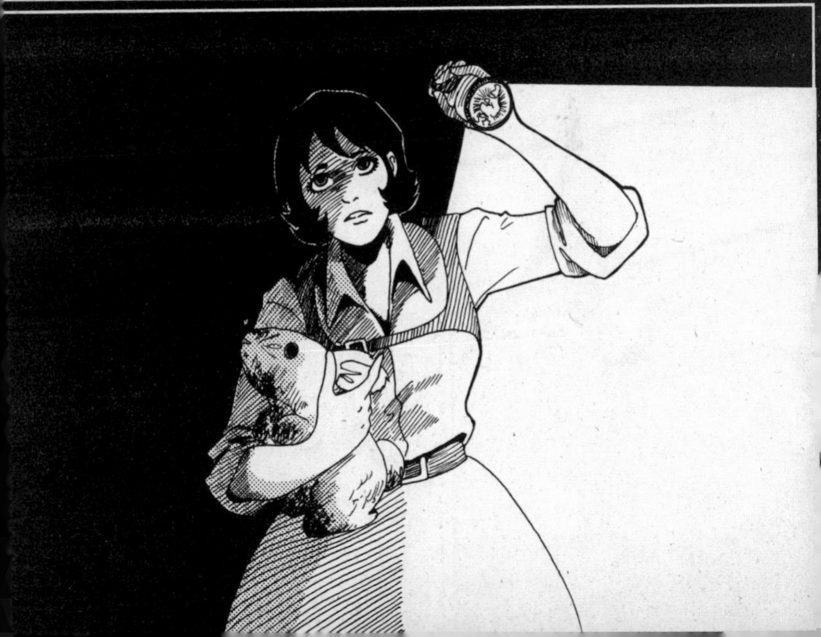

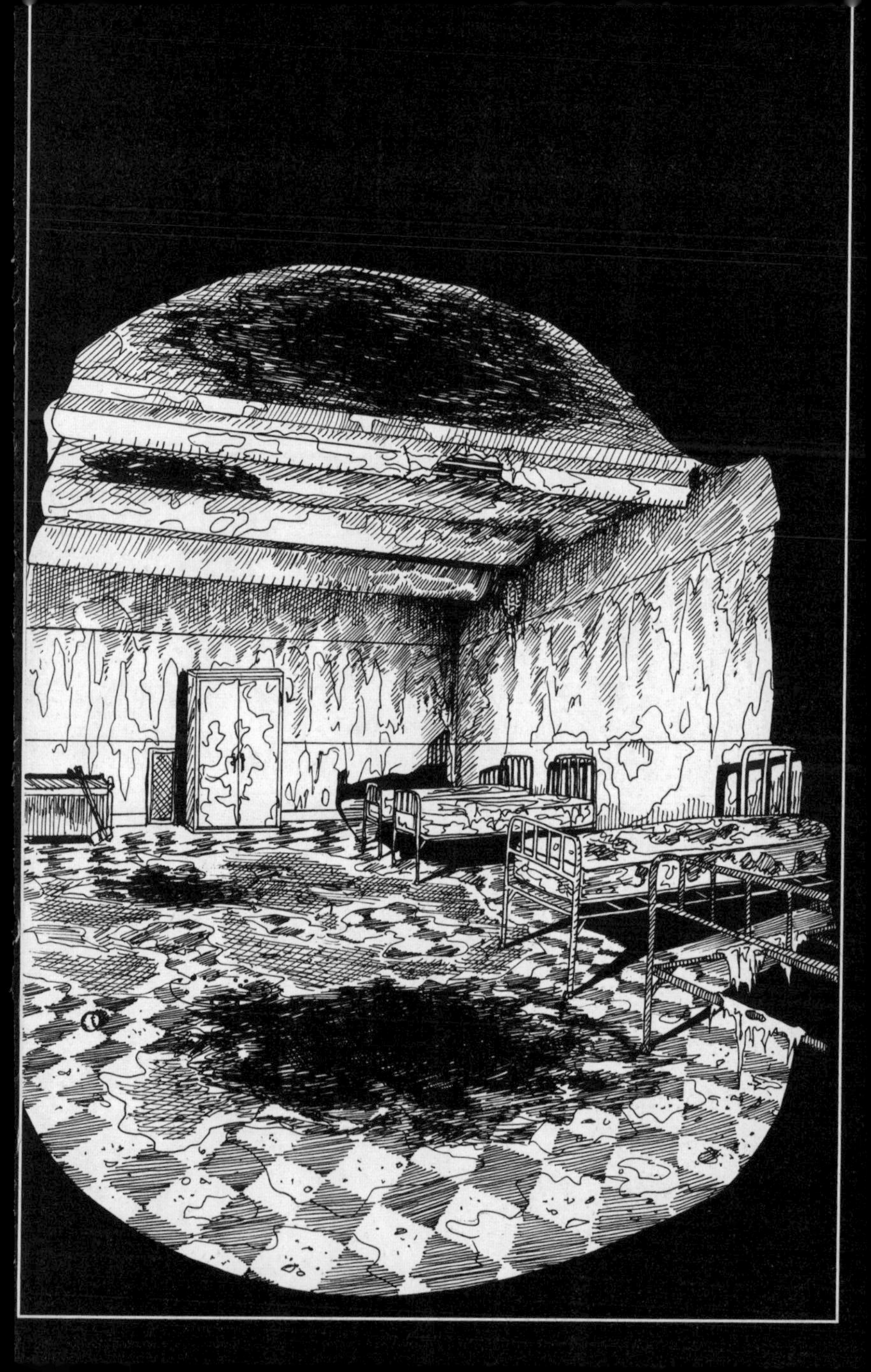

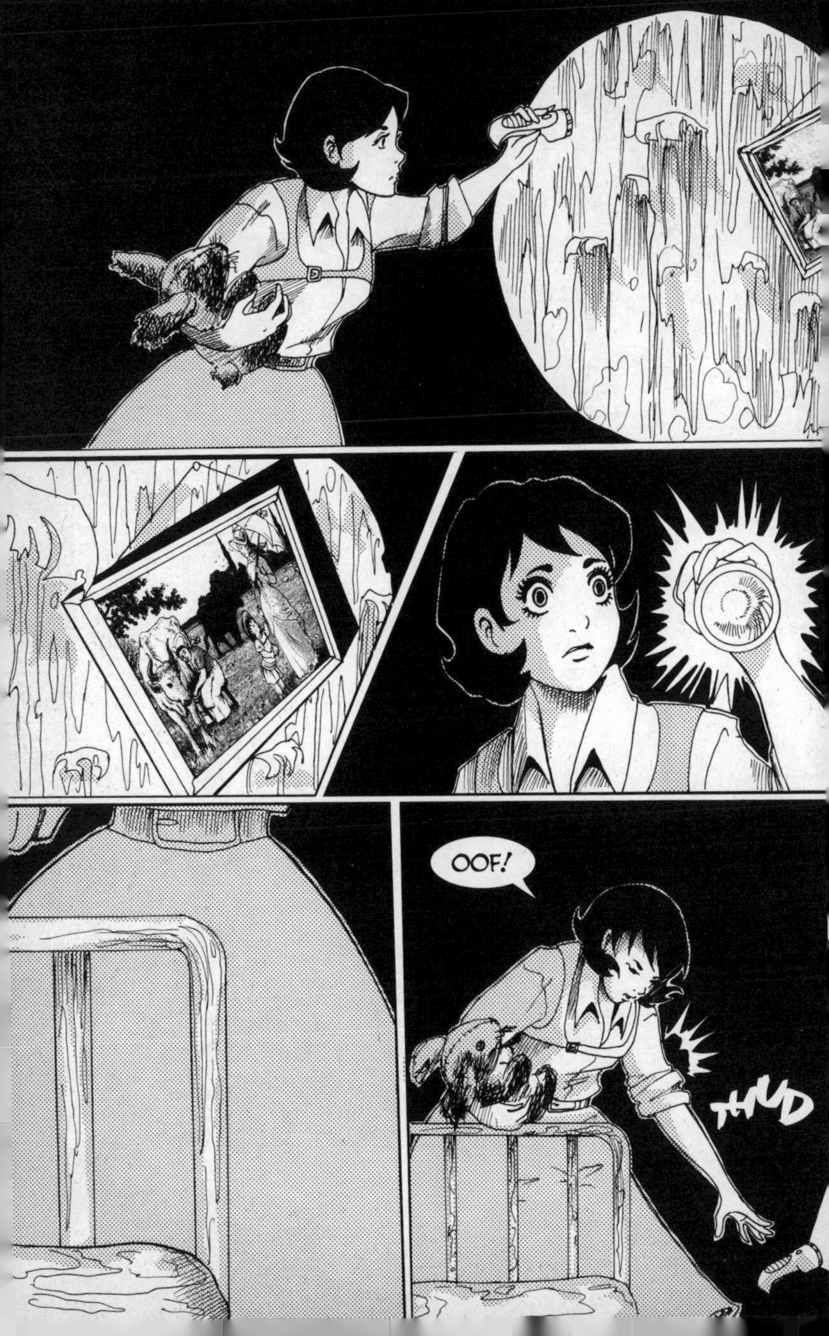
OOF!
THUD

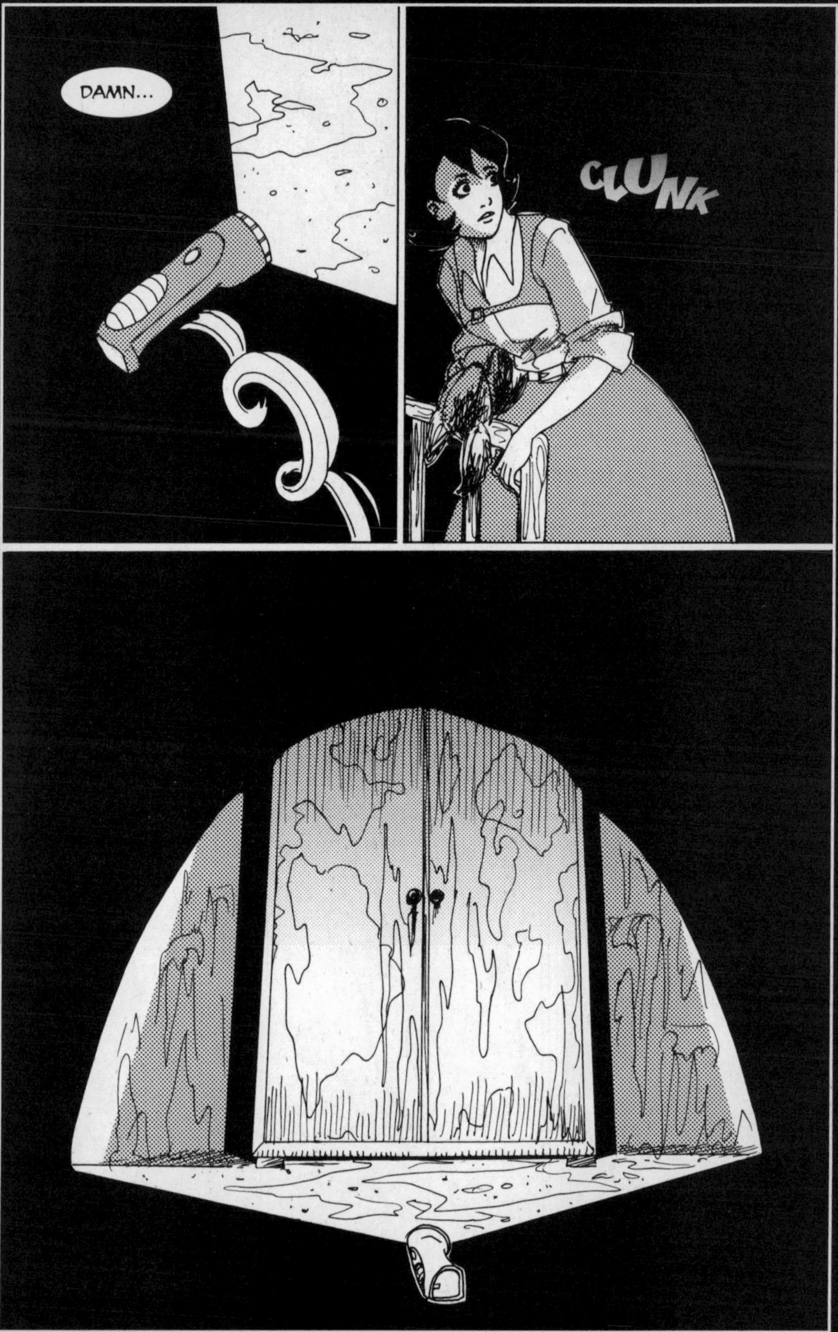
DAMN...
CLUNK

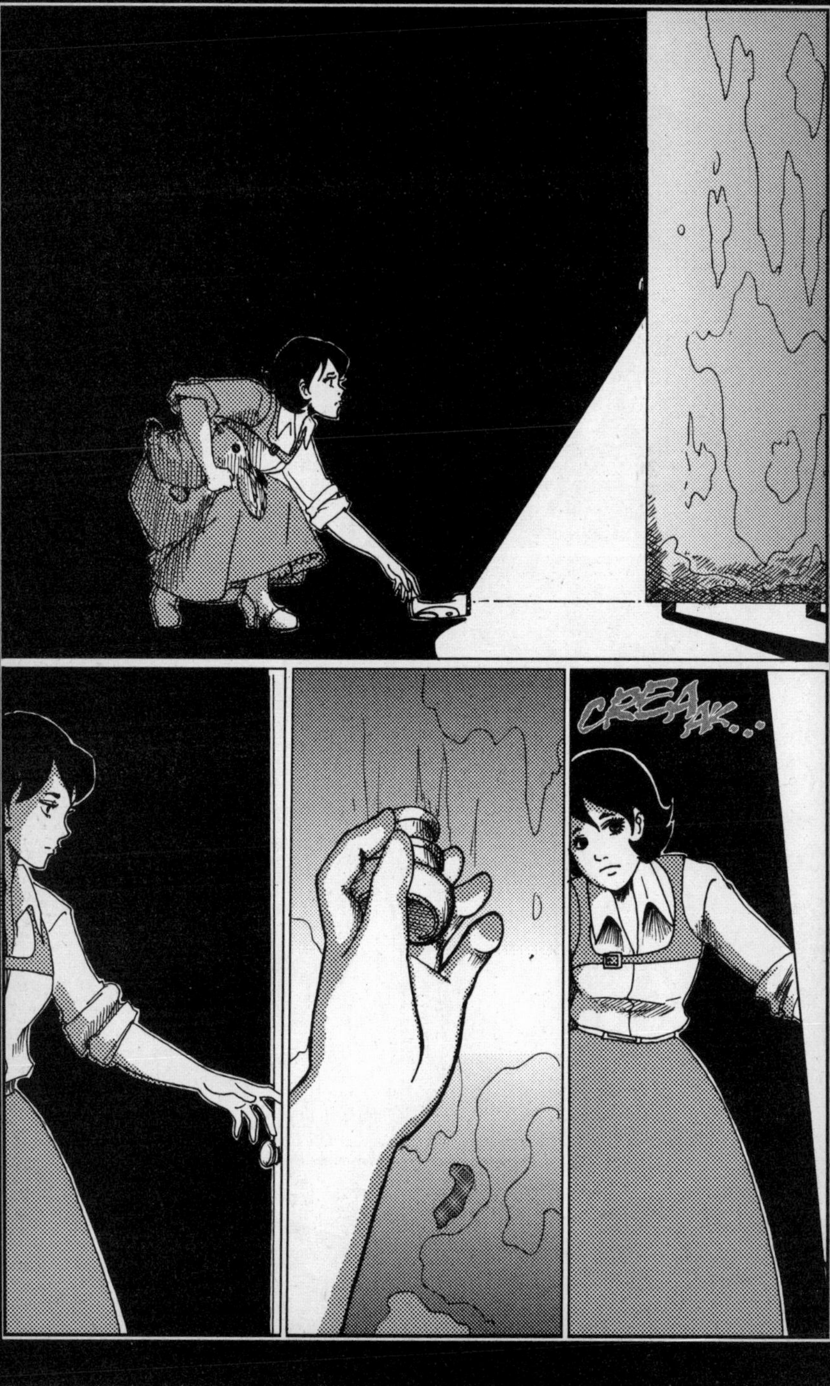
CREAAK...

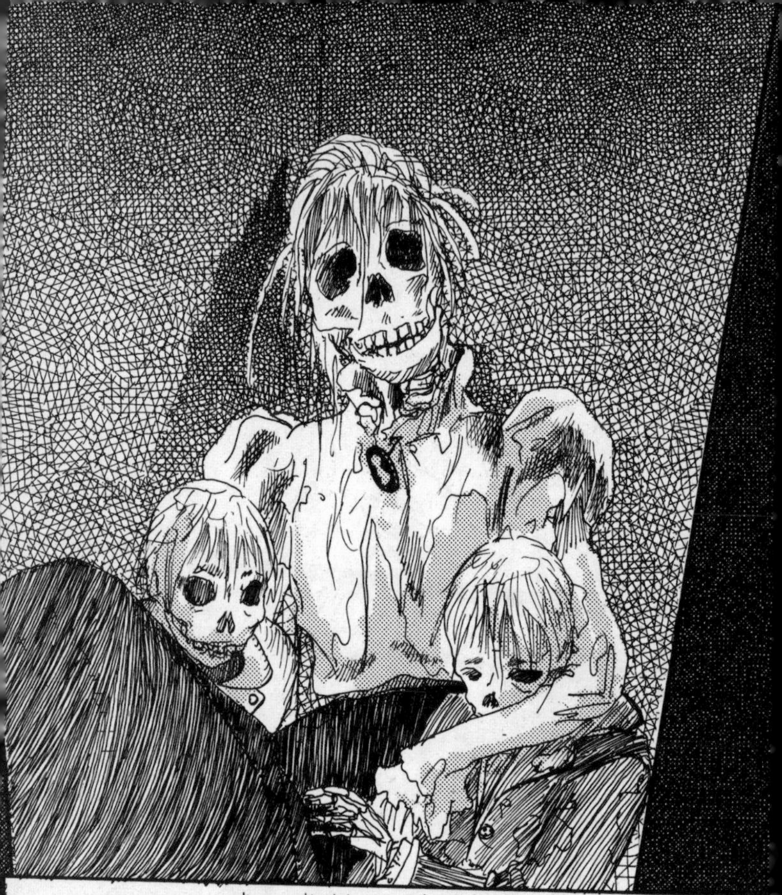

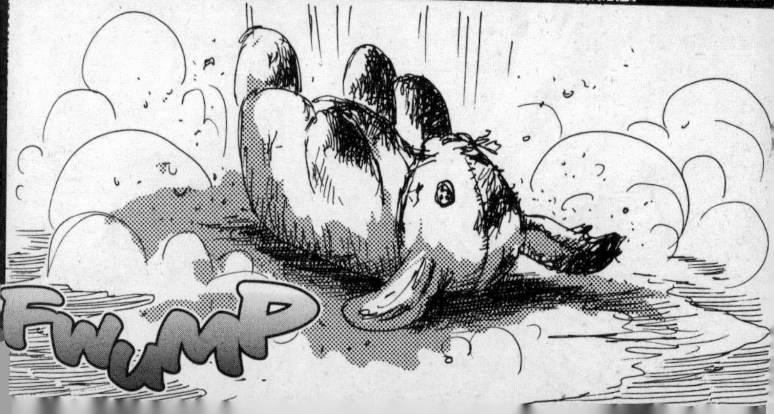
FWUMP

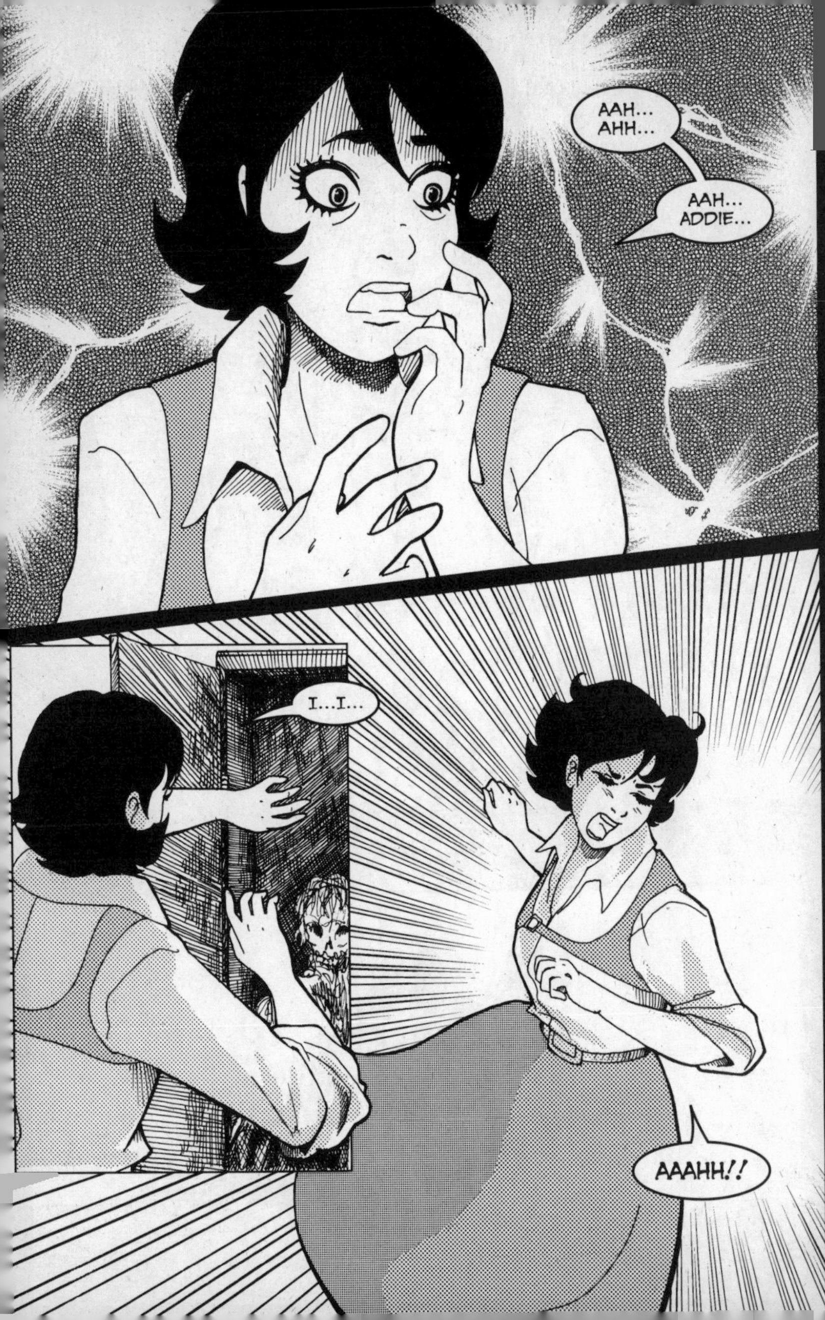
AAH... AHH...
AAH... ADDIE...
I...I...
AAAHH!!

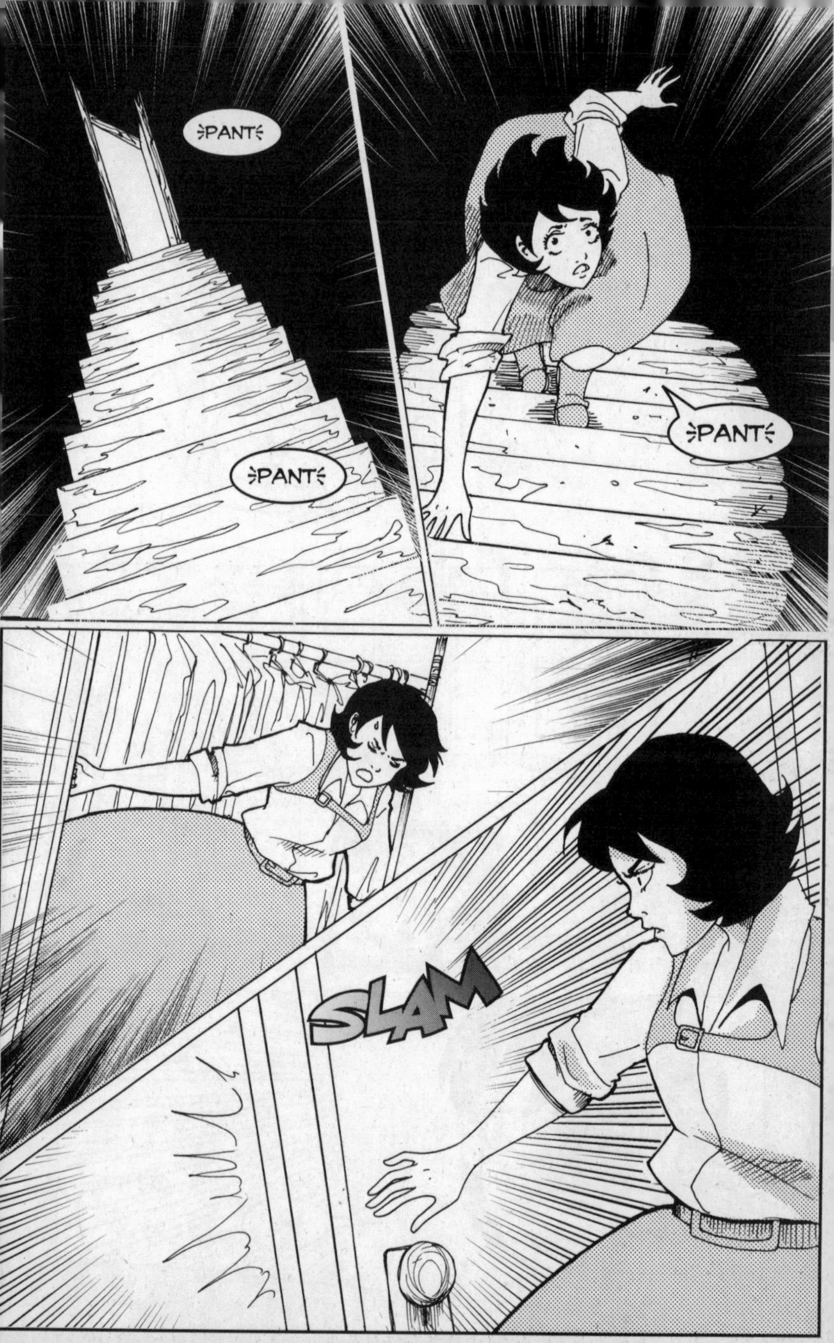
PANT
PANT
PANT
SLAM

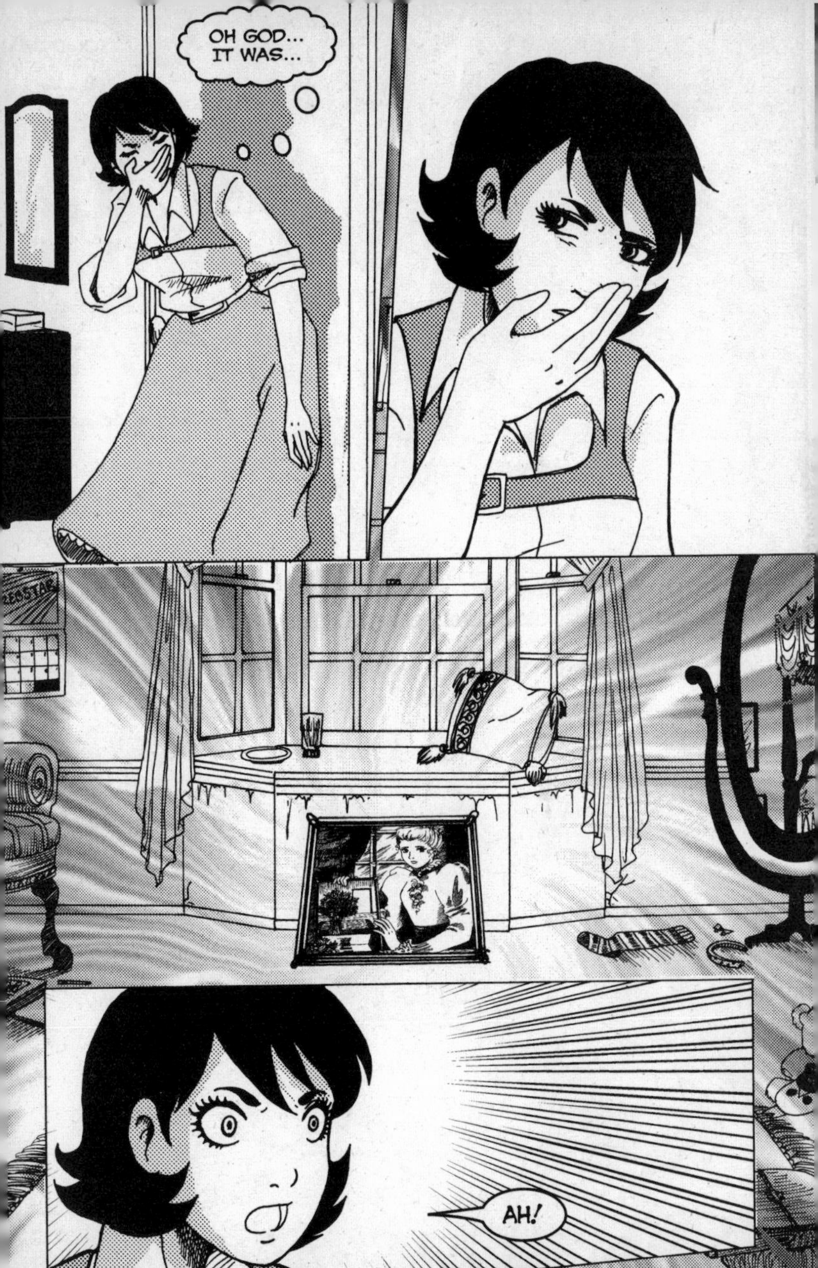
OH GOD...
IT WAS...
AH!

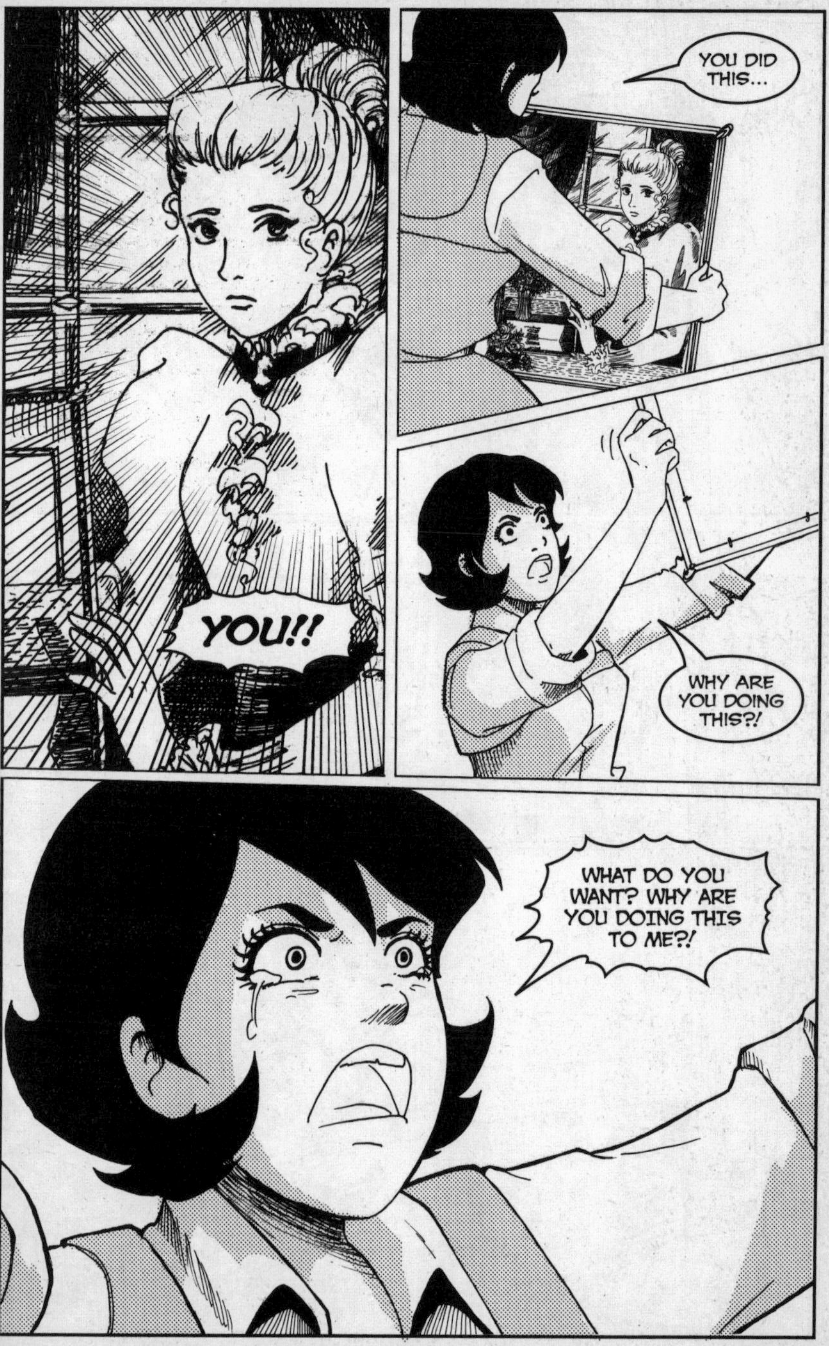
YOU!!
YOU DID THIS...
WHY ARE YOU DOING THIS?!
WHAT DO YOU WANT? WHY ARE YOU DOING THIS TO ME?!

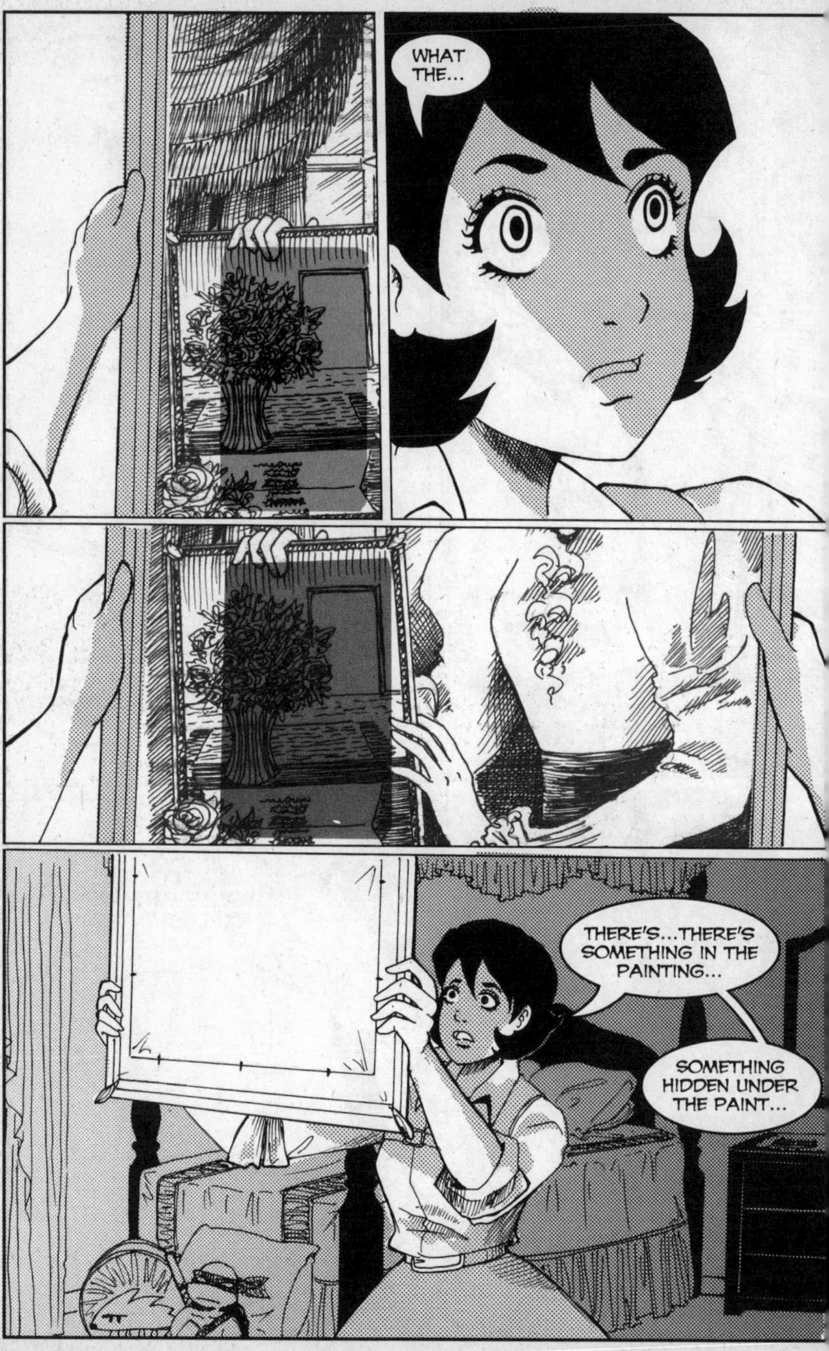
WHAT THE...
THERE'S...THERE'S SOMETHING IN THE PAINTING...
SOMETHING HIDDEN UNDER THE PAINT...

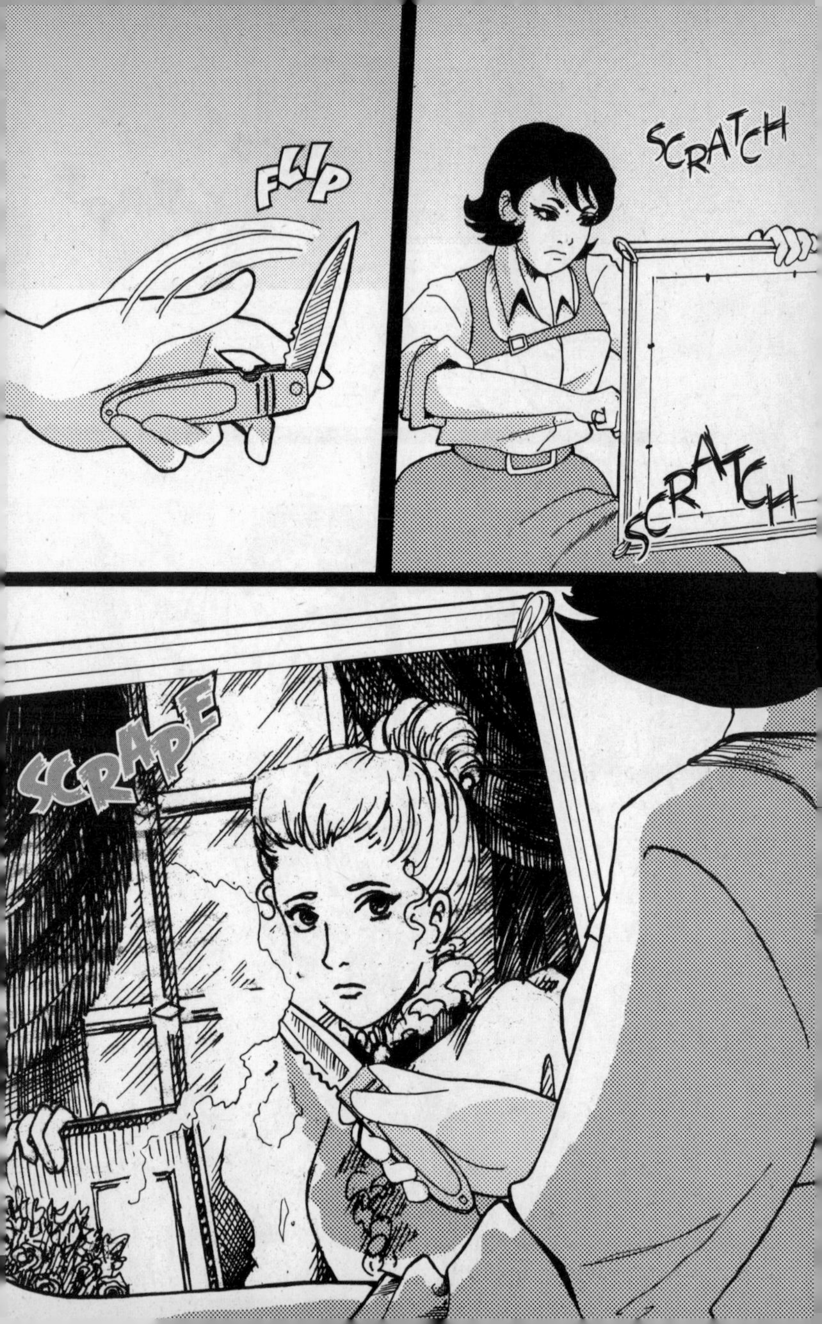
FLIP
SCRATCH
SCRATCH
SCRAPE

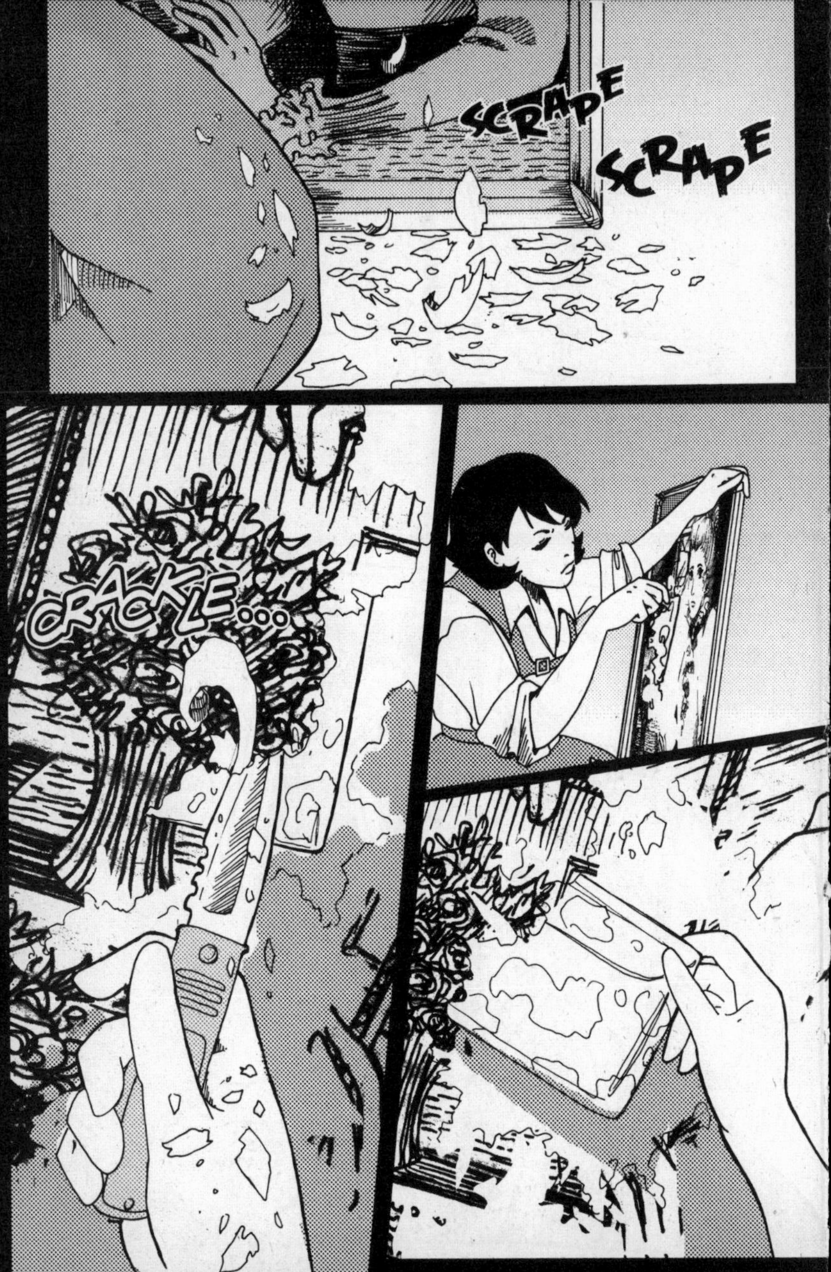
SCRAPE
SCRAPE
CRACKLE...

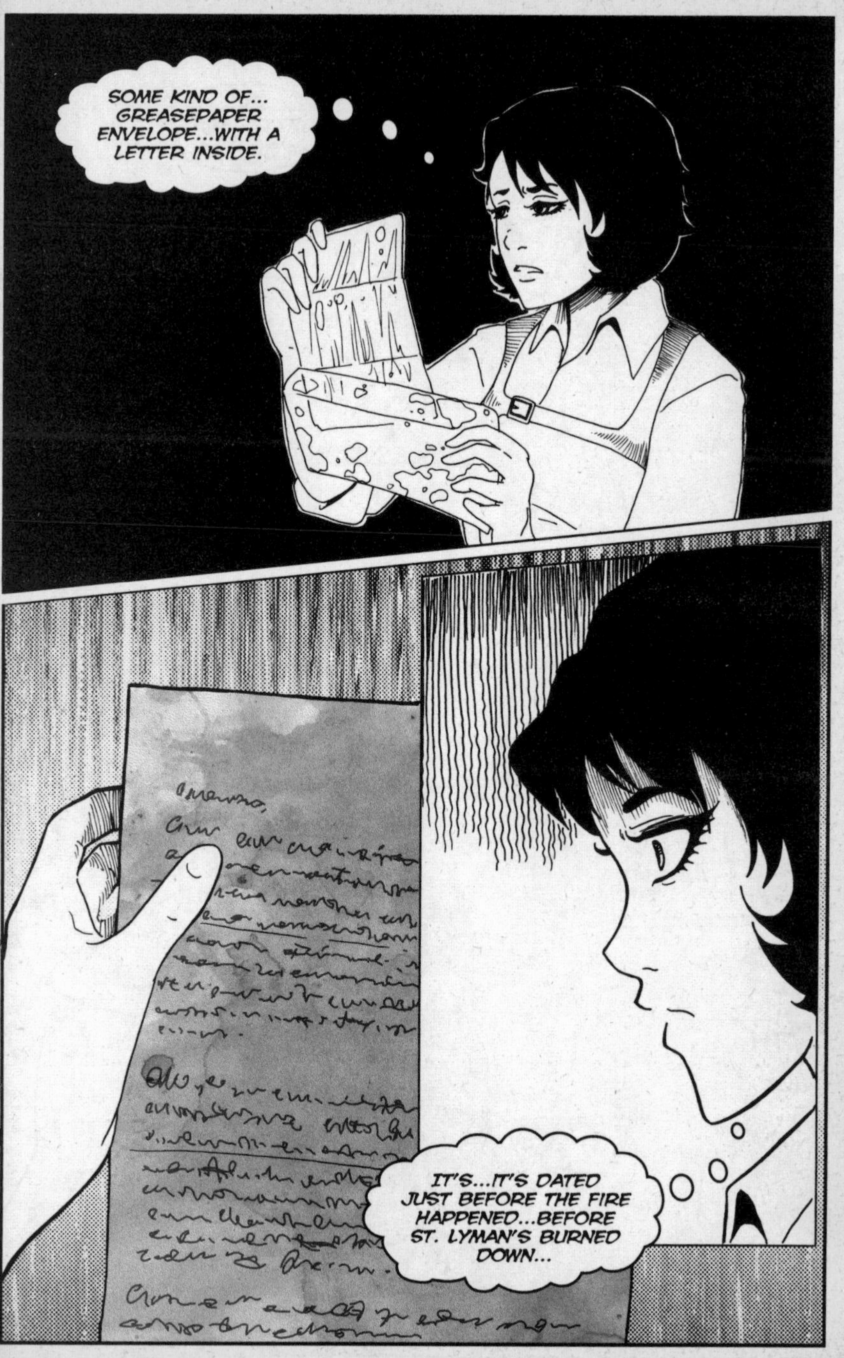
SOME KIND OF... GREASEPAPER ENVELOPE...WITH A LETTER INSIDE.
IT'S...IT'S DATED JUST BEFORE THE FIRE HAPPENED...BEFORE ST. LYMAN'S BURNED DOWN...

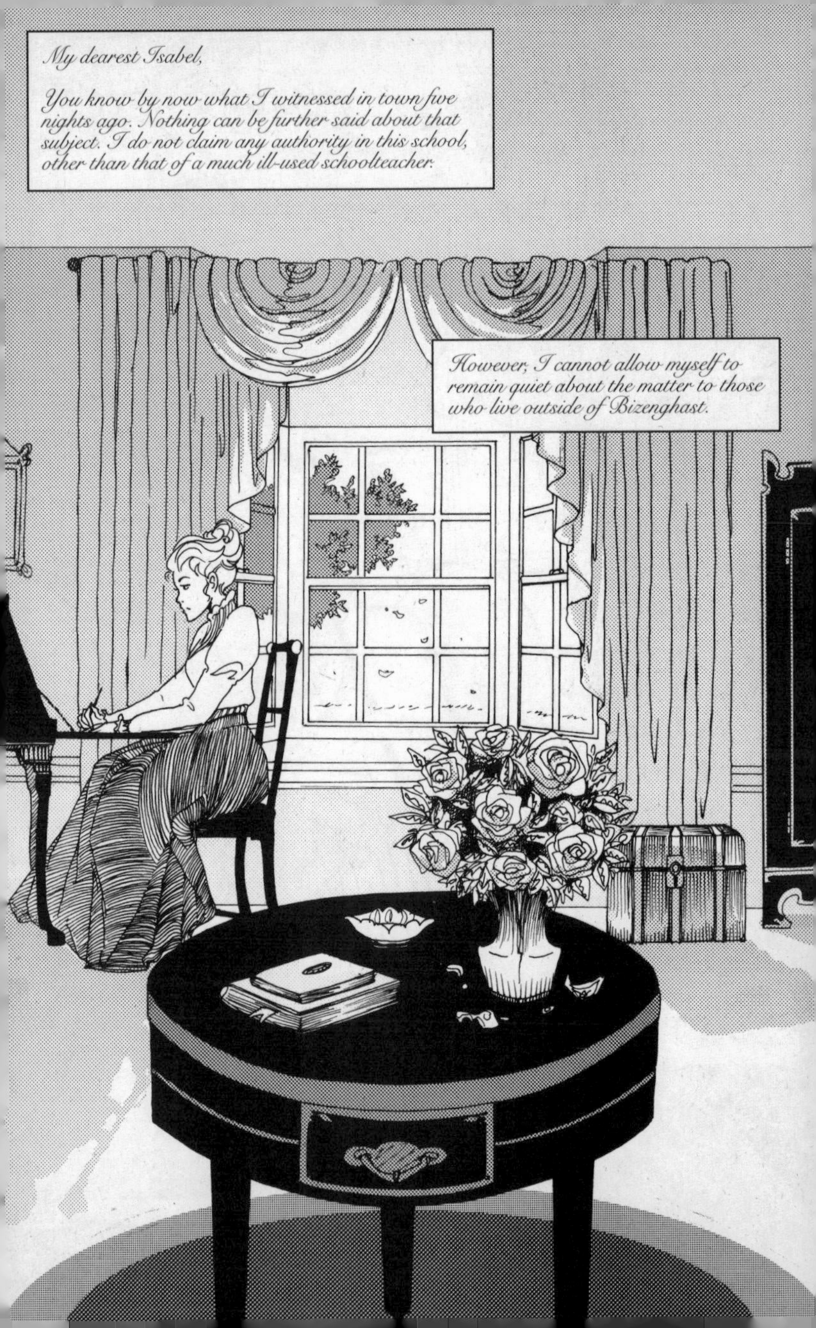
My dearest Isabel,
You know by now what I witnessed in town five nights ago. Nothing can be further said about that subject. I do not claim any authority in this school, other than that of a much ill-used schoolteacher.
However, I cannot allow myself to remain quiet about the matter to those who live outside of Bizenghast.

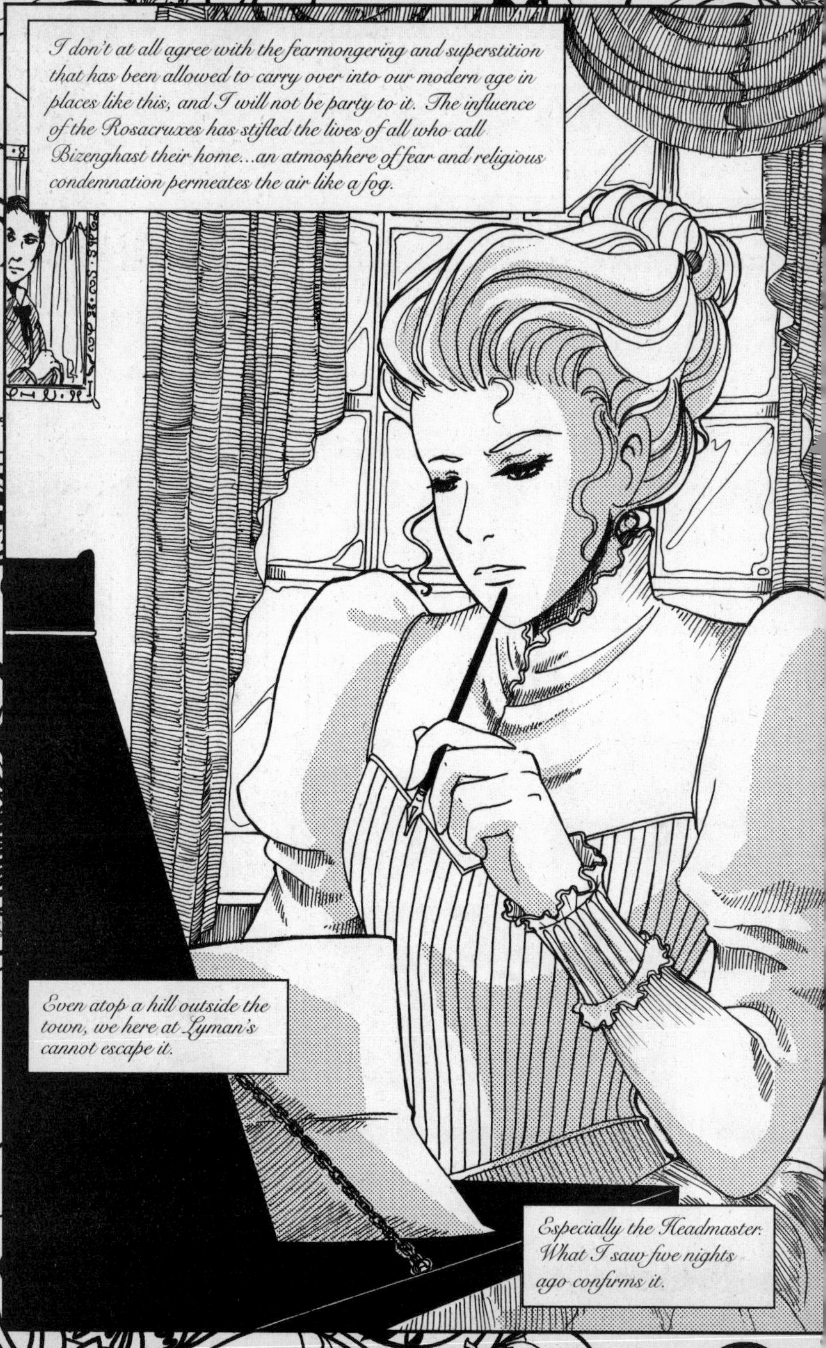
I don't at all agree with the fearmongering and superstition that has been allowed to carry over into our modern age in places like this, and I will not be party to it. The influence of the Rosacruxes has stifled the lives of all who call Bizenghast their home...an atmosphere of fear and religious condemnation permeates the air like a fog.
Even atop a hill outside the town, we here at Lyman's cannot escape it.
Especially the Headmaster. What I saw five nights ago confirms it.

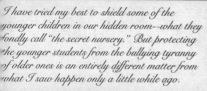

I have tried my best to shield some of the younger children in our hidden room--what they fondly call "the secret nursery." But protecting the younger students from the bullying tyranny of older ones is an entirely different matter from what I saw happen only a little while ago.

I suspect I was followed back to the school that night, though I was very careful. I can't even be certain the hidden room is still a secret.

But now I feel quite trapped. The head of the school is most certainly a close fellow of Rosacrux. I saw them together in the square that fateful night.

THE ELEPHANT BOOK

He reads all the mail leaving the school, even that of the teachers.

It was only by chance that Peter was able to carry my last letter to you, and I fear this time I won't be so fortunate.

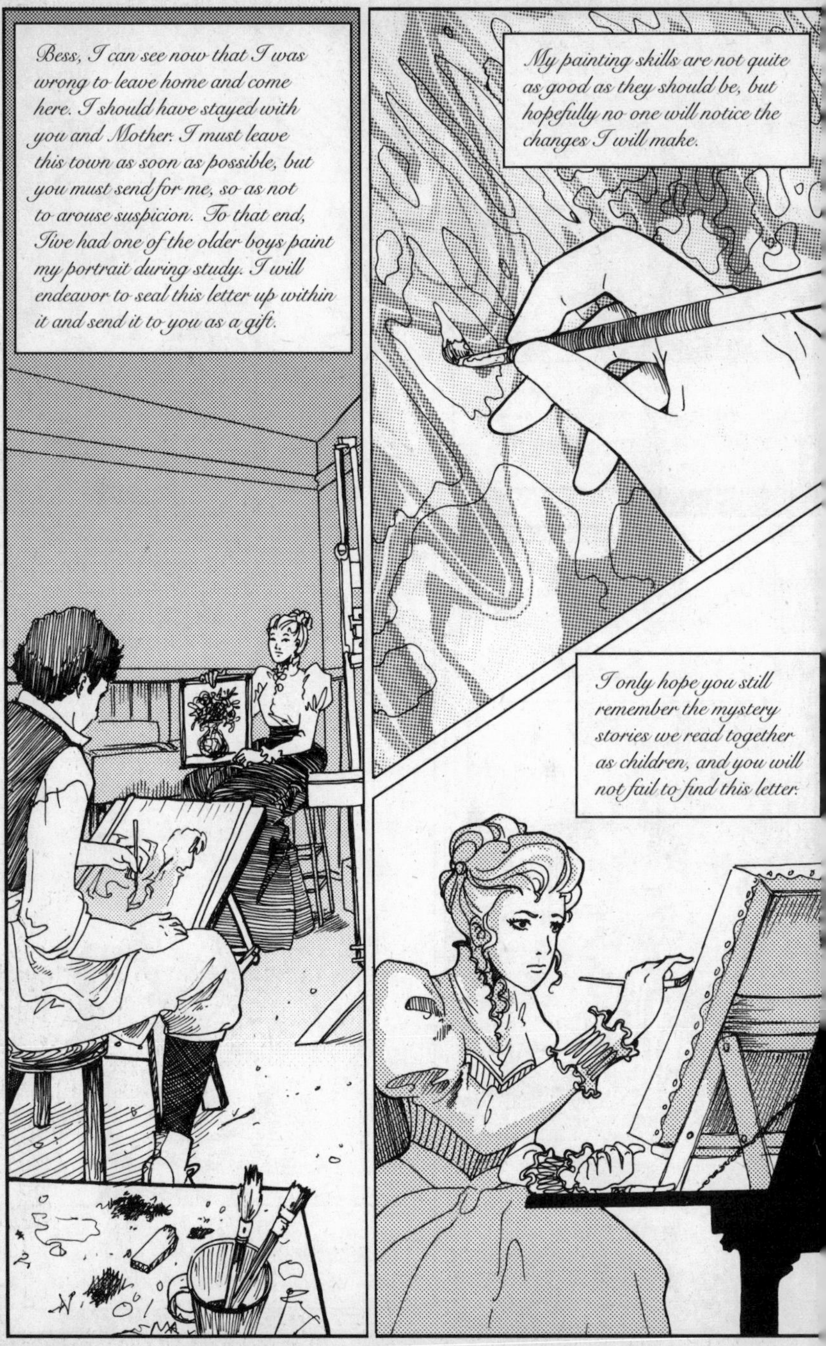
Bess, I can see now that I was wrong to leave home and come here. I should have stayed with you and Mother. I must leave this town as soon as possible, but you must send for me, so as not to arouse suspicion. To that end, I've had one of the older boys paint my portrait during study. I will endeavor to seal this letter up within it and send it to you as a gift.
My painting skills are not quite as good as they should be, but hopefully no one will notice the changes I will make.
I only hope you still remember the mystery stories we read together as children, and you will not fail to find this letter.

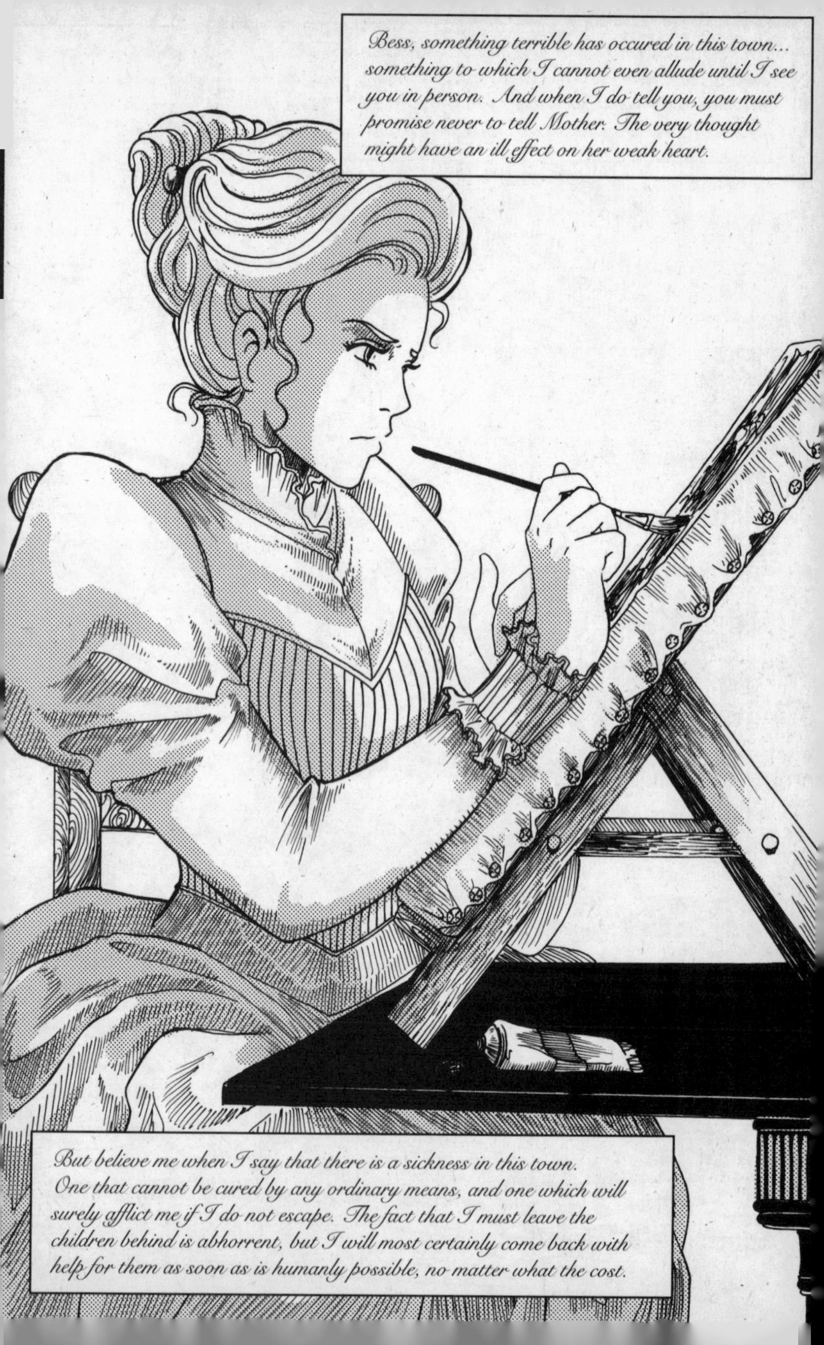
Bess, something terrible has occured in this town... something to which I cannot even allude until I see you in person. And when I do tell you, you must promise never to tell Mother. The very thought might have an ill effect on her weak heart.
But believe me when I say that there is a sickness in this town. One that cannot be cured by any ordinary means, and one which will surely afflict me if I do not escape. The fact that I must leave the children behind is abhorrent, but I will most certainly come back with help for them as soon as is humanly possible, no matter what the cost.

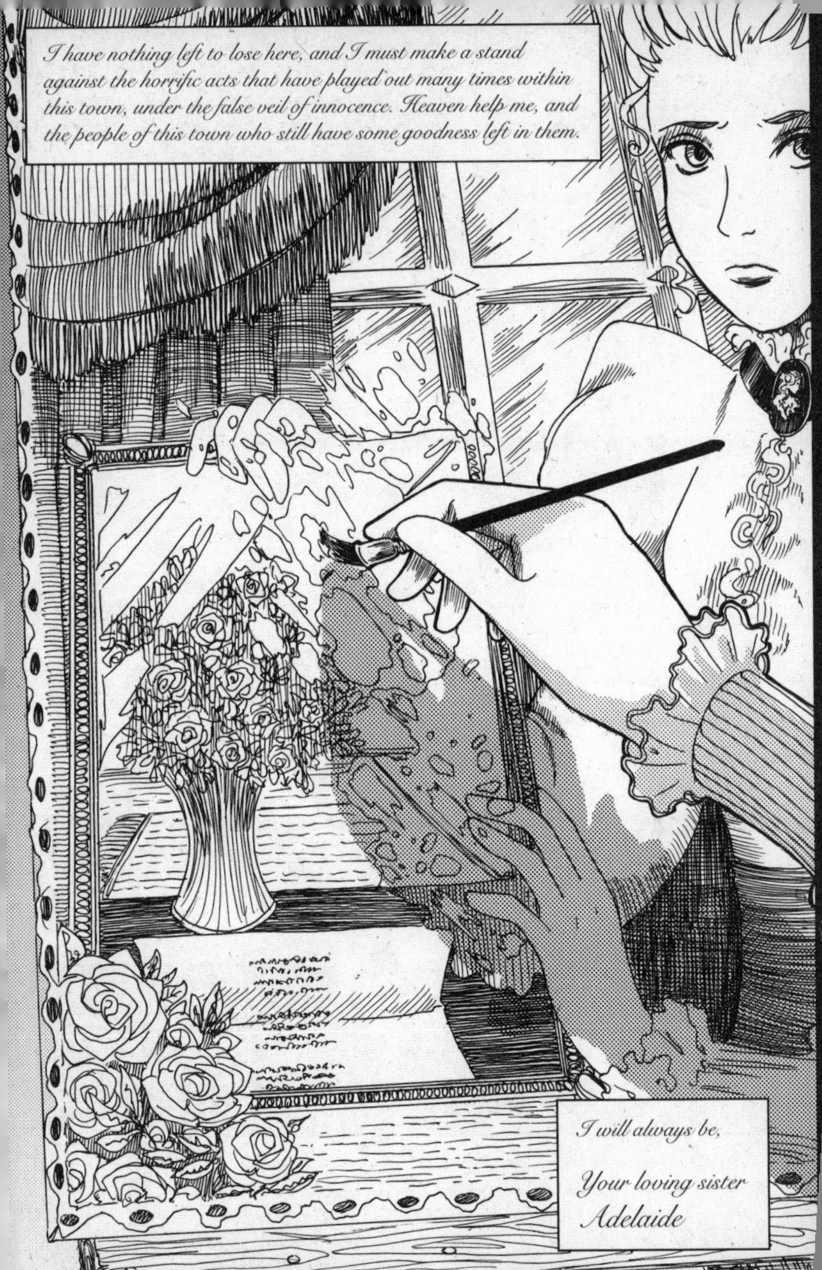
I have nothing left to lose here, and I must make a stand against the horrific acts that have played out many times within this town, under the false veil of innocence. Heaven help me, and the people of this town who still have some goodness left in them.
I will always be,
Your loving sister
Adelaide

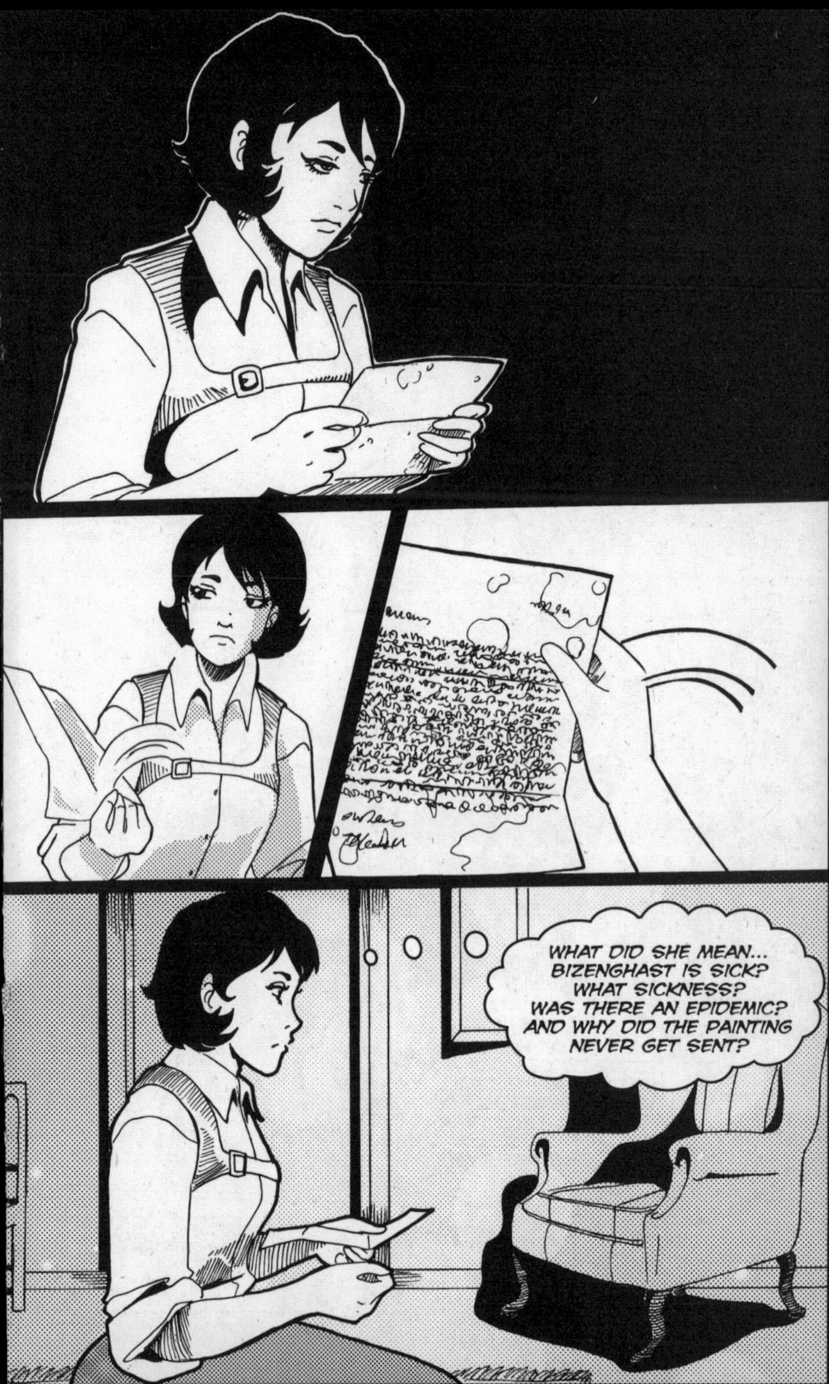
WHAT DID SHE MEAN... BIZENGHAST IS SICK? WHAT SICKNESS? WAS THERE AN EPIDEMIC? AND WHY DID THE PAINTING NEVER GET SENT?

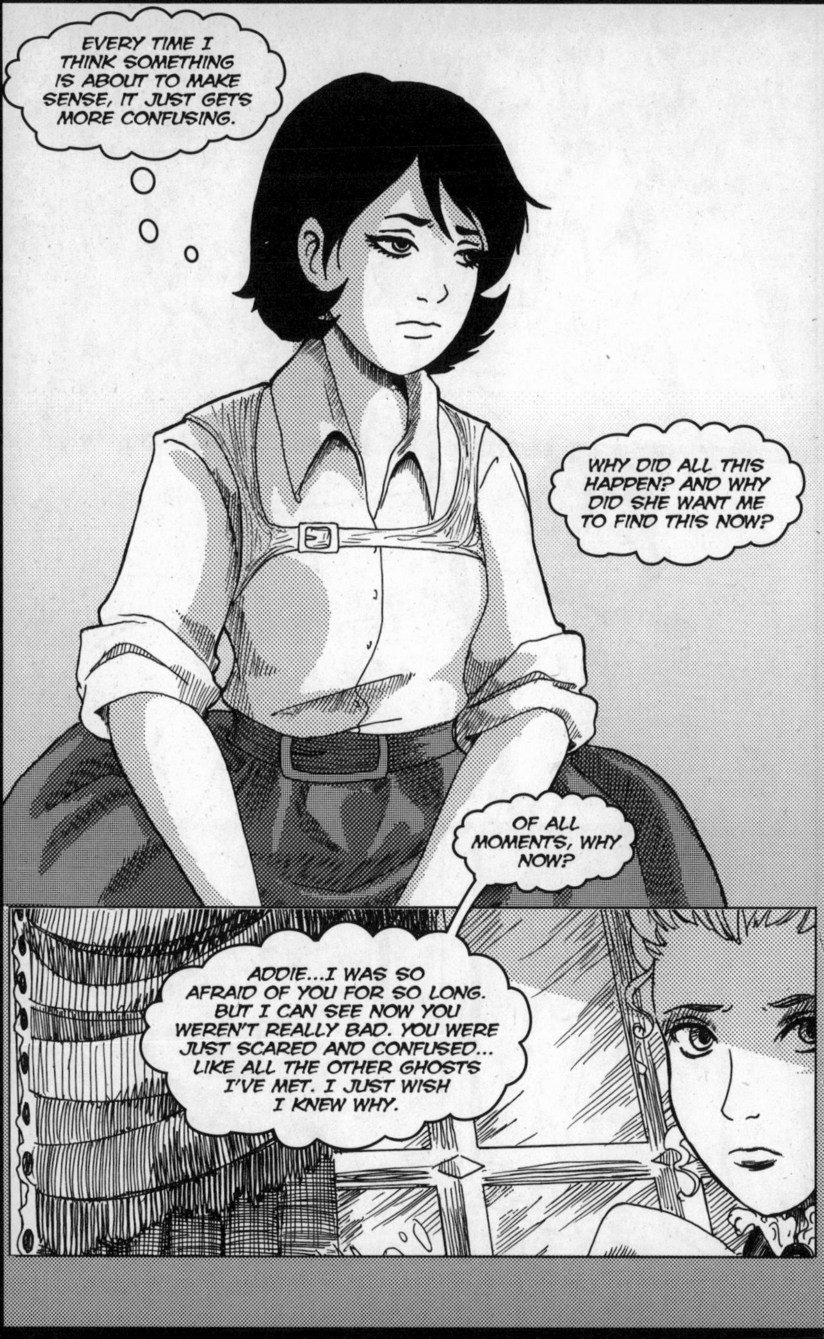
EVERY TIME I THINK SOMETHING IS ABOUT TO MAKE SENSE, IT JUST GETS MORE CONFUSING.
WHY DID ALL THIS HAPPEN? AND WHY DID SHE WANT ME TO FIND THIS NOW?
OF ALL MOMENTS, WHY NOW?
ADDIE...I WAS SO AFRAID OF YOU FOR SO LONG. BUT I CAN SEE NOW YOU WEREN'T REALLY BAD. YOU WERE JUST SCARED AND CONFUSED... LIKE ALL THE OTHER GHOSTS I'VE MET. I JUST WISH I KNEW WHY.

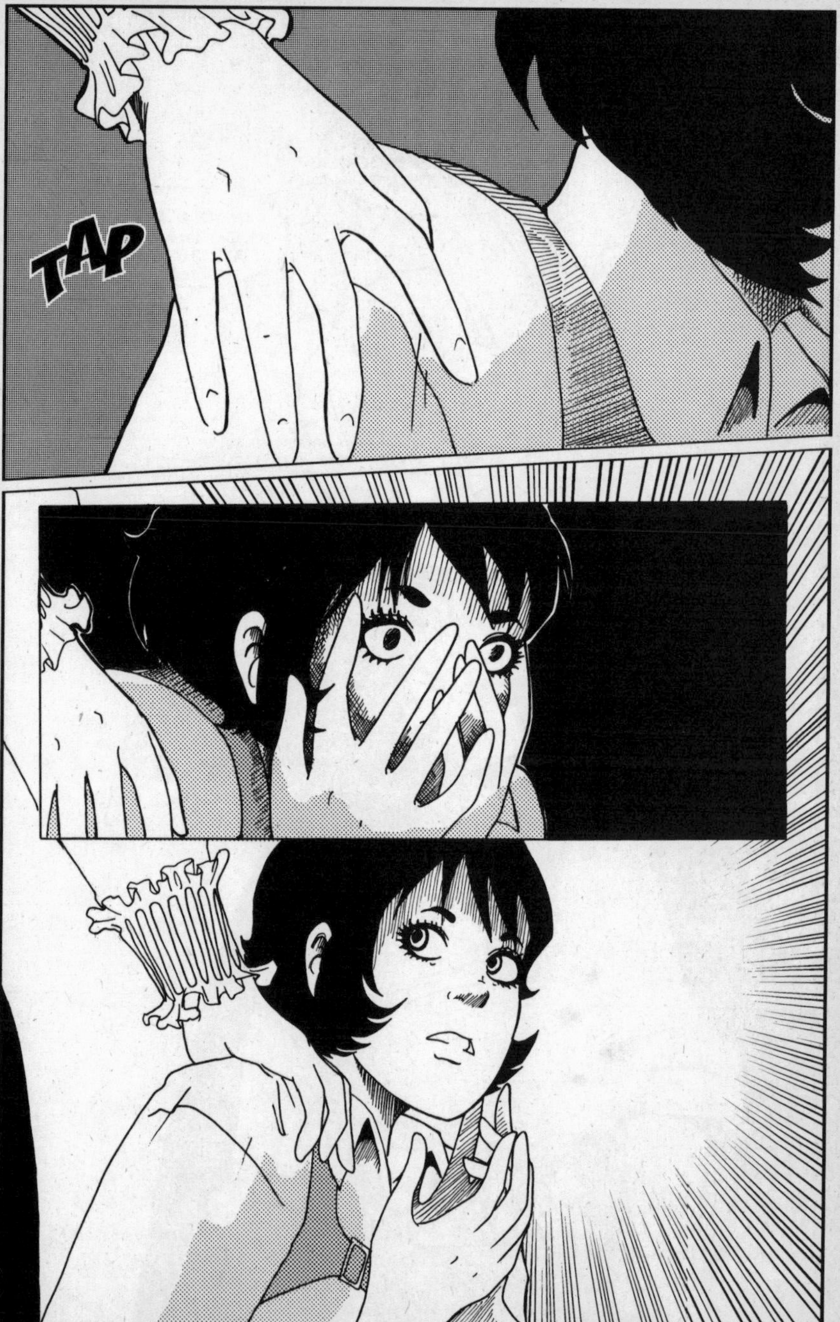
TAP

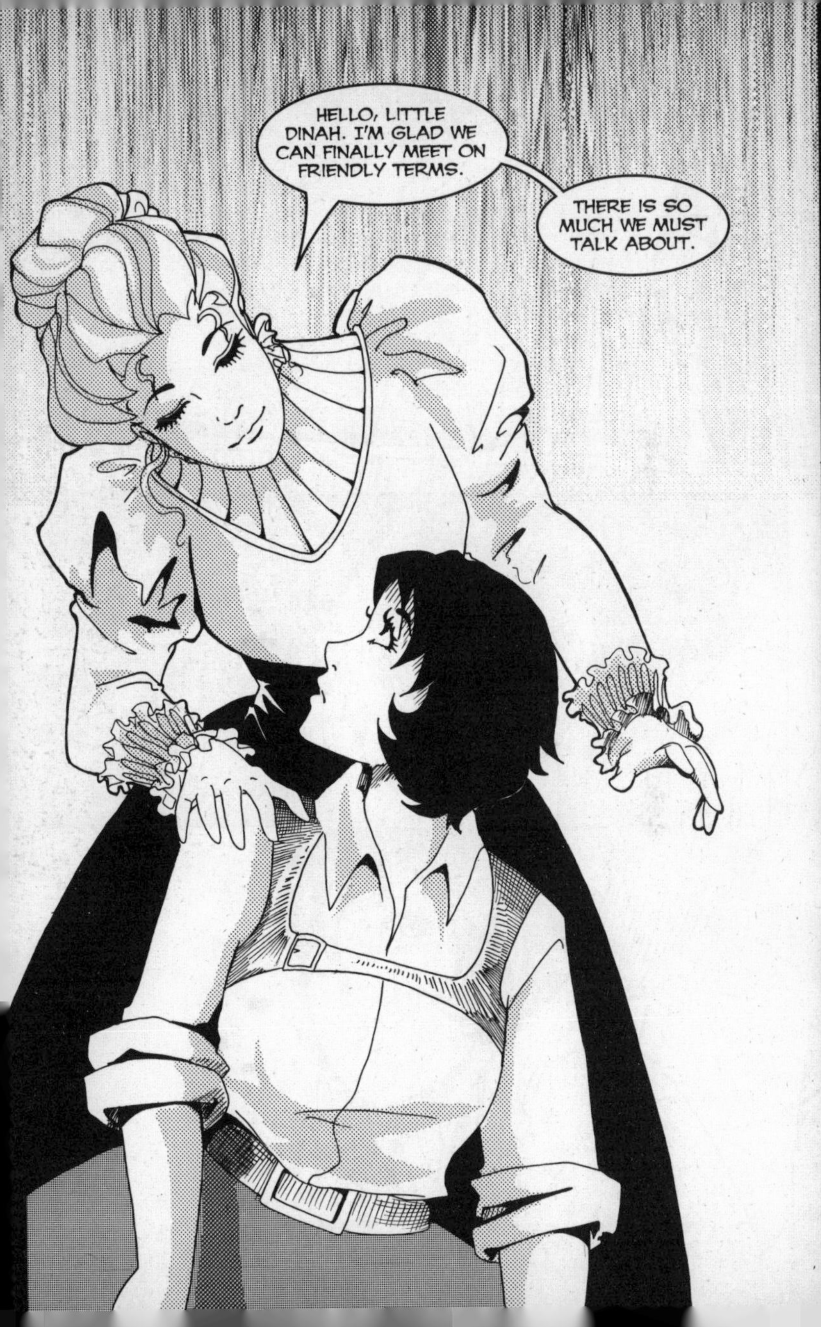
HELLO, LITTLE DINAH. I'M GLAD WE CAN FINALLY MEET ON FRIENDLY TERMS.
THERE IS SO MUCH WE MUST TALK ABOUT.

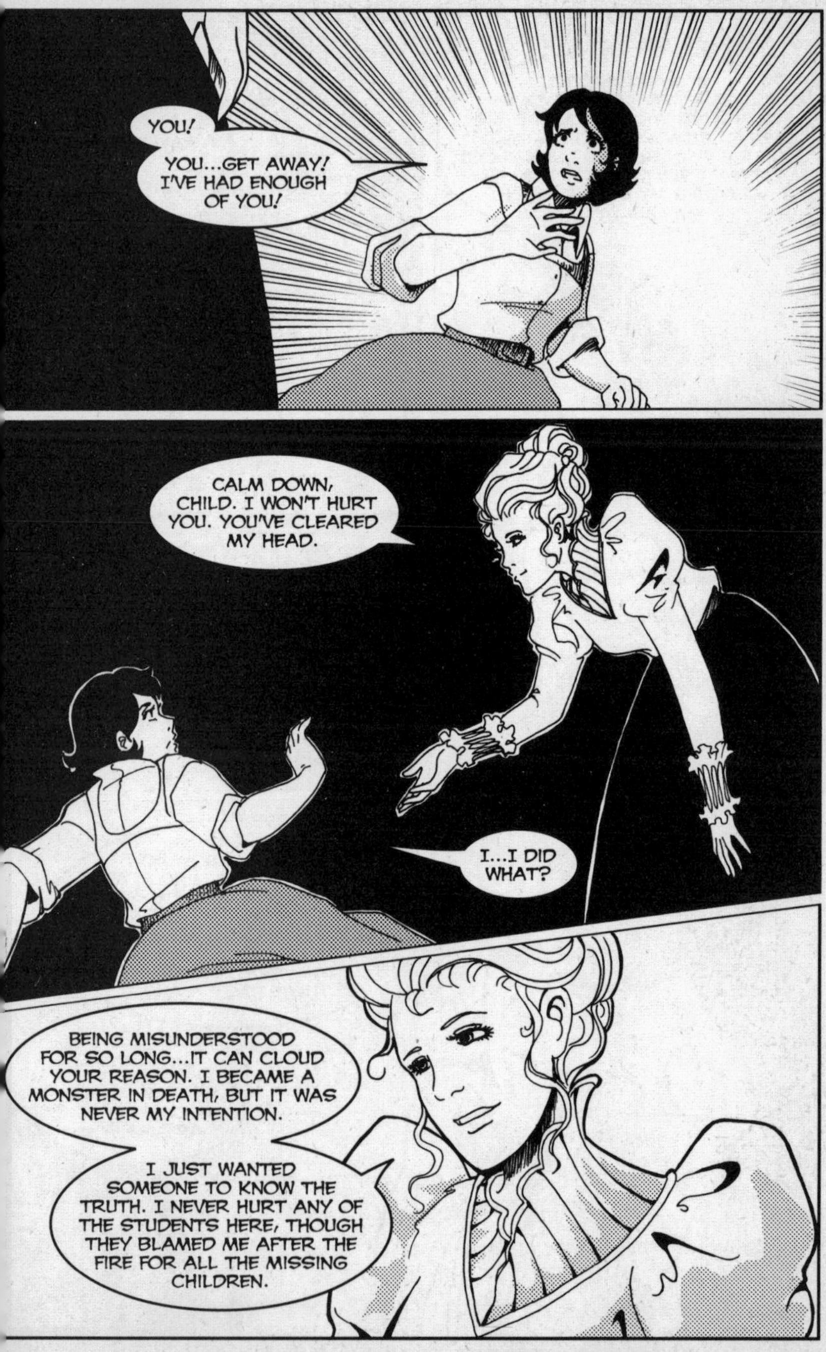
YOU!
YOU...GET AWAY! I'VE HAD ENOUGH OF YOU!
CALM DOWN, CHILD. I WON'T HURT YOU. YOU'VE CLEARED MY HEAD.
I...I DID WHAT?
BEING MISUNDERSTOOD FOR SO LONG...IT CAN CLOUD YOUR REASON. I BECAME A MONSTER IN DEATH, BUT IT WAS NEVER MY INTENTION.
I JUST WANTED SOMEONE TO KNOW THE TRUTH. I NEVER HURT ANY OF THE STUDENTS HERE, THOUGH THEY BLAMED ME AFTER THE FIRE FOR ALL THE MISSING CHILDREN.

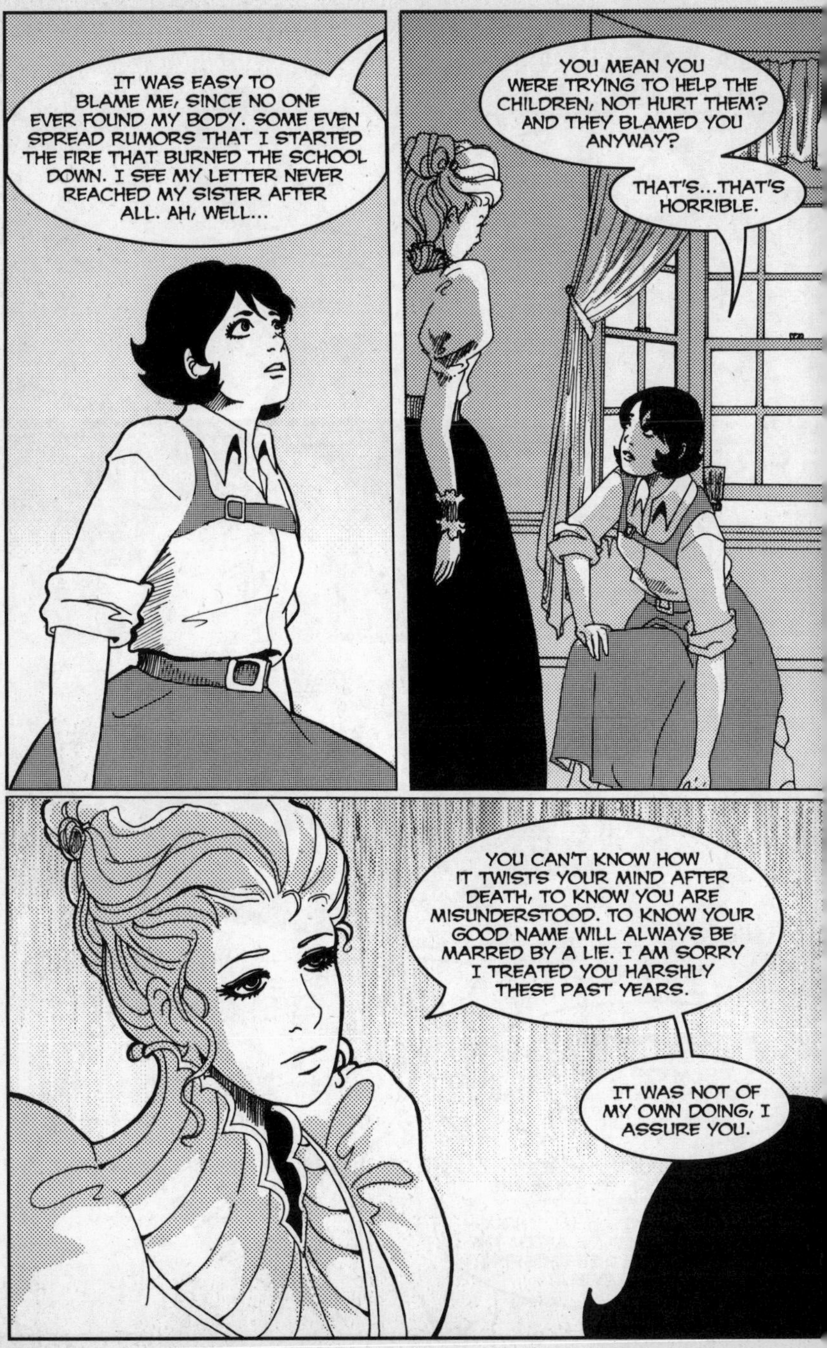
IT WAS EASY TO BLAME ME, SINCE NO ONE EVER FOUND MY BODY. SOME EVEN SPREAD RUMORS THAT I STARTED THE FIRE THAT BURNED THE SCHOOL DOWN. I SEE MY LETTER NEVER REACHED MY SISTER AFTER ALL. AH, WELL...
YOU MEAN YOU WERE TRYING TO HELP THE CHILDREN, NOT HURT THEM? AND THEY BLAMED YOU ANYWAY?
THAT'S...THAT'S HORRIBLE.
YOU CAN'T KNOW HOW IT TWISTS YOUR MIND AFTER DEATH, TO KNOW YOU ARE MISUNDERSTOOD. TO KNOW YOUR GOOD NAME WILL ALWAYS BE MARRED BY A LIE. I AM SORRY I TREATED YOU HARSHLY THESE PAST YEARS.
IT WAS NOT OF MY OWN DOING, I ASSURE YOU.

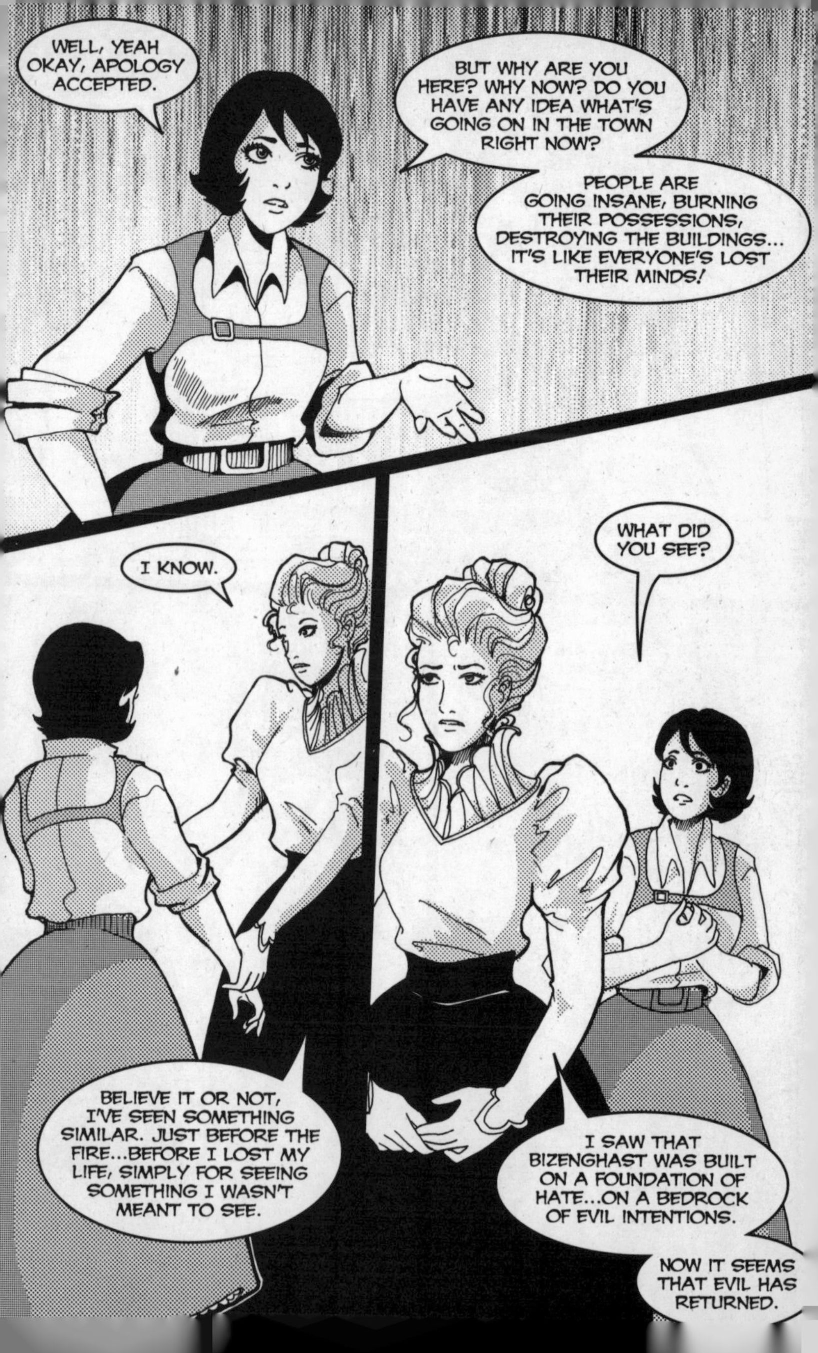
WELL, YEAH OKAY, APOLOGY ACCEPTED.
BUT WHY ARE YOU HERE? WHY NOW? DO YOU HAVE ANY IDEA WHAT'S GOING ON IN THE TOWN RIGHT NOW?
PEOPLE ARE GOING INSANE, BURNING THEIR POSSESSIONS, DESTROYING THE BUILDINGS... IT'S LIKE EVERYONE'S LOST THEIR MINDS!
I KNOW.
BELIEVE IT OR NOT, I'VE SEEN SOMETHING SIMILAR. JUST BEFORE THE FIRE...BEFORE I LOST MY LIFE, SIMPLY FOR SEEING SOMETHING I WASN'T MEANT TO SEE.
WHAT DID YOU SEE?
I SAW THAT BIZENGHAST WAS BUILT ON A FOUNDATION OF HATE...ON A BEDROCK OF EVIL INTENTIONS.
NOW IT SEEMS THAT EVIL HAS RETURNED.

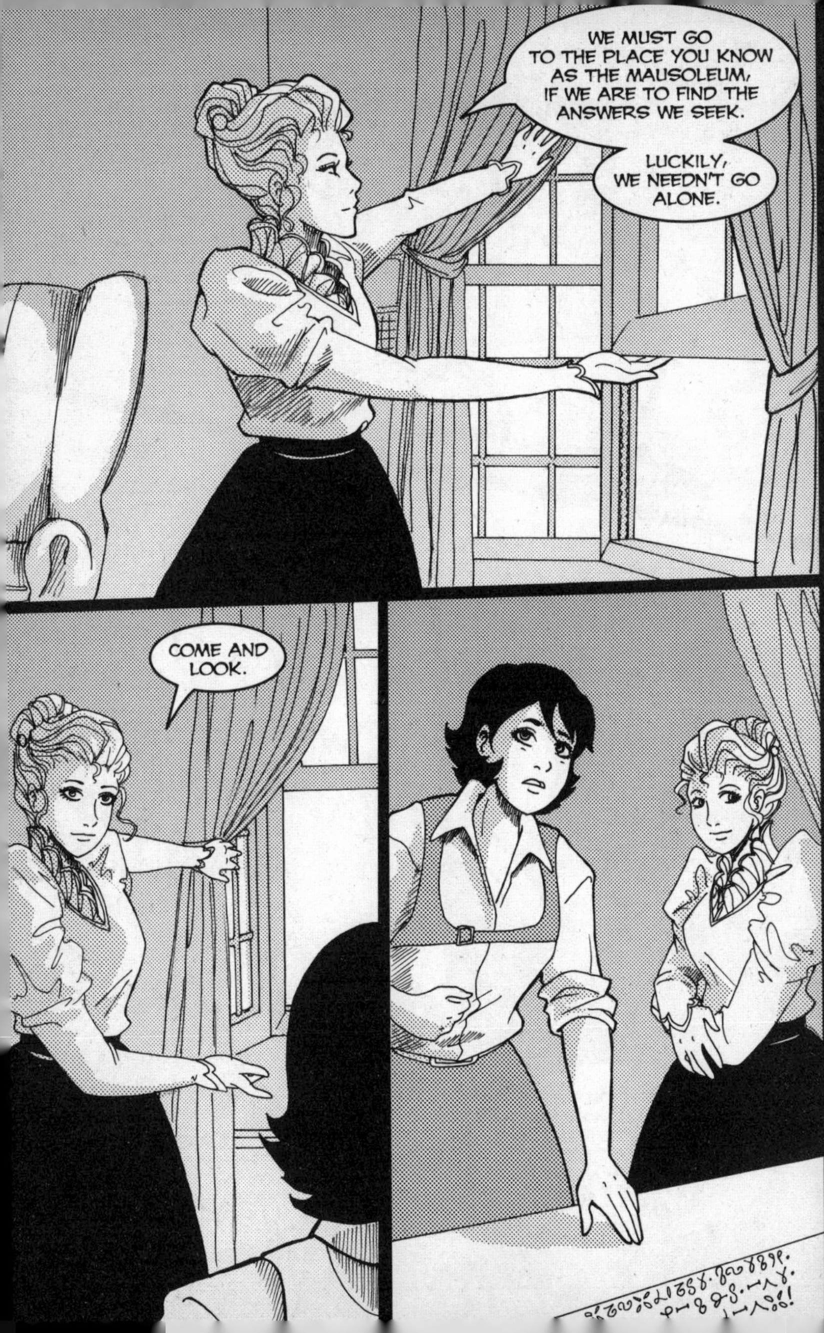
WE MUST GO TO THE PLACE YOU KNOW AS THE MAUSOLEUM, IF WE ARE TO FIND THE ANSWERS WE SEEK.
LUCKILY, WE NEEDN'T GO ALONE.
COME AND LOOK.

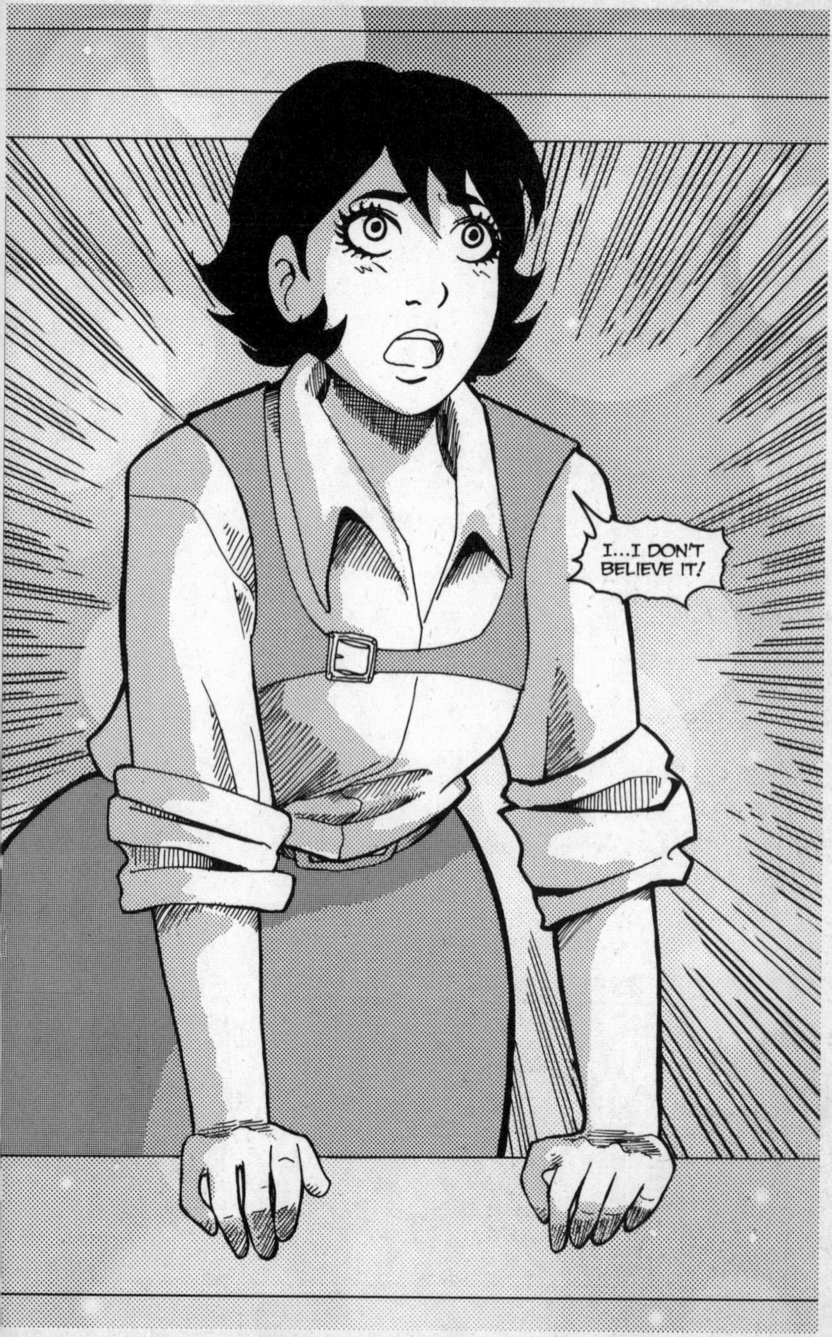
I...I DON'T BELIEVE IT!

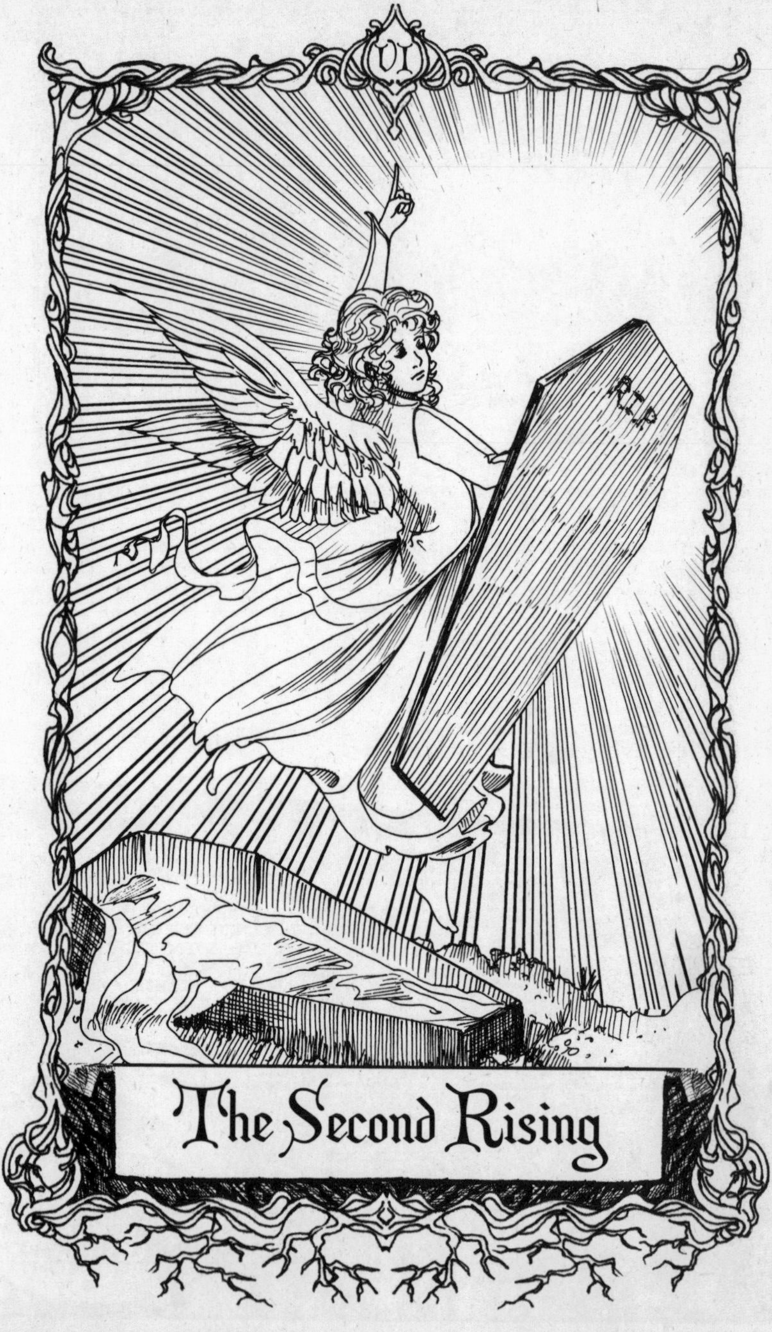
VI
R.I.P.
The Second Rising

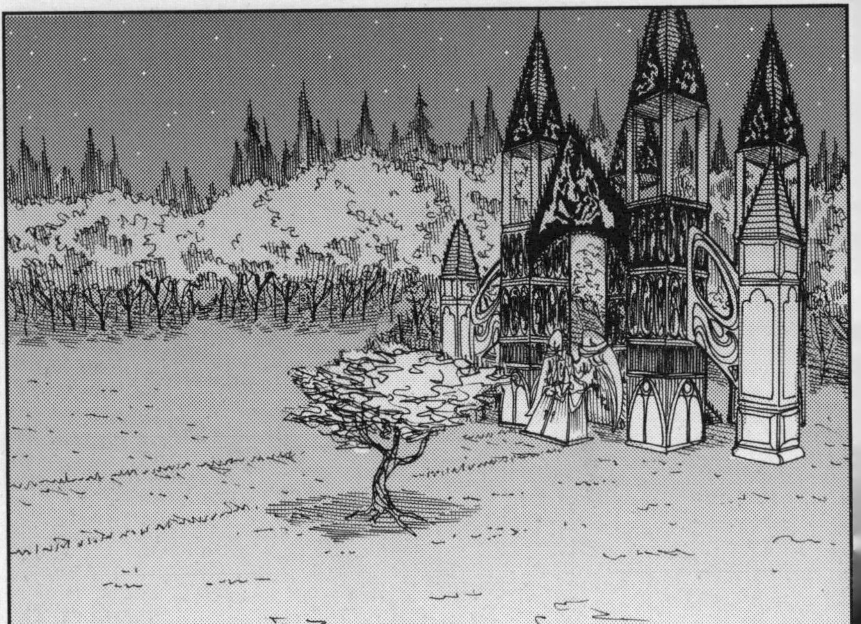

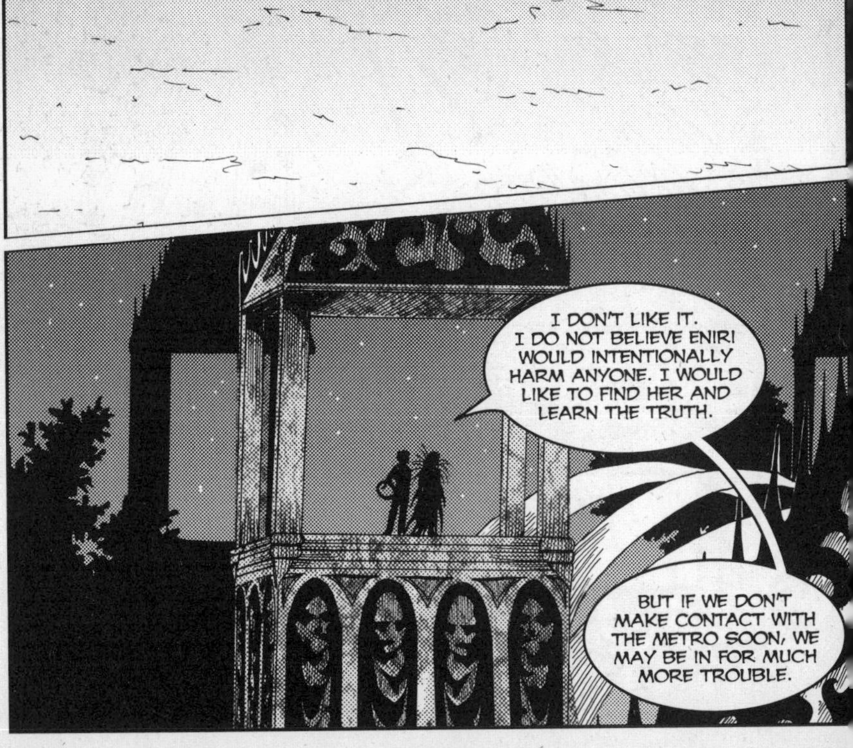
I DON'T LIKE IT. I DO NOT BELIEVE ENIRI WOULD INTENTIONALLY HARM ANYONE. I WOULD LIKE TO FIND HER AND LEARN THE TRUTH.
BUT IF WE DON'T MAKE CONTACT WITH THE METRO SOON, WE MAY BE IN FOR MUCH MORE TROUBLE.

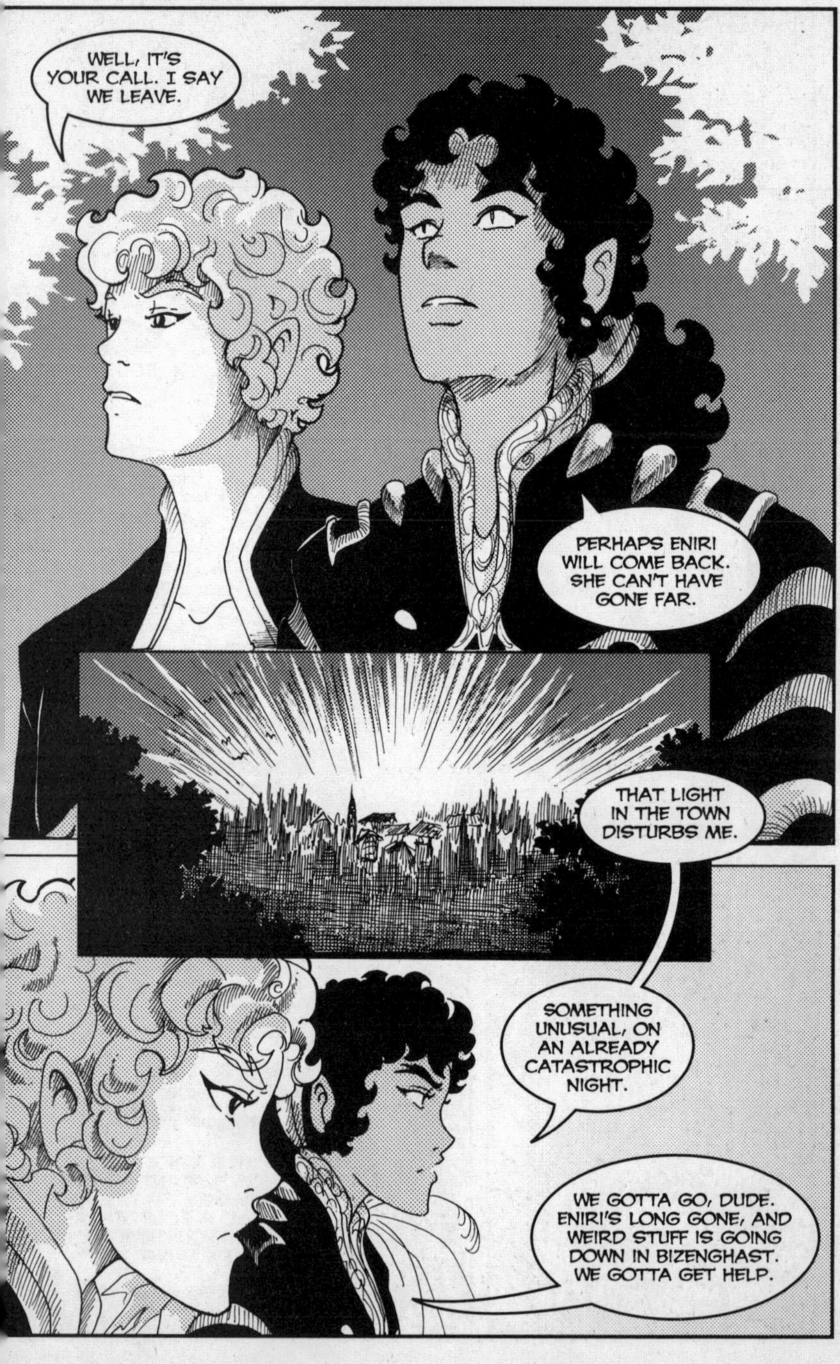
WELL, IT'S YOUR CALL. I SAY WE LEAVE.
PERHAPS ENIRI WILL COME BACK. SHE CAN'T HAVE GONE FAR.
THAT LIGHT IN THE TOWN DISTURBS ME.
SOMETHING UNUSUAL, ON AN ALREADY CATASTROPHIC NIGHT.
WE GOTTA GO, DUDE. ENIRI'S LONG GONE, AND WEIRD STUFF IS GOING DOWN IN BIZENGHAST. WE GOTTA GET HELP.

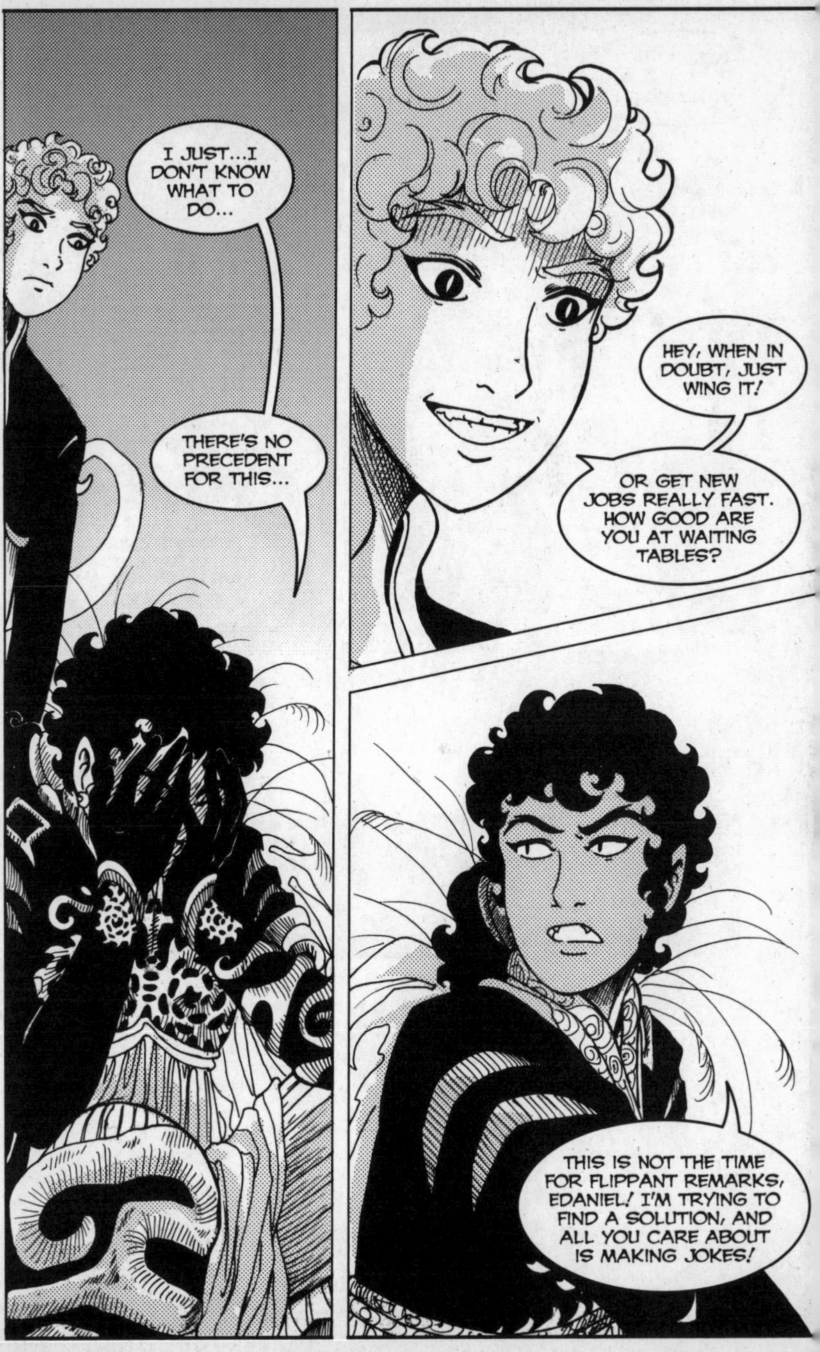
I JUST...I DON'T KNOW WHAT TO DO...
THERE'S NO PRECEDENT FOR THIS...
HEY, WHEN IN DOUBT, JUST WING IT!
OR GET NEW JOBS REALLY FAST. HOW GOOD ARE YOU AT WAITING TABLES?
THIS IS NOT THE TIME FOR FLIPPANT REMARKS, EDANIEL! I'M TRYING TO FIND A SOLUTION, AND ALL YOU CARE ABOUT IS MAKING JOKES!

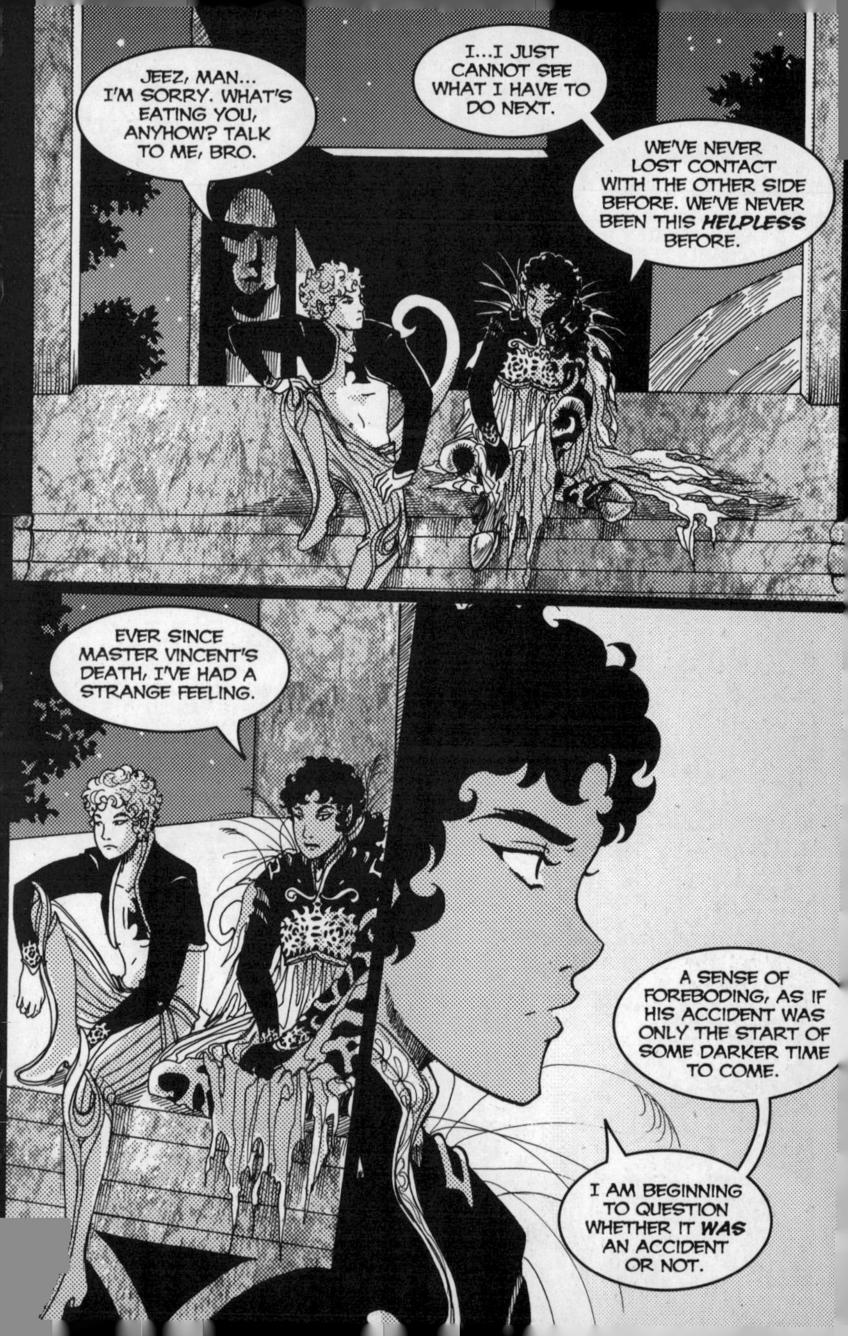
JEEZ, MAN... I'M SORRY. WHAT'S EATING YOU, ANYHOW? TALK TO ME, BRO.
I...I JUST CANNOT SEE WHAT I HAVE TO DO NEXT.
WE'VE NEVER LOST CONTACT WITH THE OTHER SIDE BEFORE. WE'VE NEVER BEEN THIS **HELPLESS** BEFORE.
EVER SINCE MASTER VINCENT'S DEATH, I'VE HAD A STRANGE FEELING.
A SENSE OF FOREBODING, AS IF HIS ACCIDENT WAS ONLY THE START OF SOME DARKER TIME TO COME.
I AM BEGINNING TO QUESTION WHETHER IT **WAS** AN ACCIDENT OR NOT.

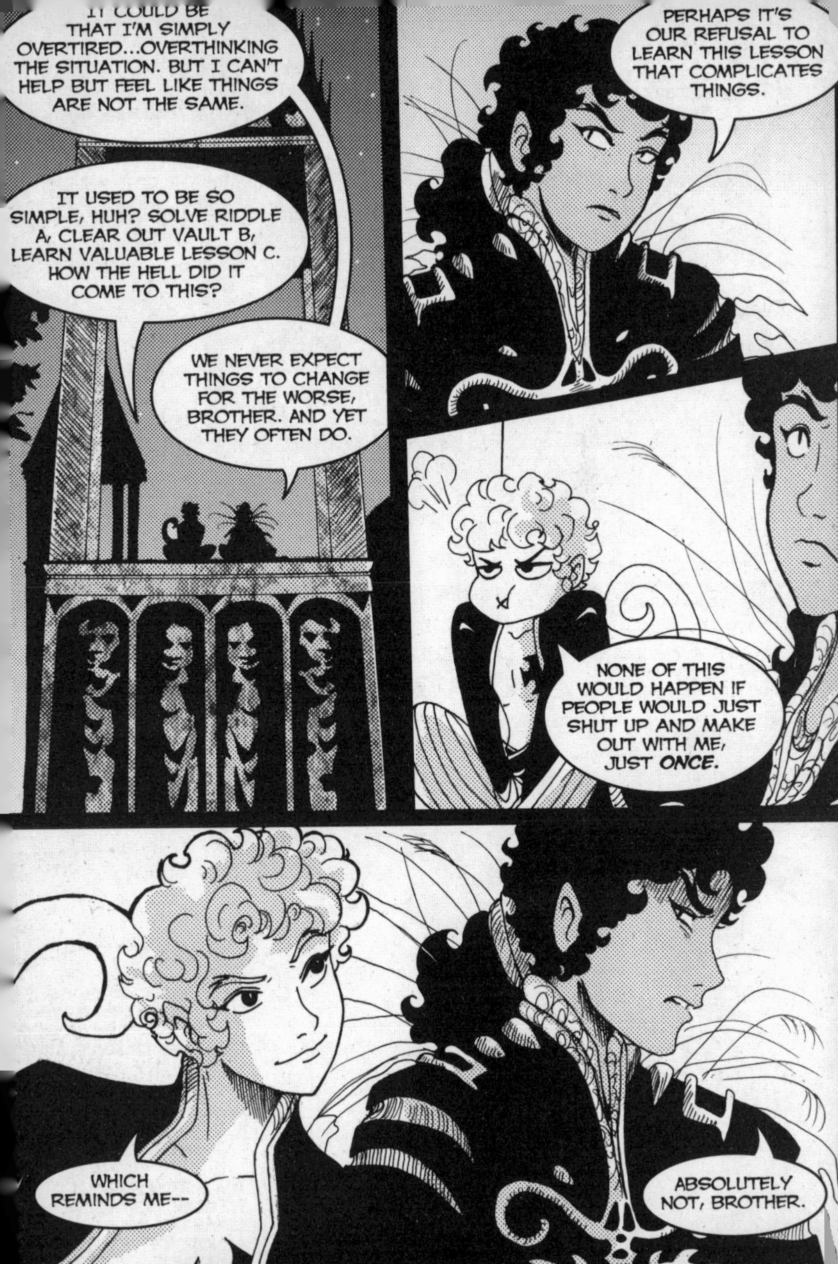
IT COULD BE THAT I'M SIMPLY OVERTIRED...OVERTHINKING THE SITUATION. BUT I CAN'T HELP BUT FEEL LIKE THINGS ARE NOT THE SAME.
IT USED TO BE SO SIMPLE, HUH? SOLVE RIDDLE A, CLEAR OUT VAULT B, LEARN VALUABLE LESSON C. HOW THE HELL DID IT COME TO THIS?
WE NEVER EXPECT THINGS TO CHANGE FOR THE WORSE, BROTHER. AND YET THEY OFTEN DO.
PERHAPS IT'S OUR REFUSAL TO LEARN THIS LESSON THAT COMPLICATES THINGS.
NONE OF THIS WOULD HAPPEN IF PEOPLE WOULD JUST SHUT UP AND MAKE OUT WITH ME, JUST *ONCE*.
WHICH REMINDS ME--
ABSOLUTELY NOT, BROTHER.

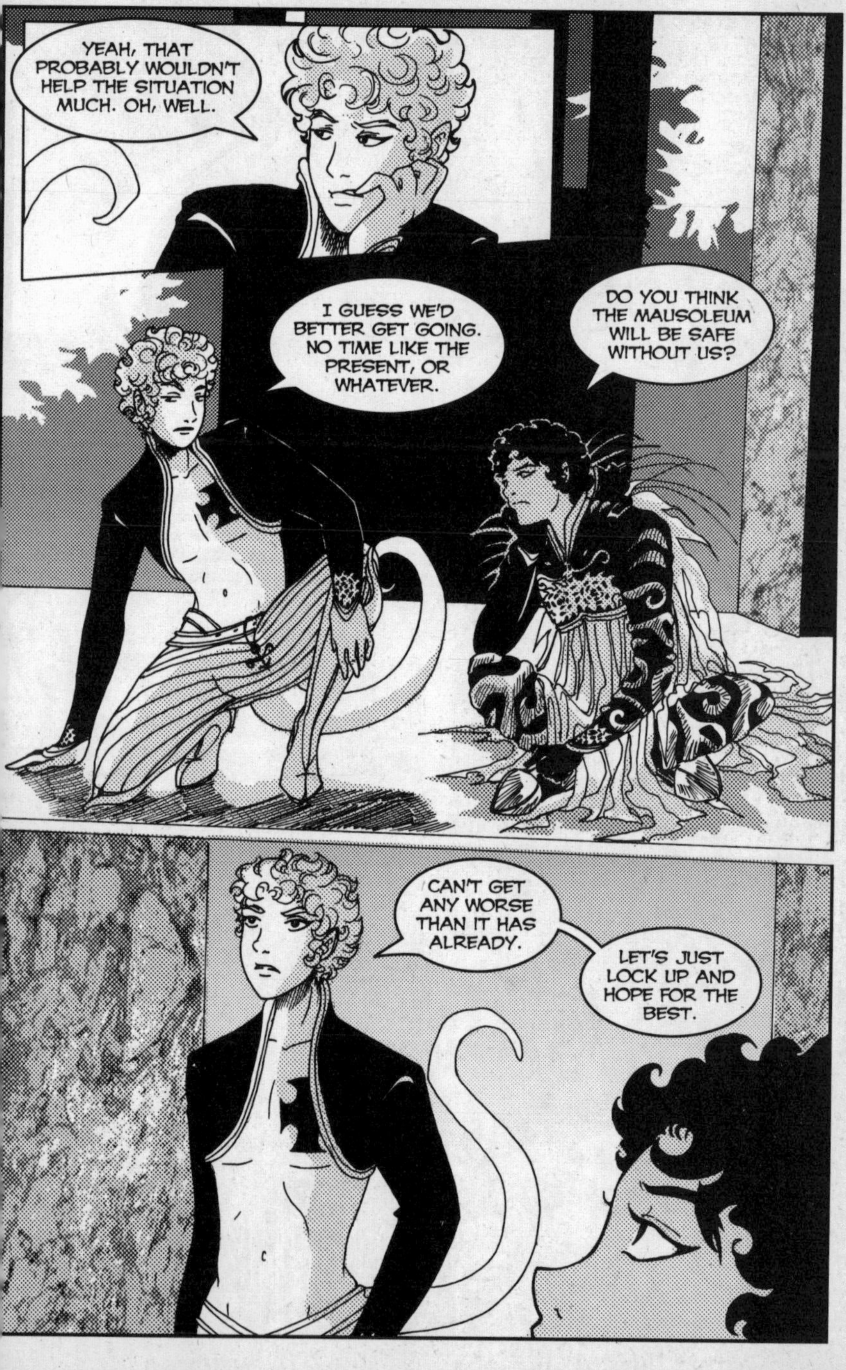
YEAH, THAT PROBABLY WOULDN'T HELP THE SITUATION MUCH. OH, WELL.
I GUESS WE'D BETTER GET GOING. NO TIME LIKE THE PRESENT, OR WHATEVER.
DO YOU THINK THE MAUSOLEUM WILL BE SAFE WITHOUT US?
CAN'T GET ANY WORSE THAN IT HAS ALREADY.
LET'S JUST LOCK UP AND HOPE FOR THE BEST.

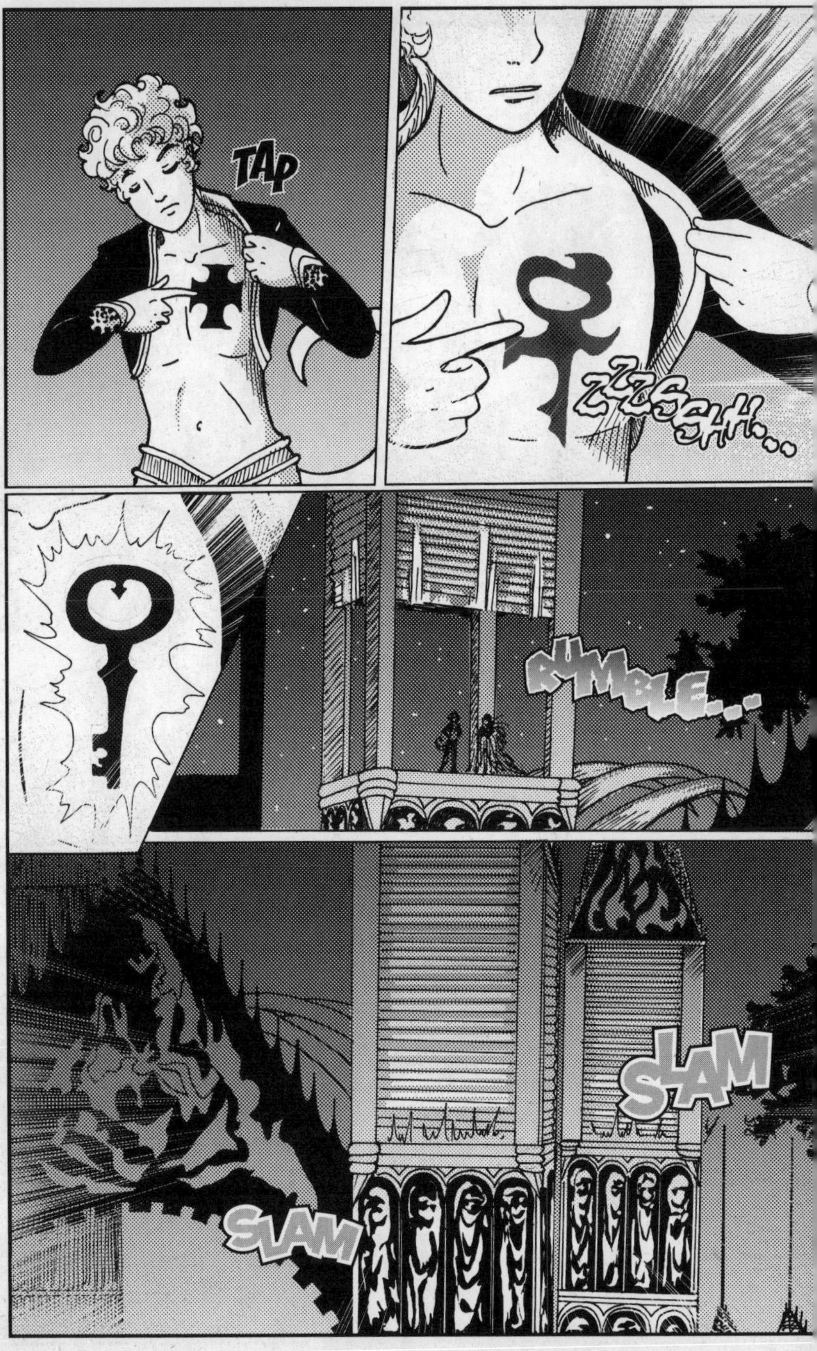
TAP
ZZZSCHH...
RUMBLE...
SLAM
SLAM

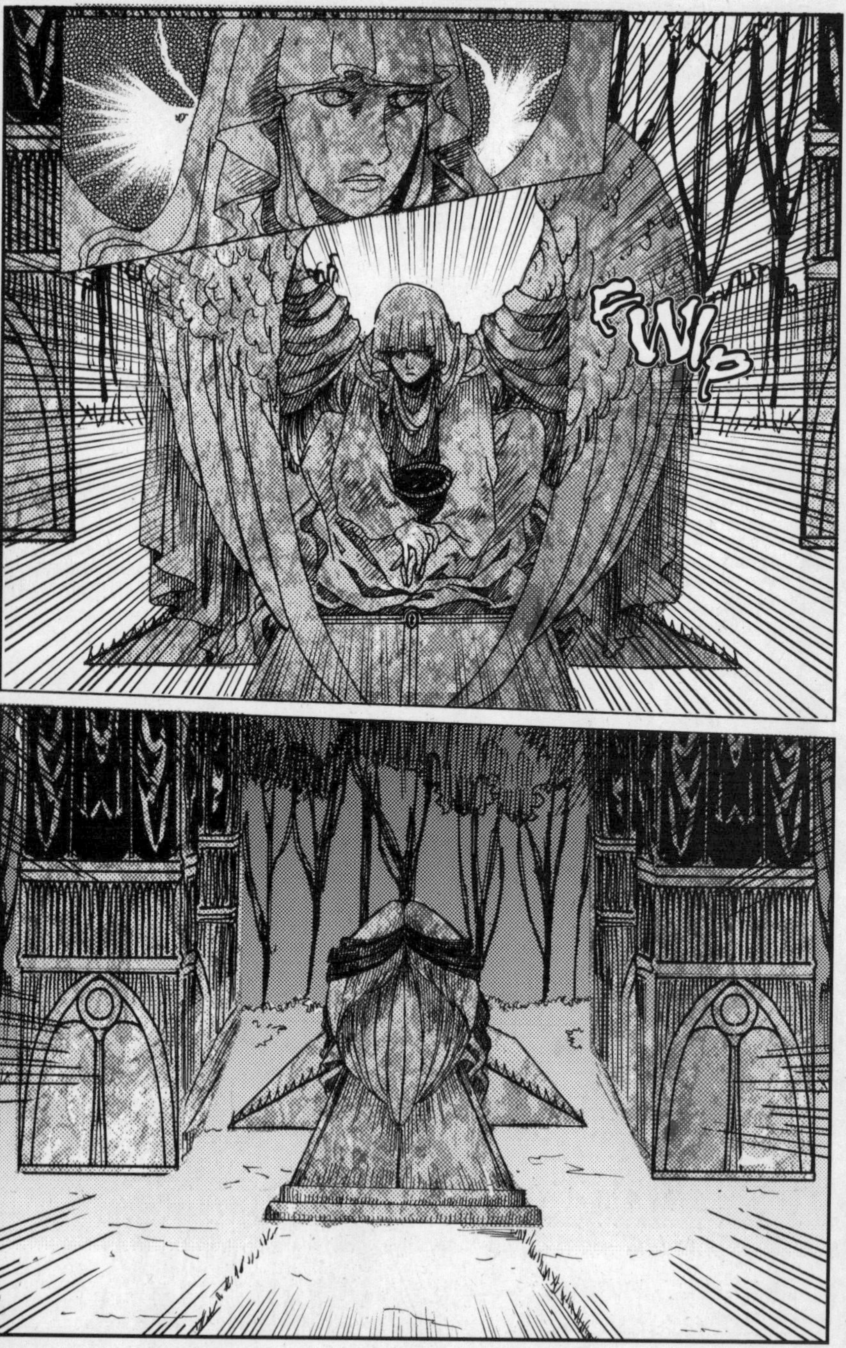
FWIP

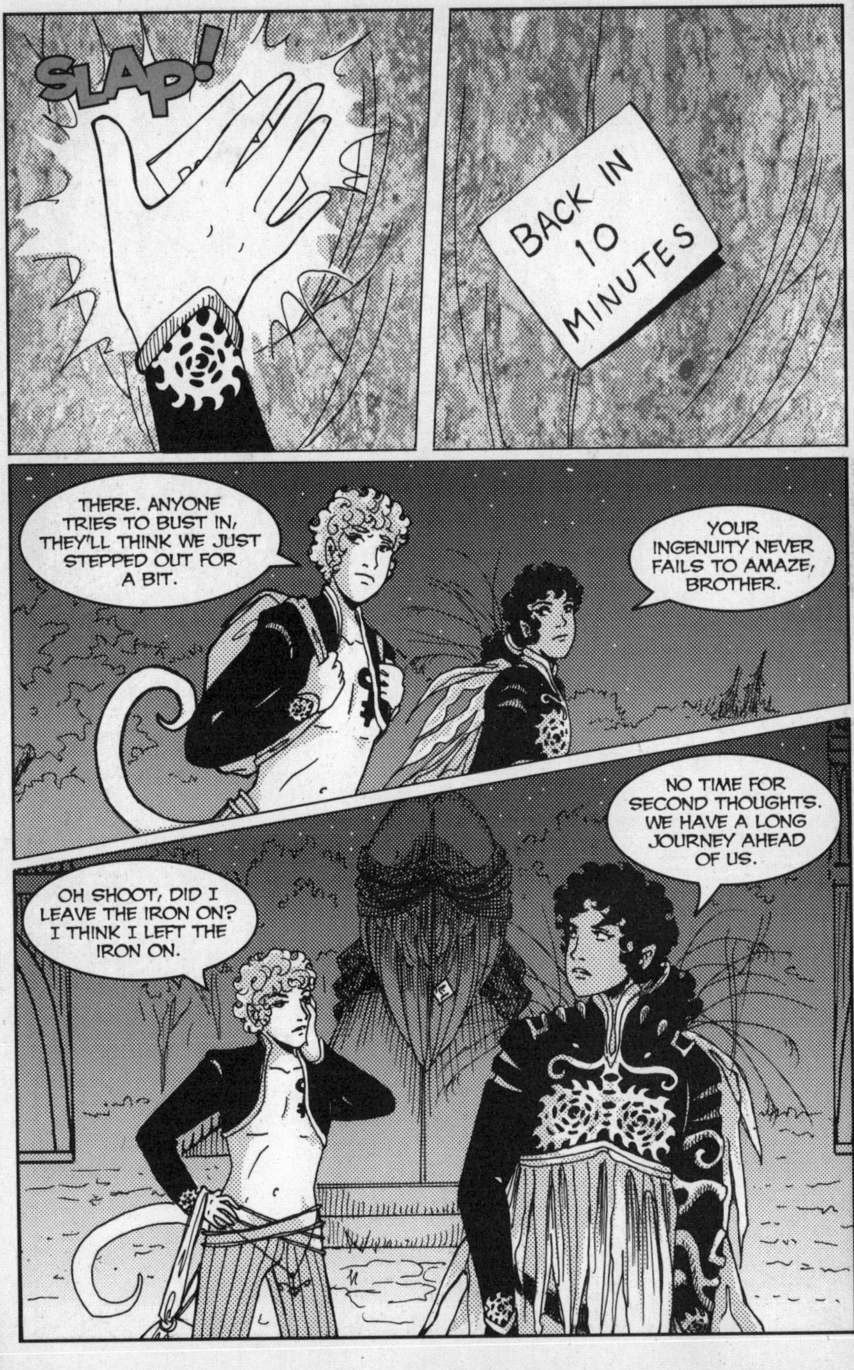
SLAP!
BACK IN 10 MINUTES
THERE. ANYONE TRIES TO BUST IN, THEY'LL THINK WE JUST STEPPED OUT FOR A BIT.
YOUR INGENUITY NEVER FAILS TO AMAZE, BROTHER.
OH SHOOT, DID I LEAVE THE IRON ON? I THINK I LEFT THE IRON ON.
NO TIME FOR SECOND THOUGHTS. WE HAVE A LONG JOURNEY AHEAD OF US.

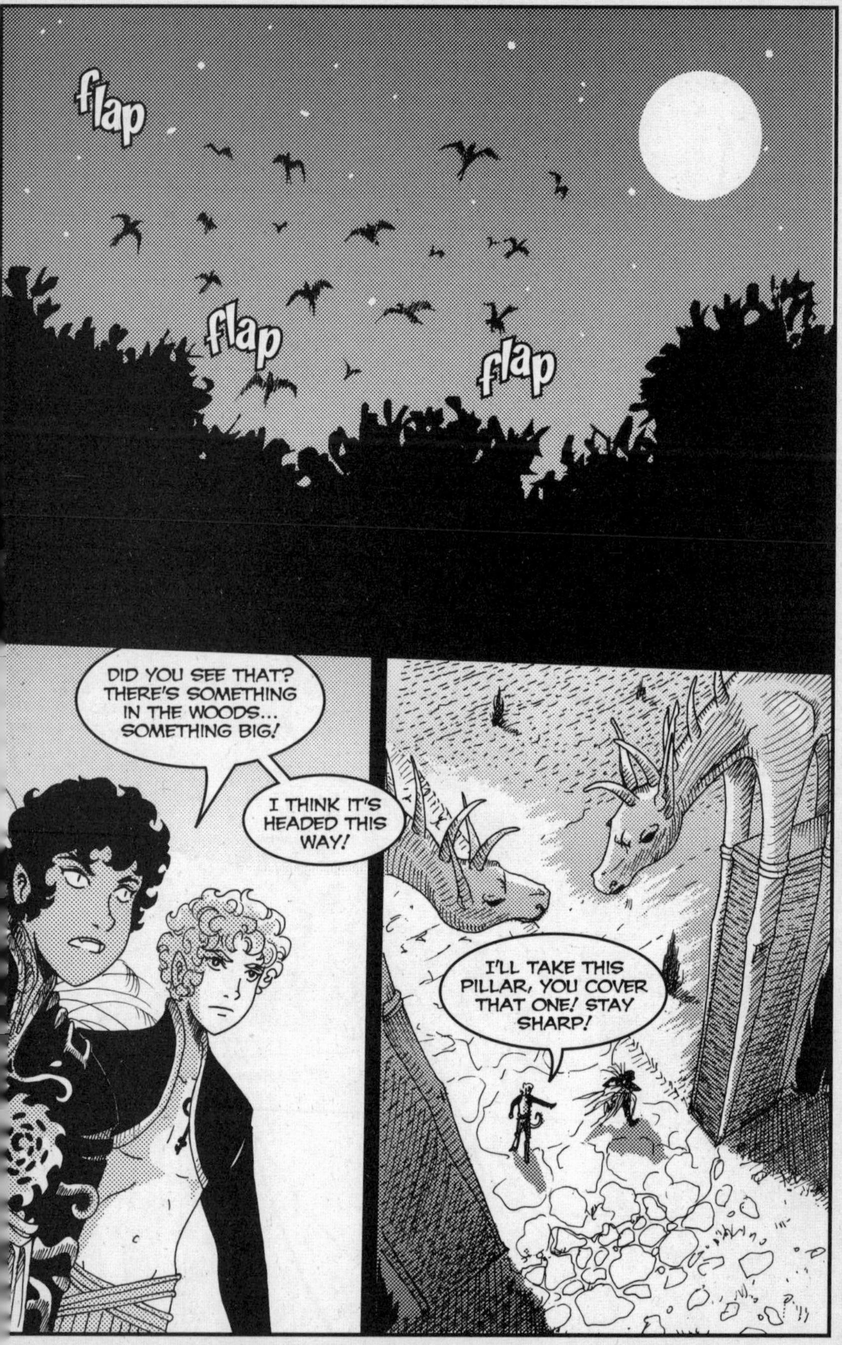
flap
flap
flap
DID YOU SEE THAT? THERE'S SOMETHING IN THE WOODS... SOMETHING BIG!
I THINK IT'S HEADED THIS WAY!
I'LL TAKE THIS PILLAR, YOU COVER THAT ONE! STAY SHARP!

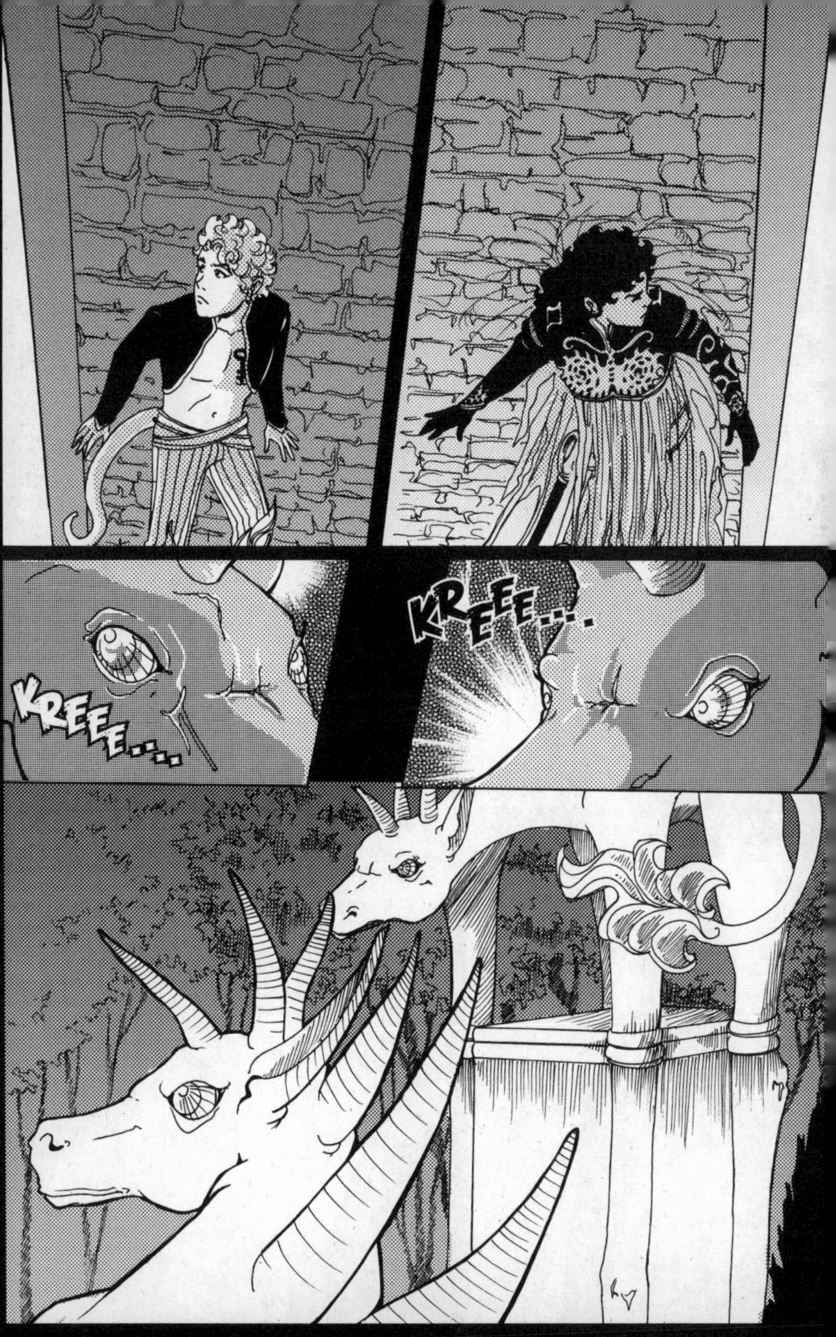
KREEEE....
KREEEE....

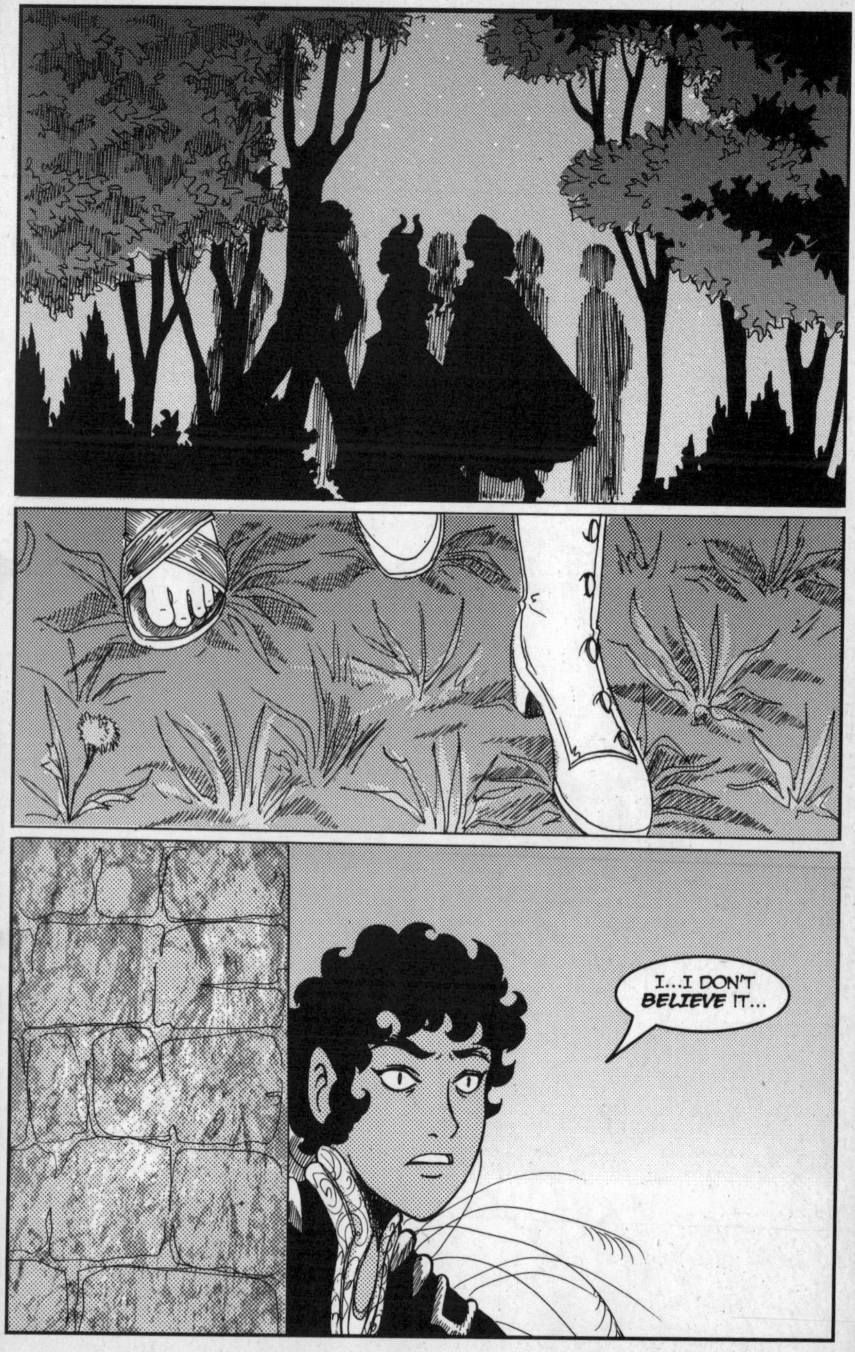
I...I DON'T BELIEVE IT...

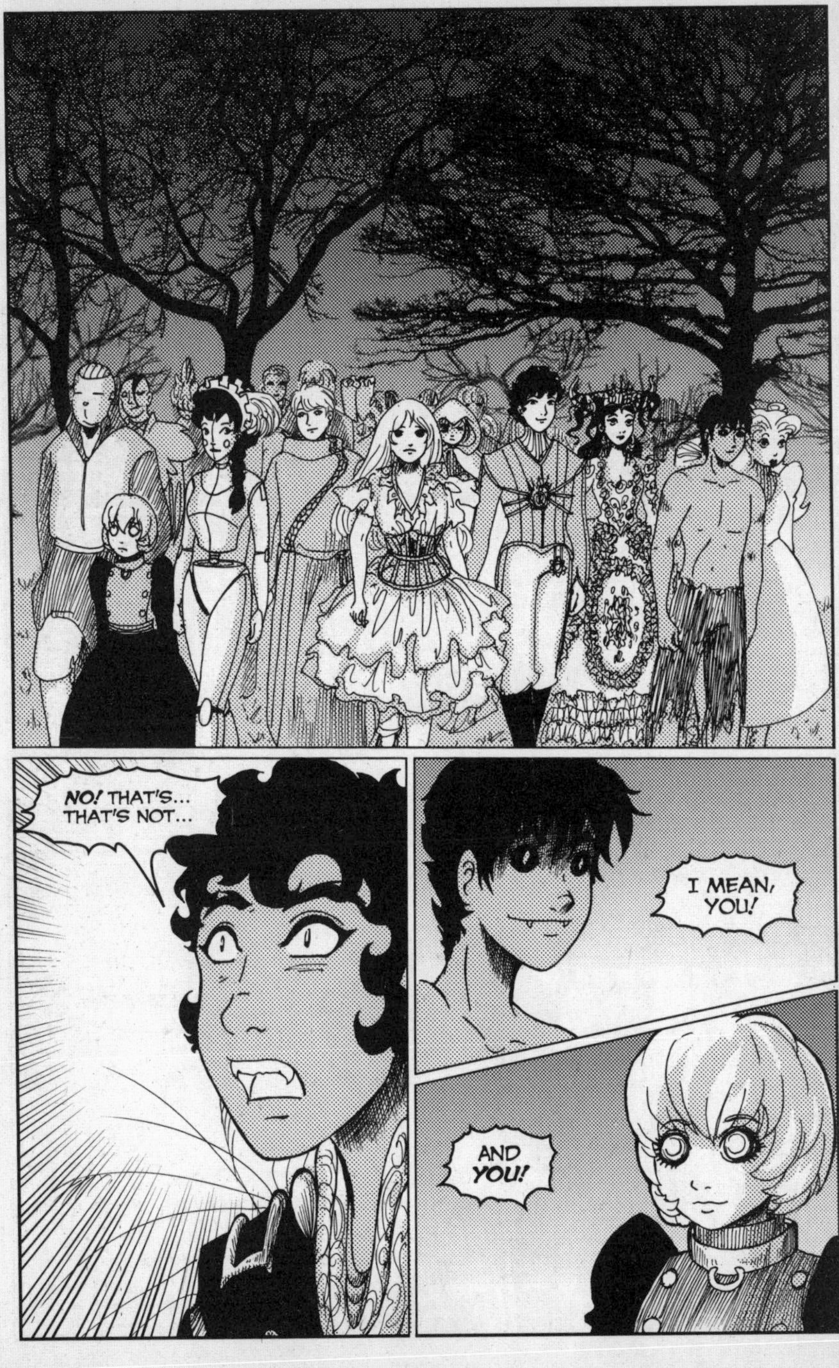
NO! THAT'S... THAT'S NOT...
I MEAN, YOU!
AND YOU!

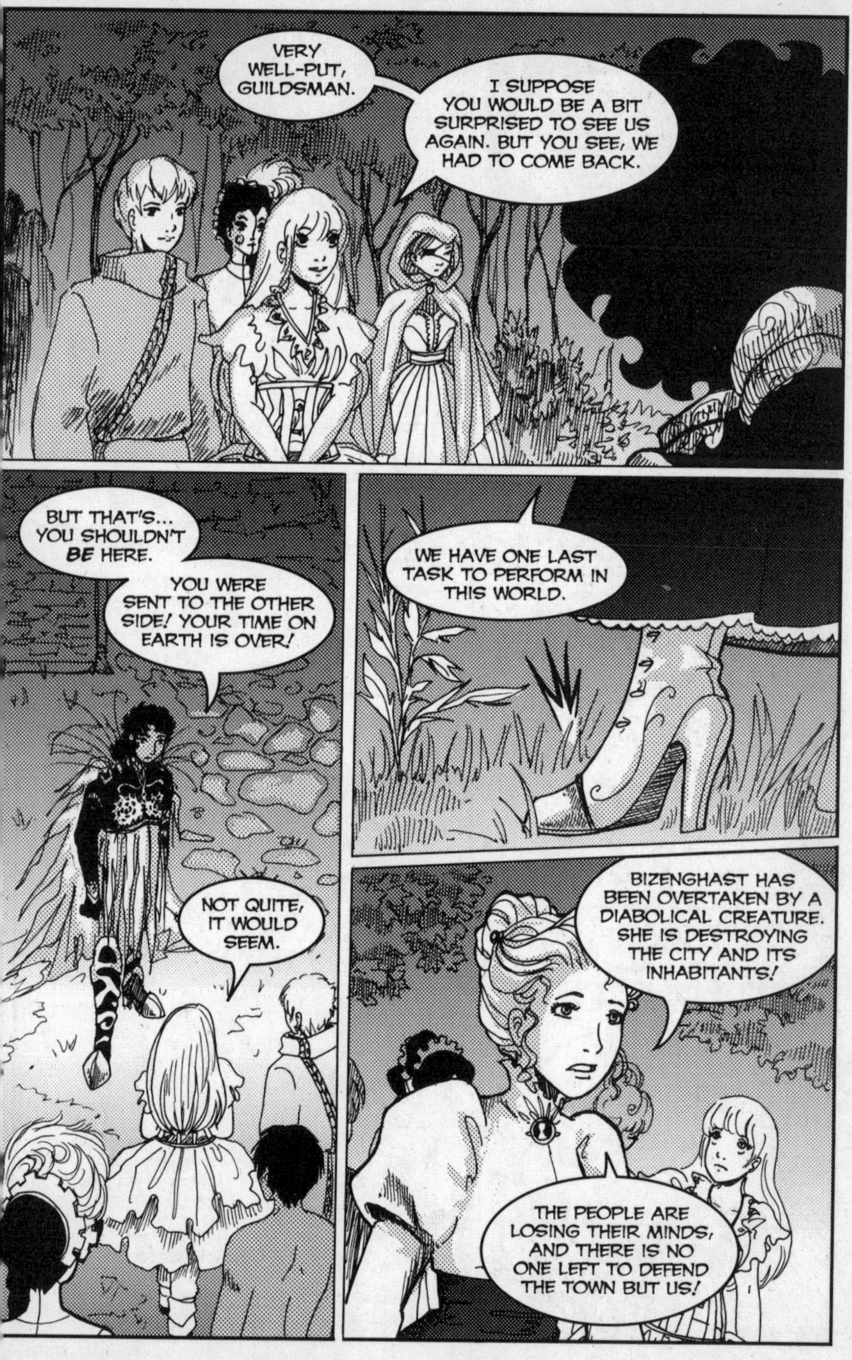
VERY WELL-PUT, GUILDSMAN.
I SUPPOSE YOU WOULD BE A BIT SURPRISED TO SEE US AGAIN. BUT YOU SEE, WE HAD TO COME BACK.
BUT THAT'S... YOU SHOULDN'T *BE* HERE.
YOU WERE SENT TO THE OTHER SIDE! YOUR TIME ON EARTH IS OVER!
NOT QUITE, IT WOULD SEEM.
WE HAVE ONE LAST TASK TO PERFORM IN THIS WORLD.
BIZENGHAST HAS BEEN OVERTAKEN BY A DIABOLICAL CREATURE. SHE IS DESTROYING THE CITY AND ITS INHABITANTS!
THE PEOPLE ARE LOSING THEIR MINDS, AND THERE IS NO ONE LEFT TO DEFEND THE TOWN BUT US!

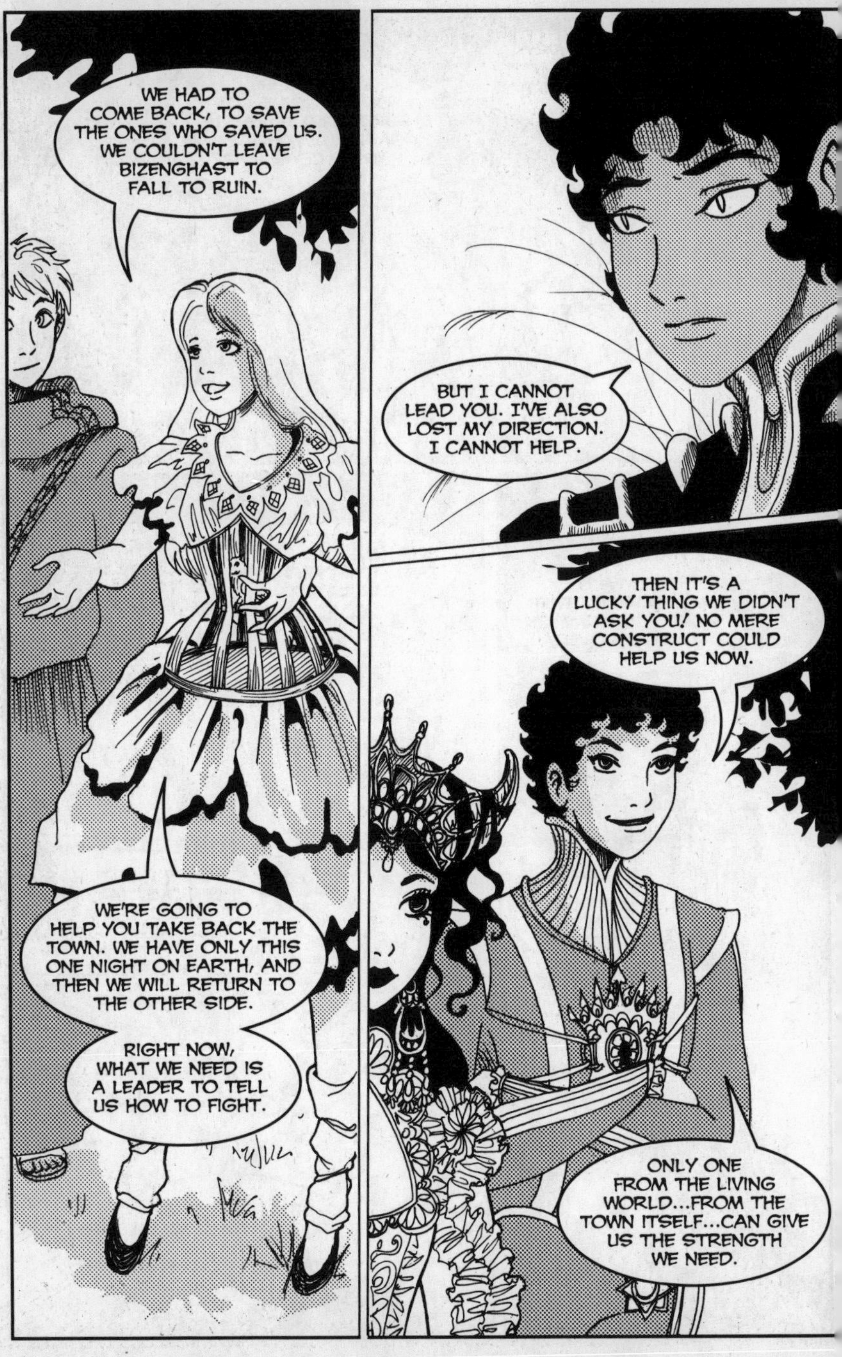
WE HAD TO COME BACK, TO SAVE THE ONES WHO SAVED US. WE COULDN'T LEAVE BIZENGHAST TO FALL TO RUIN.
WE'RE GOING TO HELP YOU TAKE BACK THE TOWN. WE HAVE ONLY THIS ONE NIGHT ON EARTH, AND THEN WE WILL RETURN TO THE OTHER SIDE.
RIGHT NOW, WHAT WE NEED IS A LEADER TO TELL US HOW TO FIGHT.
BUT I CANNOT LEAD YOU. I'VE ALSO LOST MY DIRECTION. I CANNOT HELP.
THEN IT'S A LUCKY THING WE DIDN'T ASK YOU! NO MERE CONSTRUCT COULD HELP US NOW.
ONLY ONE FROM THE LIVING WORLD...FROM THE TOWN ITSELF...CAN GIVE US THE STRENGTH WE NEED.

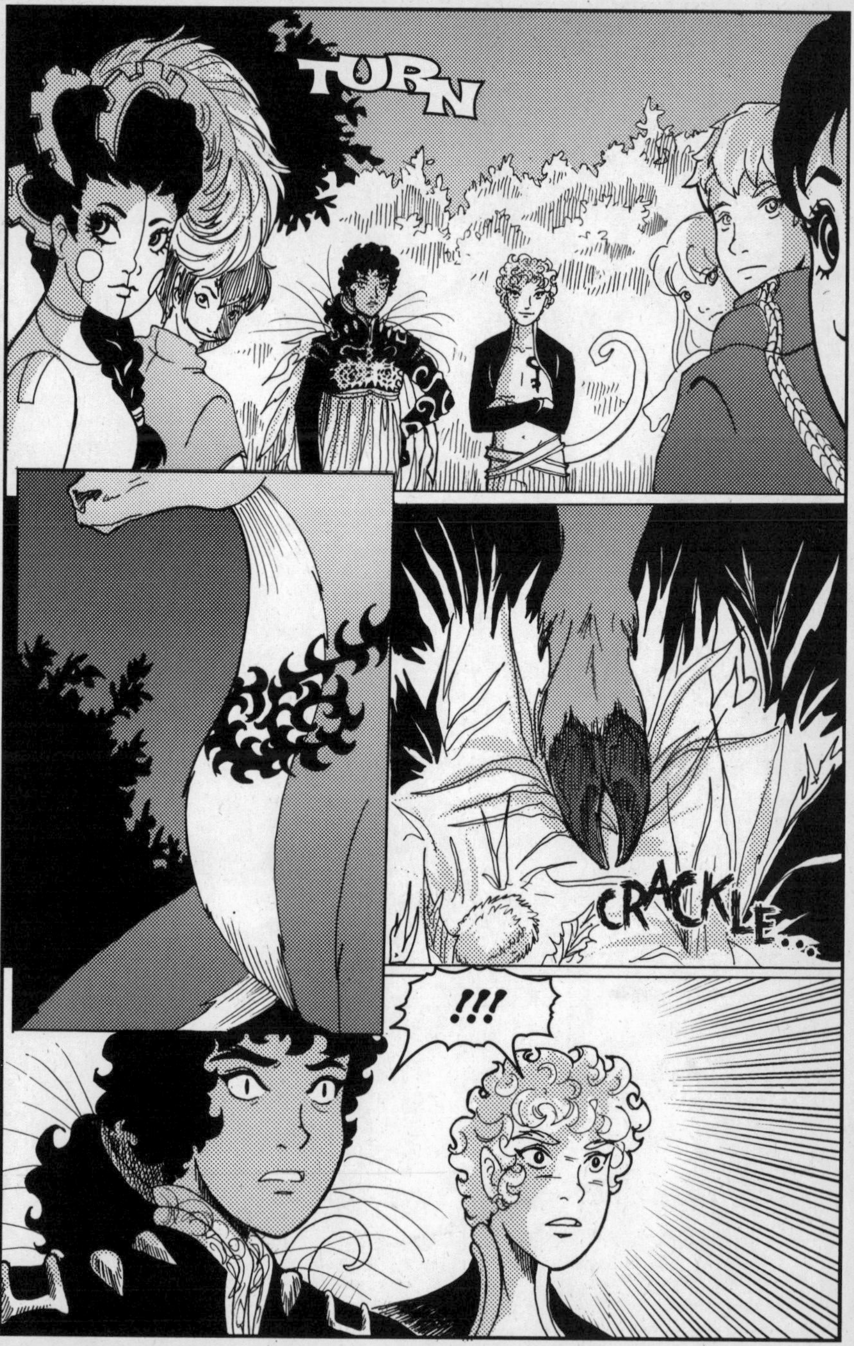
TURN
CRACKLE...
!!!

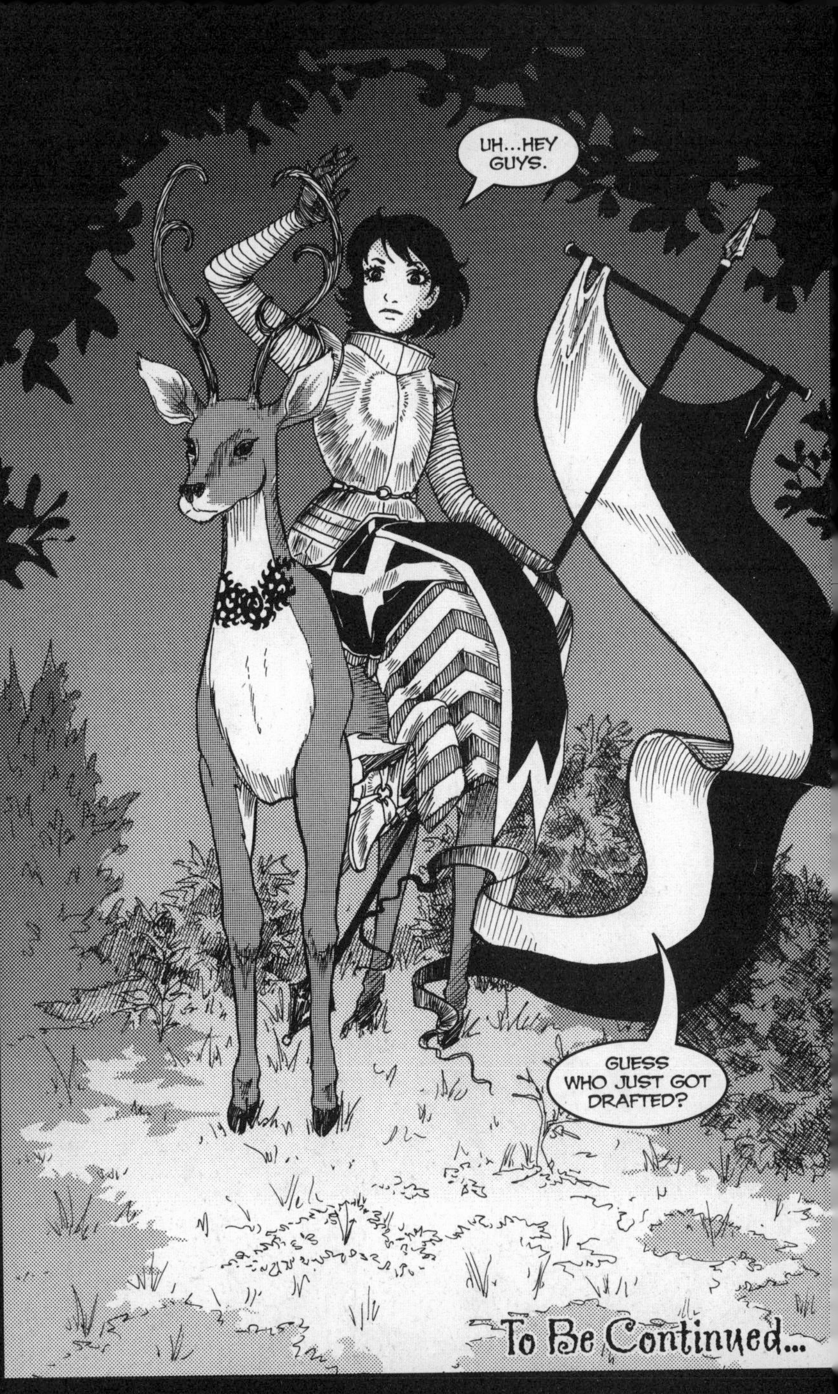
UH...HEY GUYS.
GUESS WHO JUST GOT DRAFTED?
To Be Continued...

In Volume seven of Bizenghast:

The final battle rages for the lives and souls of the inhabitants of Bizenghast, and no one is safe anymore. Shocking revelations of the town's dark history continue to emerge, and Dinah's struggle will go beyond the borders of the mausoleum, beyond Bizenghast itself... and perhaps even beyond the borders of our world...

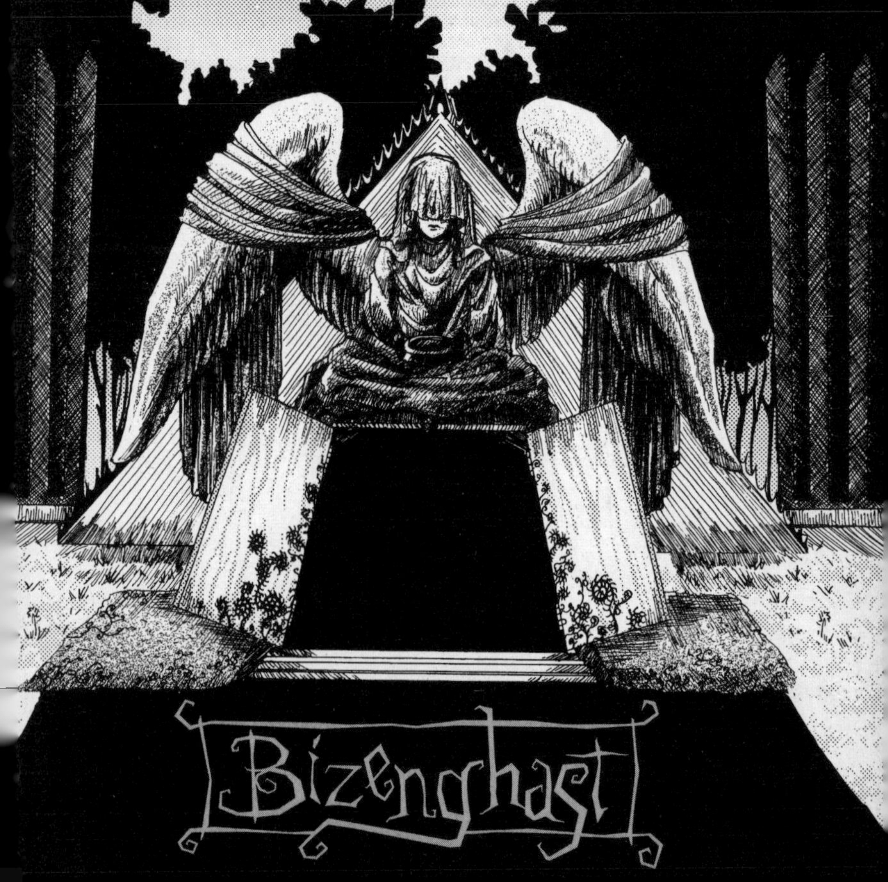
Bizenghast

What happens when your editor
asks you where that late chapter
is, and you realize that you just
spent four solid weeks trying out
new hairstyles?

You get the most inspiring and
thoroughly post-modern chapter
of Bizenghast ever written.

Presenting:
Dinah in Ghostland

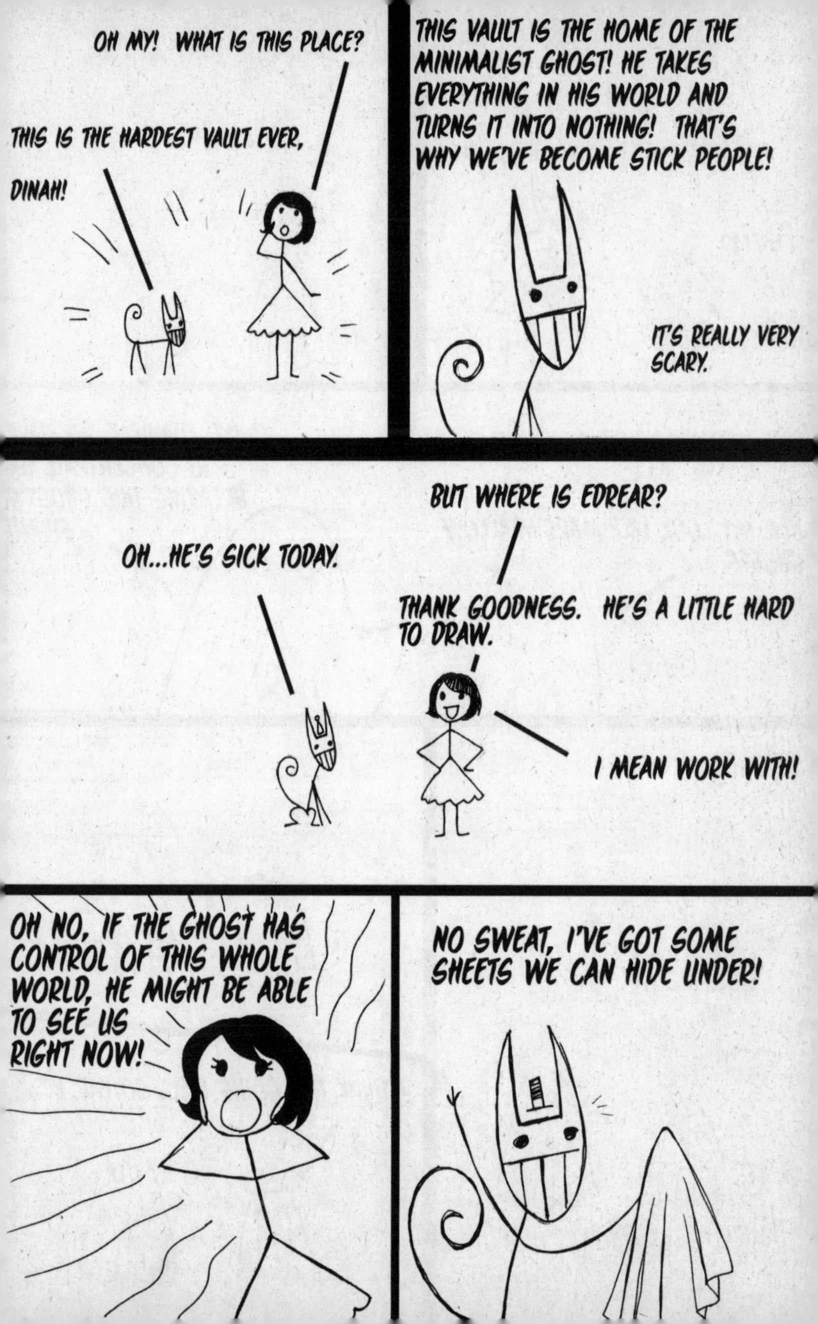
OH MY! WHAT IS THIS PLACE?
THIS IS THE HARDEST VAULT EVER, DINAH!
THIS VAULT IS THE HOME OF THE MINIMALIST GHOST! HE TAKES EVERYTHING IN HIS WORLD AND TURNS IT INTO NOTHING! THAT'S WHY WE'VE BECOME STICK PEOPLE!
IT'S REALLY VERY SCARY.
OH...HE'S SICK TODAY.
BUT WHERE IS EDREAR?
THANK GOODNESS. HE'S A LITTLE HARD TO DRAW.
I MEAN WORK WITH!
OH NO, IF THE GHOST HAS CONTROL OF THIS WHOLE WORLD, HE MIGHT BE ABLE TO SEE US RIGHT NOW!
NO SWEAT, I'VE GOT SOME SHEETS WE CAN HIDE UNDER!

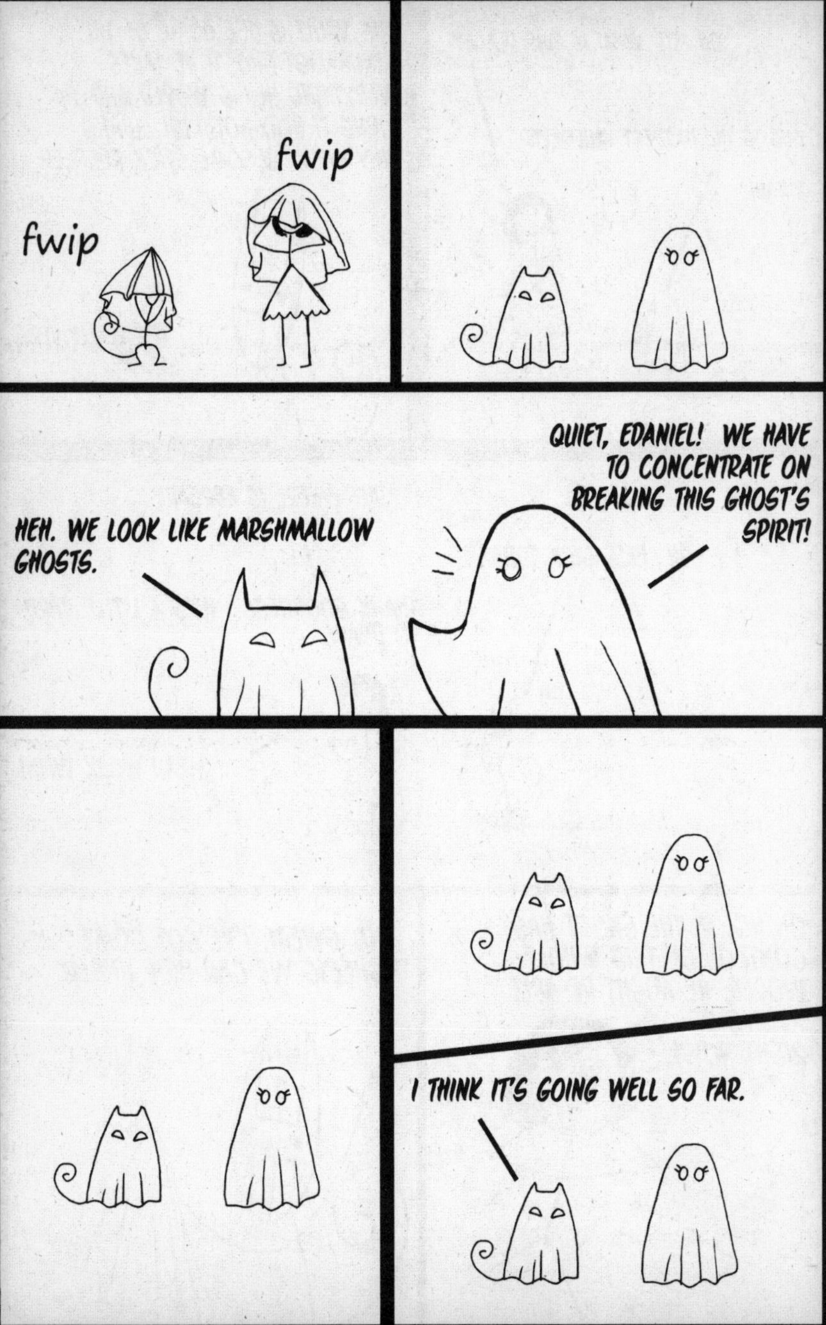
fwip
fwip
HEH. WE LOOK LIKE MARSHMALLOW GHOSTS.
QUIET, EDANIEL! WE HAVE TO CONCENTRATE ON BREAKING THIS GHOST'S SPIRIT!
I THINK IT'S GOING WELL SO FAR.

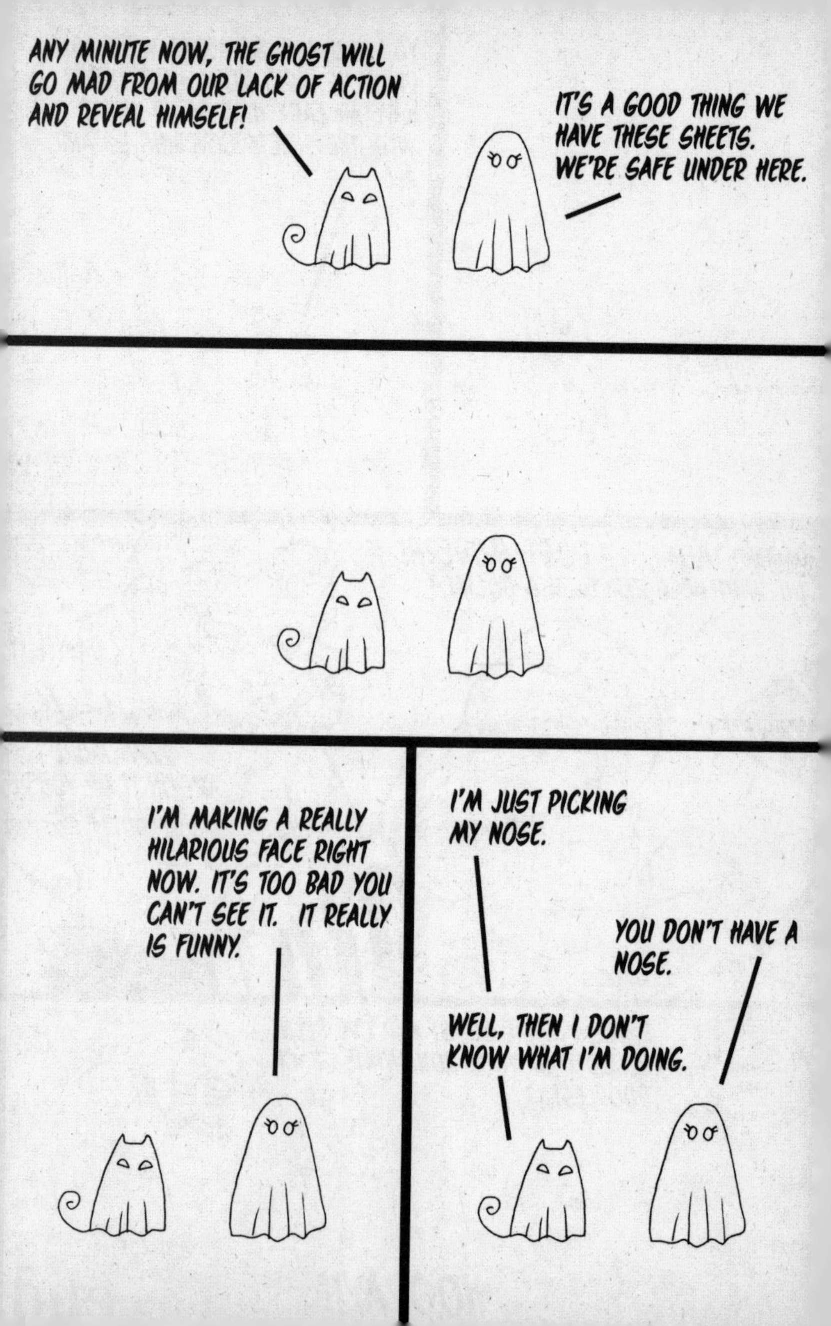

ANY MINUTE NOW, THE GHOST WILL GO MAD FROM OUR LACK OF ACTION AND REVEAL HIMSELF!
IT'S A GOOD THING WE HAVE THESE SHEETS. WE'RE SAFE UNDER HERE.
I'M MAKING A REALLY HILARIOUS FACE RIGHT NOW. IT'S TOO BAD YOU CAN'T SEE IT. IT REALLY IS FUNNY.
I'M JUST PICKING MY NOSE.
YOU DON'T HAVE A NOSE.
WELL, THEN I DON'T KNOW WHAT I'M DOING.

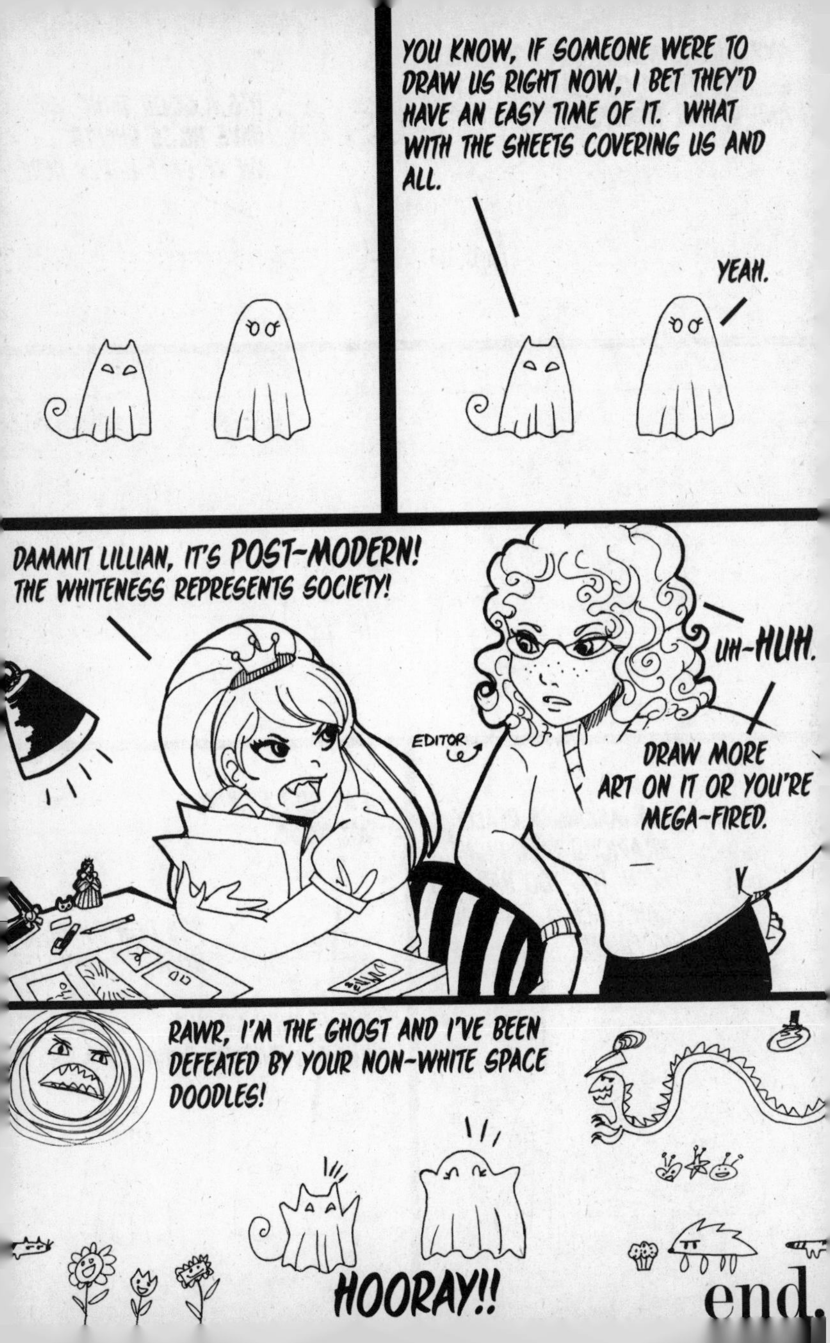
YOU KNOW, IF SOMEONE WERE TO DRAW US RIGHT NOW, I BET THEY'D HAVE AN EASY TIME OF IT. WHAT WITH THE SHEETS COVERING US AND ALL.
YEAH.
DAMMIT LILLIAN, IT'S POST-MODERN! THE WHITENESS REPRESENTS SOCIETY!
UH-HUH.
EDITOR
DRAW MORE ART ON IT OR YOU'RE MEGA-FIRED.
RAWR, I'M THE GHOST AND I'VE BEEN DEFEATED BY YOUR NON-WHITE SPACE DOODLES!
HOORAY!!
end.

# THE OCTOPUS CONTEST

Over on my DeviantArt gallery, I recently held a contest for readers to submit art for the back of this volume of Bizenghast.  The catch?  They had to involve at least one character from the series, wearing or otherwise interacting with an octopus.

Here's what you came up with!

The Octopus's Garden

The Octopus' Garden
by
http://Eu-4iA.deviantart.com

Bizenghast Octofest
by
http//Mmystery.deviantart.com

Bizenghast Octopi
by
http://shiezka.deviantart.com

Octopi Contest

by

http://decomposerdoll.deviantart.com

BZG Octopus Adventures

by

http://vampirepumpkin.devaintart.com

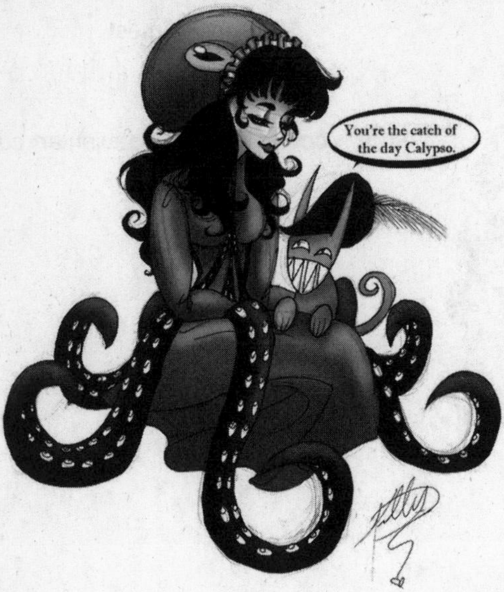
You're the catch of the day Calypso.

Dinah and Edaniel

by

http://theroseofmanga.deviantart.com

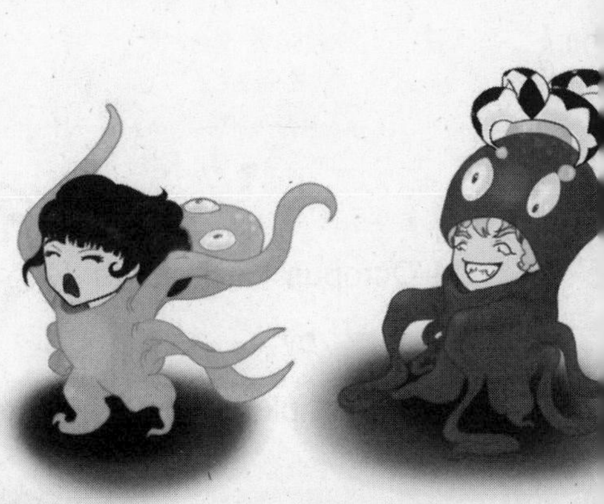

Edaniel Scares Dinah

by

http://antoinette721.deviantart.com

OctoEdaniel

by

http://pechan.deviantart.com

Kraken Ahoy, Boys

by

http://Tsuki-Noa.deviantart.com

Snuggly Octopi Love

by

http://mercuryfox22.deviantart.com

*Rosette and Ironbound* 🖤

Octopus Play Time

by

http://Hemlocks.deviantart.com

COMING SOON . . .

# BIZENGHAST:
# THE NOVEL

The first volume of this exciting new series
will arrive in stores in August 2008!

A  Prose Novel

TOKYOPOP Inc.
5900 Wilshire Boulevard, Suite 2000
Los Angeles, CA 90036
www.TOKYOPOP.com

| STORY | Shawn Thorgersen |
| ILLUSTRATIONS | M. Alice LeGrow |
| INTERIOR DESIGN | John Lo |
| LAYOUT ARTIST | Michael Paolilli |
| SENIOR EDITOR | Jenna Winterberg |
| EDITOR | Michelle Prather |
| PRE-PRESS SUPERVISOR | Lucas Rivera |
| DIGITAL IMAGING MANAGER | Chris Buford |
| ART DIRECTOR | Al-Insan Lashley |
| CREATIVE DIRECTOR | Anne Marie Horne |
| MANAGING EDITOR | Vy Nguyen |
| EDITOR-IN-CHIEF | Rob Tokar |
| PUBLISHER | Mike Kiley |
| PRESIDENT AND COO | John Parker |
| CEO AND CHIEF CREATIVE OFFICER | Stu Levy |

# The Sickness

**D**r. Morstan's stuff—Dinah couldn't remember the fancy name for it, though she knew the medication by its distinct taste of chalk dust—had been running its course through her ever since he'd arrived to treat her an hour or so earlier. Or maybe it was longer than that . . . the chalk stuff made time drip, drip along, as slow and strained as her heavy eyelids.

She lay in bed, her long curls splayed beneath her, dark rivers on the white shores of her aunt's linens. Outside her bedroom, the day had started: A cloudy morning had come to Bizenghast, the decrepit, all-but-forgotten mill town Dinah had called home since . . . how long had it been now? The doctor's stuff made it hard to think. . . . Biting her lip until she left small red marks, she focused as much as the prescription would allow. How long, she thought . . . how long had she been here?

The answer materialized through the mists of her clouded mind: She'd been in Bizenghast since . . . yes, that was it: since the sudden bursting of a tire.

That's how the newspaper reporter had described it: "The sudden bursting of a tire."

Right. She took a breath. The medication must have been weakening. More breathing and more thinking, that was the trick. Dinah tried to remember that old newspaper clipping.

She'd read it only once—after all, she'd been riding in the back of the car when the accident happened, so she didn't need an article to tell her about an incident that had left her bumped and bruised . . . and her mother and father far worse. It had been—yes, now she recalled—seven years had passed since the accident. She had been eight years old, and up until then, it had never occurred to her that sometimes, parents die and leave their children all alone.

Weak as it was, that chalk stuff, that liquid Morpheus, beckoned her to sleep—but if she forced her blue eyes to remain open, and if she kept her thoughts whirring, she could escape its lulling whisper. Sometimes, though, her mind raced ahead of her, revealing memories she'd prefer to forget. Memories, for instance, of that night in Drury, when she'd heard the tire rupture, sharp like a pistol shot, the screeching—she'd felt her mother's hand fire back to safeguard Dinah as the sedan's wheels screeched and the headlights set the double-yellow lines of the highway alight until oncoming high beams washed the whole view into blinding white light, a light that seemed like heaven—until Dinah had awakened later, here on earth once more.

As her mind cleared, she could see the newspaper clipping again. At the age of twelve, she'd found it in a shoebox under her aunt's bed: a jagged-edged strip cut with a shaking hand and blunt scissors. Dinah remembered hating the reporter; in six words he'd summarized the moment when her life had cracked in two. But the part of the clipping that had hit her, smacked her, dropped her to her knees—was this:

*"I just don't understand how it happened," said firefighter Neil Redmond. "The busted tire we found was brand new with no defects or puncturing. It didn't even burst in a way you'd expect a tire would. It had a tiny puncture in it like a dart."*

How interesting! How curious! What's more, the reporter had added: "Police are investigating the scene for signs of foul play."

Dinah sat up. A lock of her hair fell in her face. Her gown had crept up during her rest, so she tugged it down over her knees. I'm awake, she thought to herself. Most times, she just poured the chalk stuff down the drain, but whenever Dr. Morstan was here, he watched her take it. Now, though, she was coherent; the memory of that night—the shock, rush, crash so fast you can't scream—had snapped her into a semblance of focus.

Foul play? No. Dinah knew there had been no foul play, and she'd known it all the seven years since moving from her parents' home in Pennsylvania to this Massachusetts graveyard town. It hadn't been foul play or fate that had caused the accident. Forget fate.

It had been random chance. Chaos, if you like. Dumb luck. A cruddy roll of the die.

She took a final breath, flipped off the bedcovers, and ran across her bedroom floor. It was a wide expanse; her bedroom had been a convalescent chamber back when the property was St. Lyman's School for Boys. After the accident, her aunt had received the deed and moved from Colorado; she'd renovated the place to provide a home for her and Dinah, whom she placed in the healing room, as it came with a bathroom and was safely stationed on the first floor. In other words, it was the perfect spot for her newly inherited, troubled child.

Dinah sat by the phone and dialed, twining the black cord in her pale fingers; these days, with Aunt Jane keeping her from attending school or leaving home for the most part due to her "illness," Dinah rarely saw the sun. Through the thin walls (Dinah suspected that some of the renovations had been done on the cheap), she could hear Dr. Morstan talking to Aunt Jane. Most of it sounded like mumbles, but she pieced together a few words—

words like "hospital" and "testing" and "for her safety." Now, she knew she'd beaten the medication. She was getting nervous again, which was partly what the stuff was supposed to prevent.

Likely, Aunt Jane hated having to assume responsibility for Dinah since the accident, and certainly believed there was something very wrong with her niece. Vincent, on the other hand . . .

Just when she thought she might get stuck talking to his voicemail, Vincent picked up. She listened to his breath; likely, he was outside somewhere, perhaps riding the outskirts of town on his bicycle. His breath, and then his voice, soothed her. She knew so few people here—heck, there were only sixty-four residents in the whole town, including herself, Aunt Jane, and Vincent. Vincent struck Dinah as the closest she'd ever come to meeting an adventurer; he was brave, he liked to explore the abandoned homes in town, and—the bottom line was—when he came around, the *other* inhabitants of the former St. Lyman's school, the ones only Dinah could see, left her alone.

"Hello?" he said. She imagined Vincent standing on a hill somewhere, his blond hair glistening with sweat from bicycling, but light and long enough to blow in the chill wind. Possibly, he had some interesting gadgets in his pockets, ripped from one of the local buildings. That's how he looked when she'd met him two years ago. He'd been dared to explore the weird old Lyman's school, and he'd arrived with an antenna knotted to his bicycle and some crown molding strapped to his back, as a knight might have strapped his sword. Vincent had startled her, but perhaps she'd startled him, too; he'd discovered her filling what likely resembled a miniature grave in the yard. She'd felt certain she'd scared the boy away, but two weeks later, Vincent had returned with a discovered copy of *Le Petit Prince,* salvaged from some of the town's other ruins. Dinah was thirteen at the time; she couldn't have guessed that this boy might become her dearest companion.

"Come over," Dinah answered. She paused, listening through the thin wall separating her bedroom from the foyer. Sometimes, Dr. Morstan stopped in simply to drop off meds, or for a quick exchange of paperwork along with a brief update—not this time. "I need you here. Dr. Morstan hasn't left yet."

On the other end, Vincent took a deep breath. His breathing slowed. "What do you want me to do? He and your aunt hate me."

"But they know!" she said, and then her voice fell to a whisper. There was no way she could allow Aunt Jane or Dr. Morstan to hear this next part: "They know about the ghosts!"

"Don't worry. I'll make him leave. I'll tell him what he wants to hear."

"Please hurry." She felt helpless—like a fair maiden on a faded movie poster, grasping the brave hero as he valiantly shields her from black-hearted villains. She hated the feeling almost as much as she hated the chalk stuff, but what could she do? She had no power. No authority. And anyway, what difference would it make if she *did* try something? Random chance could happen along and ruin things anyway. Forget that. So, she might as well leave it to Vincent, who was much better at taking care of things than she was.

"Hurry up," she said, "before he sends me away!"

She hung up the phone and listened. They were quiet on the other side of the wall. Had they overheard her conversation? She sidled to the wall that separated her bedroom from the main hall and cupped her hand to eavesdrop, trying to imagine what they were doing in such silence. In her mind's eye, she saw Dr. Morstan, a pale, bespectacled man in his late thirties, sporting a goatee. Likely, he felt it was fashionable, but Dinah often wondered whether he was just attempting to look like a legitimate psychiatrist—a young, hip, Freud, maybe. At Aunt Jane's request, he had been studying Dinah to ascertain the cause

of her "fits," as he called them. Thus far, he'd discovered precious little—only that whatever had been troubling her through the years since her parents' passing and the move to her aunt's property often had left her screaming and bruised. He'd seen the fits himself, so any suspicion toward Aunt Jane had been quashed. He'd even tested her for the usual diagnosis, epilepsy, but that had come back negative. No, this was something else, and he hadn't figured it out yet, which is why Dr. Morstan had recently made his worst suggestion—that Dinah be removed to a hospital, where she could be better tested and treated.

When she'd heard that, she imagined towering white walls, wrinkled clothes reeking of bleach, and long, disinfected linoleum hallways spied through the reinforced glass square of solitary rooms. What an awful deal of the cards that would be, she thought. To be without parents was bad enough. To live in Bizenghast—which was, to her, the rotting cadaver of some colonist's dead vision—was to wilt alongside it. But to be alone, without even her aunt, or Vincent, her single friend, that would be the end for her. She'd never go to the hospital if she could help it, even if it somehow learning to cope with house full of ghosts.

If only Dr. Morstan could see what she saw. If only he could see the Walkers on the lawn, the shapes within the shadows here in her aunt's home . . . if he could see the governess, the matron ghost that would discipline Dinah, and realize that the creaks in the ancient floorboards were *not* the damned house settling, then he would know everything he needed to, and she wouldn't have to go to some hospital.

But the truth was that only Dinah saw these things. And in moments like these, staring at cracks in spackled walls, the eight-year-old inside her, who had been happy before the sudden bursting of a tire, wondered whether the new Dinah actually saw ghosts, or was simply mad as a hatter.

"Hurry, Vincent," she whispered.

★★★

The boy rode as quickly as he could, considering the chain on his bike sounded like it was going to rattle off and twirl around the rear wheel if he pedaled any faster over these dirt roads.

There, he saw it: The rusted, broken archway outside Dinah's home, informing any soul who came this way that this was St. Lyman's School for Boys. He'd always wanted to rip a chunk off that sign, partly as a souvenir, partly because a good hunk of iron presented so many possibilities. But this was Dinah's home, and even if her aunt didn't much like him, Vincent wasn't about to do wrong by Dinah.

He rode beneath the arch and past the brick walls, which were thick enough, he mused, to keep any of the old Lyman's boys from escaping, assuming the school still had a sturdy gate at the front (which it didn't). Vincent let his momentum take him the rest of the way, watching as the old school-turned-home grew large and looming, like a nightmare creature, in his vision. As was true of most of the buildings in town, Dinah's place needed work, and the boy wondered how long it would be before the ivy grew over the windows and covered the sharp rooftops.

Still, he loved his hometown of Bizenghast, and what some might label hopeless or strange, he called captivating, because you never knew how a thing might be if you fixed it up just right.

He could hear them talking about Dinah on the other side of the front door. Giving the bell-pull a good yank should hush up Aunt Jane, he figured, so he did just that. He grinned—she'd muttered something about killing him just as Dr. Morstan opened the door.

The doctor looked down his nose at Vincent the way some teachers did when they wanted to feel authoritative. Well, it wasn't going to work here. This doctor was a quack as far as Vincent was

concerned, and even if he *did* know what he was doing, he was still hurting Dinah, and Vincent couldn't let that continue.

"Vincent," Dr. Morstan said, "what are you doing here?"

With as much innocence as he could muster, Vincent answered. "I came to see Dinah. Can I go inside?"

"Just a minute. Did Dinah . . ." At this, the doctor looked over his shoulder, glancing at Aunt Jane. "Has she had any fits lately?"

*Fits?* Vincent thought. Lying, he knew, was all about what you let stream through your head while speaking. To really, really, get out a good lie, it was important to actually *think* along the lines of what you spoke. So, Vincent thought, *This doctor IS off his rocker, asking such a ridiculous and bizarre question* (which wasn't hard for him to do). "Sir?" he answered, as if completely shocked by the question. He nearly believed himself.

"Fits, Vincent. Has she been well?"

For an instant, Vincent faltered. Deceiving him, his mind returned to a scene not two days past, when he'd nearly had to wrestle Dinah down from whatever phantom force had been troubling her. She'd grabbed the canopy of her bed and held on for dear life, screaming loud enough that Aunt Jane could have heard from anywhere in the large house, had she been home.

When he finally brought his mind back to the present, he realized he might not be able to craft a good lie again.

"Vincent?"

"Um, she's fine. She's been just fine." *Dammit*, he thought. *I don't even believe me.*

And neither, evidently, did Dr. Morstan. "Truthfully, Vincent. Are you quite sure of that?"

Again, his memories ruined a perfectly good deception. He struggled to move past an image of holding Dinah; she'd been cold to the touch, deathly white, eyes flared open as though to absorb a giant, terrible secret. And as much as he'd tried, he couldn't pull

her hands down from her face until her . . . well, until her fit had passed.

Vincent looked to Aunt Jane. She was youngish and attractive (for a thirty-something-year old, anyway), with brown hair, lighter than Dinah's, fashioned in a short bob. Her curled ends made her appear youthful, but the way she furled her eyebrows and pressed her lips while talking about Dinah aged her. Sometimes, Vincent pitied her, although she preferred he not come around. After all, she wasn't a mother, hadn't planned on being one, but was nonetheless put in a hard spot. Tough break.

*That's it,* he thought. He shifted his focus to thinking of her—to using sympathy as a grounding point for a little lie that could help Dinah. So, was he quite sure that Dinah was just fine? *Focus,* he thought. "Sure as I'm standing here, sir," he said, and left the spot a trifle too quickly to fully drive home the point. No matter, though: He'd gotten past Dinah's guardians, and that was the real objective. They weren't his biggest fans, but nothing he could have said was going to change that, anyway.

He paused in the hallway, waiting to see if they would follow him. Dr. Morstan spoke first: "Well, fits or no," he said to Aunt Jane, "those cuts and bruises didn't make themselves."

Aunt Jane answered, incredulous. "Are you suggesting *they* did it?"

"Come now, Jane . . . we both know there's no such thing as ghosts."

With that, Vincent walked the short hall to Dinah's room. *So,* he thought, *they wondered about it, too.* While sneaking around inside abandoned homes these last few years, he'd had his share of scares: floors that bottomed out, rooftops that caved, and the occasional shadow that looked remarkably like an old owner staring at him as he looted the place. But truthfully, he'd never seen a ghost—not that he'd mind it if he did. Dinah said she saw them, and who was he to disagree? It didn't much trouble him, because in the end, he

alone could help ease Dinah's troubles, and that was the thing that mattered to Vincent.

He opened her door, and saw her—she was a year younger than he was, and she always dressed, well, differently than the girls in school; it was always something elaborate with Dinah. But his favorite thing, upon seeing her for the first time each day, was her eyes—her blue eyes, wide and sad, waiting for him to give her a hand. And he would—any day she needed him, he'd be there.

***

## TO BE CONTINUED . . .

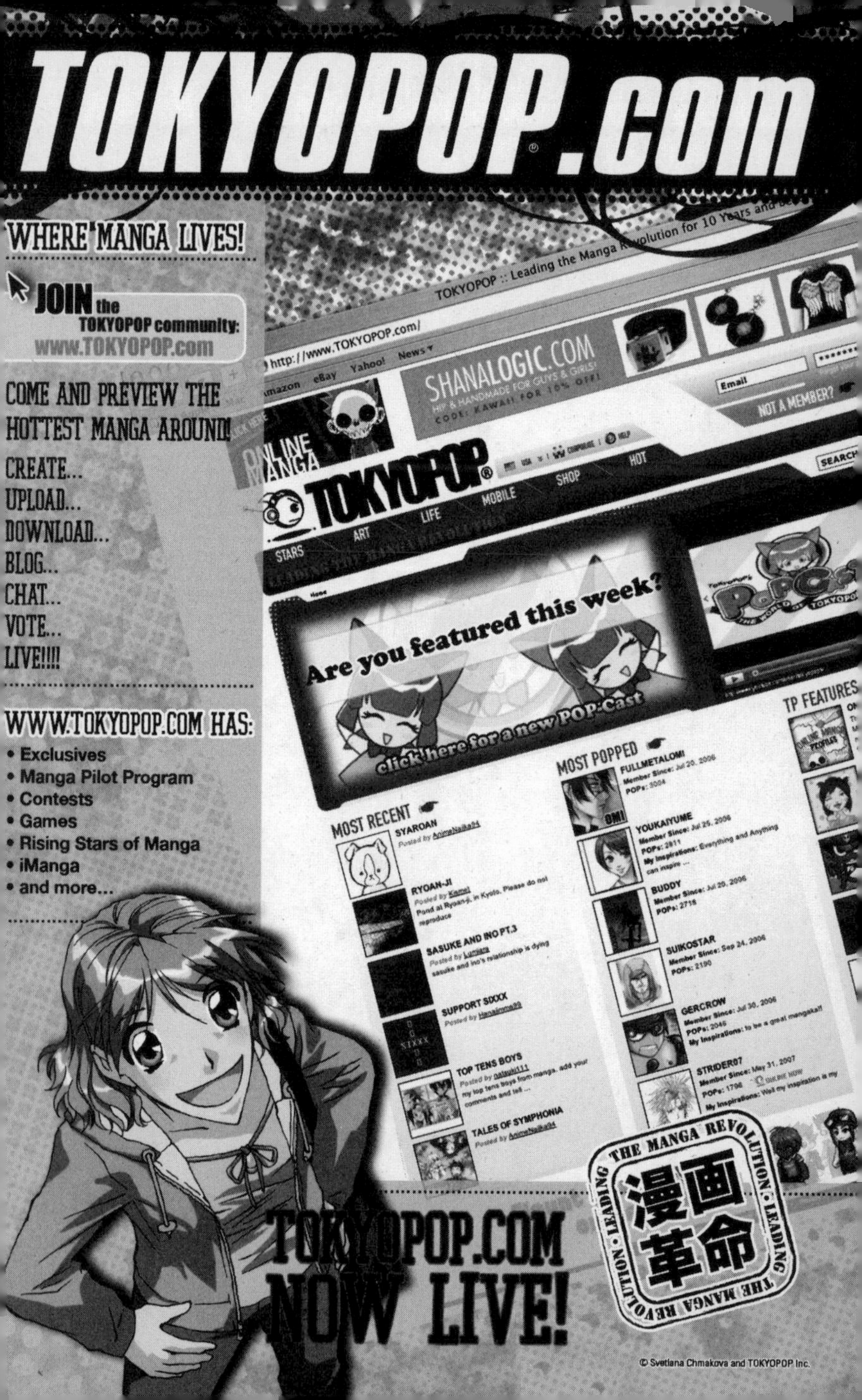
TOKYOPOP.com
WHERE MANGA LIVES!
JOIN the TOKYOPOP community:
www.TOKYOPOP.com
COME AND PREVIEW THE HOTTEST MANGA AROUND!
CREATE...
UPLOAD...
DOWNLOAD...
BLOG...
CHAT...
VOTE...
LIVE!!!!
WWW.TOKYOPOP.COM HAS:
• Exclusives
• Manga Pilot Program
• Contests
• Games
• Rising Stars of Manga
• iManga
• and more...
TOKYOPOP :: Leading the Manga Revolution for 10 Years and be
http://www.TOKYOPOP.com/
SHANALOGIC.COM
NOT A MEMBER?
ONLINE MANGA
TOKYOPOP
STARS
ART
LIFE
MOBILE
SHOP
HOT
SEARCH
Are you featured this week?
click here for a new POP-Cast
TP FEATURES
MOST POPPED
MOST RECENT
SYAROAN
RYOAN-JI
SASUKE AND INO PT.3
SUPPORT SIXXX
TOP TENS BOYS
TALES OF SYMPHONIA
FULLMETALOMI
YOUKAIYUME
BUDDY
SUIKOSTAR
GERCROW
STRIDER07
TOKYOPOP.COM NOW LIVE!
LEADING · THE MANGA REVOLUTION ·
漫画革命
© Svetlana Chmakova and TOKYOPOP Inc.

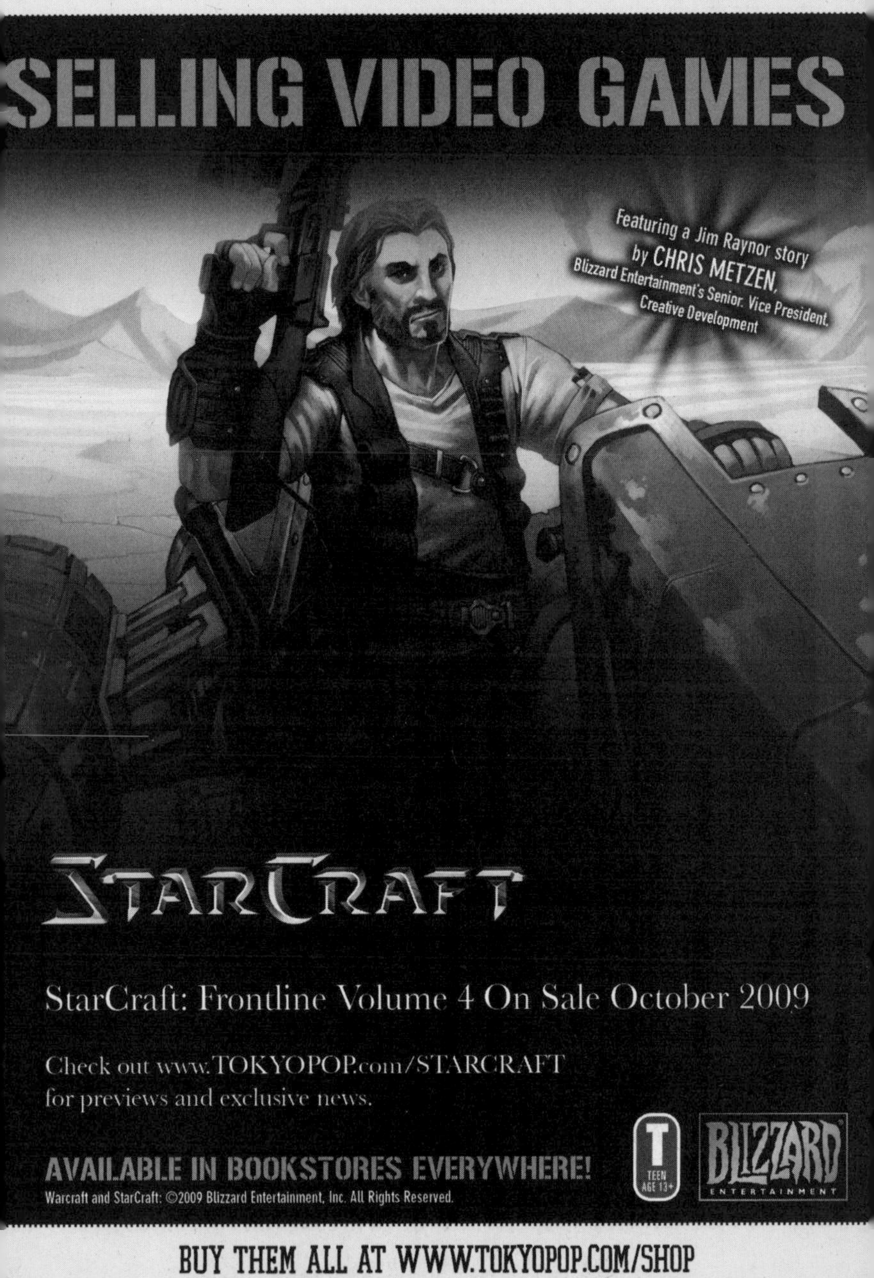
SELLING VIDEO GAMES
Featuring a Jim Raynor story by CHRIS METZEN, Blizzard Entertainment's Senior. Vice President, Creative Development
STARCRAFT
StarCraft: Frontline Volume 4 On Sale October 2009
Check out www.TOKYOPOP.com/STARCRAFT for previews and exclusive news.
AVAILABLE IN BOOKSTORES EVERYWHERE!
Warcraft and StarCraft: ©2009 Blizzard Entertainment, Inc. All Rights Reserved.
T TEEN AGE 13+
BLIZZARD ENTERTAINMENT

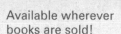

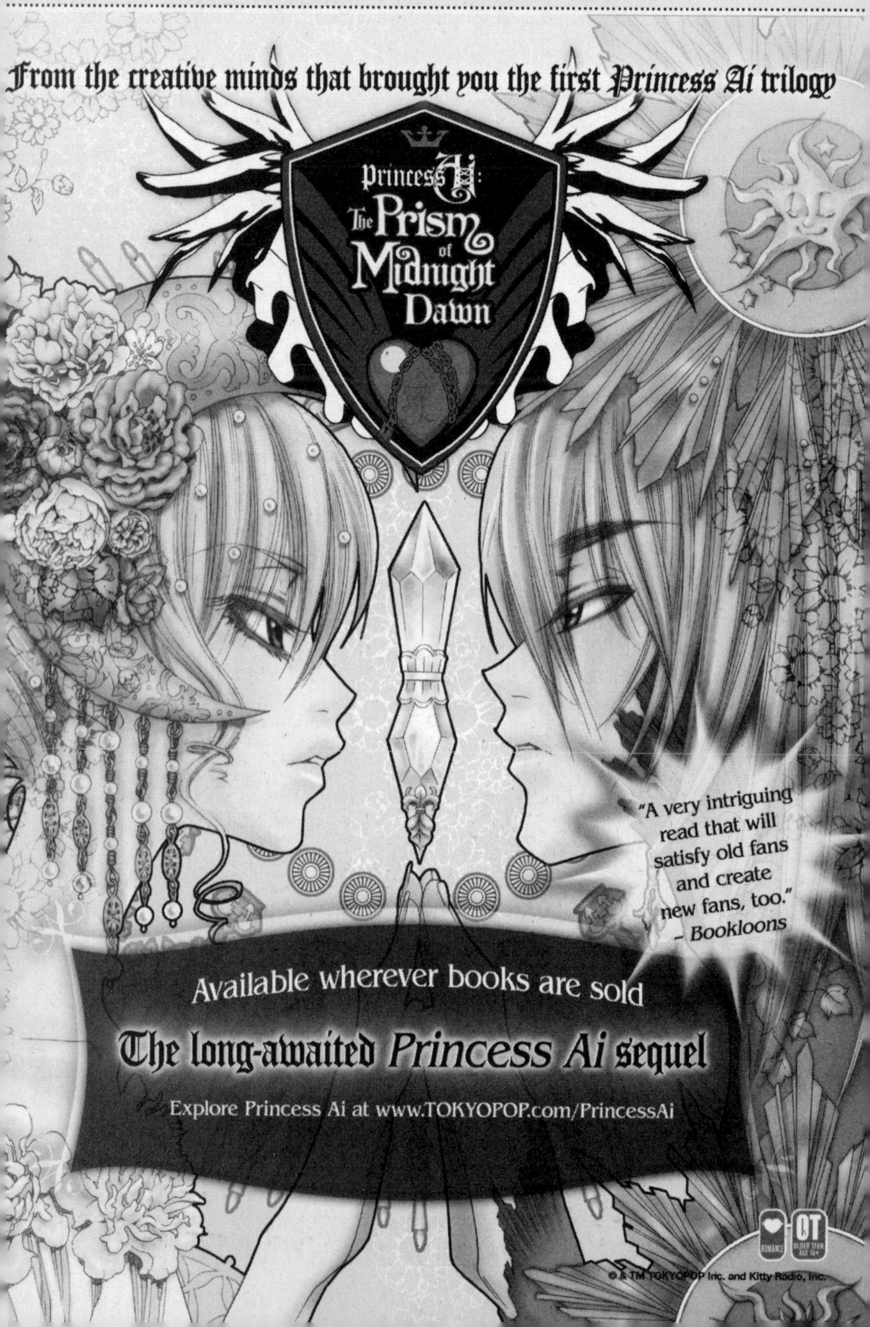

From the creative minds that brought you the first Princess Ai trilogy
Princess Ai: The Prism of Midnight Dawn
"A very intriguing read that will satisfy old fans and create new fans, too."
– Bookloons
Available wherever books are sold
The long-awaited Princess Ai sequel
Explore Princess Ai at www.TOKYOPOP.com/PrincessAi
© & TM TOKYOPOP Inc. and Kitty Radio, Inc.

## The class president has a little secret she's keeping from the sexy bad boy in school...

It's love at first fight in this shojo romantic comedy—with a hilarious spin on geek culture and... student government?!

As President of the Student Council, the overachieving feminist Misaki really socks it to the boys in an attempt to make the former all-boys' school attract a more female student body. But what will she do when the hottest boy in class finds out Misaki's after-school gig is in a maid café?!